CW01666981

PASSPORT TO CAMBRIDGE PROFICIENCY

Student's Book

Jeremy Walenn

MACMILLAN PUBLISHERS

ela

First published 1992

Published by MACMILLAN PUBLISHERS LIMITED
London and Basingstoke

ISBN 0 - 333 - 56495 - 2

Printed in Singapore

A catalogue record for this book is available from the British Library.

Acknowledgements

Designed by Arc Design.

Illustrations by: Sarah Cottrill (Penguin Visual Concepts), Simon Davis, Jo Sumner, Richard Wileman.

Photographs by: Steven Ashton, Sarah Hannant, Living Proof, Josie Williams.

The publishers would like to thank the following for permission to reproduce photographs and advertisements:

Barclays Bank plc, Casio Electronics Company Ltd, Honda UK, IWC International Watch Company AG, Northern Ireland Tourist Board, Outward Bound Trust, Zefa.

The publishers would like to thank the following for permission to reproduce texts:

American Express, Arlington Books, Bantam Books, BBC Enterprises Ltd, Jonathan Cape, Chatto and Windus, Elle Magazine, the Estate of Frieda Lawrence Ravagli, Faber and Faber, Samuel French Ltd, Hamish Hamilton Ltd, William Heinemann Ltd, Hodder and Stoughton Publishers, Macdonald and Co, Macmillan Publishers Ltd, John Murray Publishers Ltd, Octopus Publishing Group Library, Laurence Pollinger Ltd, Margaret Ramsay Ltd, Julian Rathbone, Time Life, Times Newspapers, Weidenfeld and Nicholson.

Contents

There's no success like failure and failure's no success at all.

Bob Dylan

Speaking

1 What criteria are used to judge success and failure?

1 Look at the statements below and decide where you would place each of them on the scale below. Number them 0 – 5 in the boxes provided.

2 Give reasons for your decisions and discuss your conclusions with a partner.

Failure	←——→				Success
0	1	2	3	4	5

- ☐ Studying your favourite subject at university but being unable to get a job.
- ☐ Studying a subject that you hate but which enables you to get a highly paid job.
- ☐ Writing a book which is critically acclaimed but sells very few copies.
- ☐ Writing a book which has no literary merit but sells a million copies.
- ☐ Buying an artistic masterpiece and selling it shortly afterwards at a huge profit.
- ☐ Buying an undiscovered artistic masterpiece at a bargain price and keeping it to admire.
- ☐ Doing a job which is highly stressful and highly paid.
- ☐ Inheriting a lot of money, giving up work, and enjoying a life of leisure and pleasure.
- ☐ Passing an examination which required very little work.
- ☐ Failing an examination but learning a lot in the process.
- ☐ Achieving ambitions at the expense of losing friends.
- ☐ Keeping friends by not achieving ambitions.

2 Look at the statements below. Is the argument correct? If not, is it logical?

All successful people go to university.
John didn't go to university.
Therefore John isn't successful.

Listening

1 Listen to these people talking about their education and how they see it in the light of what they have achieved since. Identify them and number them in the order in which they speak.

- ☐ a person who has benefited from going to university
- ☐ a person who has not benefited from going to university
- ☐ a person who could have gone to university but didn't and regrets this
- ☐ a person who has no regrets about not going to university
- ☐ a person who thinks education for its own sake is a complete waste of time
- ☐ a person who left school with few qualifications but did an Open University degree

2 Make notes on each speaker as shown below.

```
Speaker: …

Did / Did not go to university.

Regrets / Does not regret this.

Has / Has not done other further education courses.

Present position: …

Happy / Unhappy with present position. Why? …

Positive / Negative attitude towards education.
Give details: …
```

3 Which speaker reflects most closely your atttitude towards and experience of education? Discuss this with a partner. Then report your partner's views on education to the class.

Use of English

Look at the sentences and explanations below.

I would have gone if I'd had the chance.
The speaker indicates that there was a lack of opportunity which, despite the motivation, prevented the speaker from achieving an aim.

I wouldn't have gone even if I'd had the chance.
The speaker indicates that the opportunity was not there but even if it had been, there was still no motivation.

I could have gone if I'd wanted to.
The opportunity was there but there was no motivation.

I couldn't have gone even if I'd wanted to.
There was no opportunity and therefore the question of motivation did not arise.

Think about these differences in meaning. Then complete sentences 1 – 8 appropriately.

1 The police ... the thief but they decided not to for a while, in the hope that she would lead them to the mastermind behind the crime.
2 The police ... the house for the missing necklace if they hadn't had a warrant giving them authorisation.
3 Charlie Allsort ... that novel, as he simply hasn't got the talent.
4 Selina ... to that office party, had she been invited, as she can't stand the sight of her colleagues.
5 Rebecca, the second Mrs de Winter, ... Max de Winter if she had known the truth about his first wife.
6 Cinderella ... to the ball without the help of her fairy godmother.
7 Blofeld ... Bond on many occasions, but he was always thwarted by the spy's amazing powers of survival.
8 Superman may have looked dead but nobody ... him because his body was protected by supernatural forces.

Speaking

Work with a partner. Using the structures in the previous exercise, respond to each of the following situations appropriately.

1 You have been turned down for a job that you applied for although you knew you didn't have the right experience or qualifications.
2 Because you were having a shower you did not hear the doorbell. The person who rang was a door-to-door salesman. You never answer the door to salesmen.
3 You live close to a stadium where there was a free rock concert but you didn't go as it was being shown live on television.
4 Although you have the necessary equipment, you consider it both immoral and illegal to make copies of videotapes. A friend who knows your views asks someone else to do it.

Reading and listening

This extract is taken from *Educating Rita*, a play by Willy Russell. It is set in a university city in the north of England and involves two main characters, Rita and Frank. Rita, whose real name is Susan but who, for effect, has taken the first name of the popular romantic novelist Rita Mae Brown, has enrolled on an Open University course in English Literature. Under this system, students without the qualifications normally required to enter a conventional university can still study for a degree.

At the moment Rita is working as a hairdresser and is married. There is considerable social and family pressure on her to have a baby, which she is resisting. Frank, her tutor, has talent both as a teacher and as a poet, but his judgement is apparently impaired by continual alcohol abuse.

1 Listen to their first meeting. Read the text. Which of these characteristics could describe (a) Rita (b) Frank?

Write (a) or (b) in the appropriate boxes.

- ☐ intellectual
- ☐ arrogant
- ☐ reserved
- ☐ strong-willed
- ☐ talkative
- ☐ witty
- ☐ calm
- ☐ good-natured
- ☐ uncultured
- ☐ bossy
- ☐ well-read
- ☐ culturally aware

2 Listen to the passage again and complete each statement appropriately.

1 Frank has decided to work for the Open University because
a he wants to meet real students.
b it is no different from an ordinary university.
c he needs the money.
d it will help with his research.

2 Frank at first refuses Rita's offer of a cigarette because he
a doesn't like tobacco.
b has promised to give up smoking.
c has never smoked.
d only smokes cigars.

3 Rita believes that Frank won't think the poem by Roger McGough is any good because
a he won't understand it.
b it is about death.
c it isn't about reality.
d he will understand it.

4 Rita believes that Scotch whisky
a is good for the brain.
b is bad for the brain.
c makes you careful.
d has a very bad effect on her.

Speaking

Discuss with your partner your initial impressions of Frank and Rita. Note them down.

Listening

1 The story has now moved on. As a result of Rita's studies, the relationship between her and Frank has changed.

As you listen to this extract, look back at the characteristics you originally used to describe Frank and Rita. Discuss with your partner whether they should be modified. For example:

Is Frank less arrogant?
Is Rita more talkative?

2 Discuss with your partner what changes have taken place in the relationship between Frank and Rita.

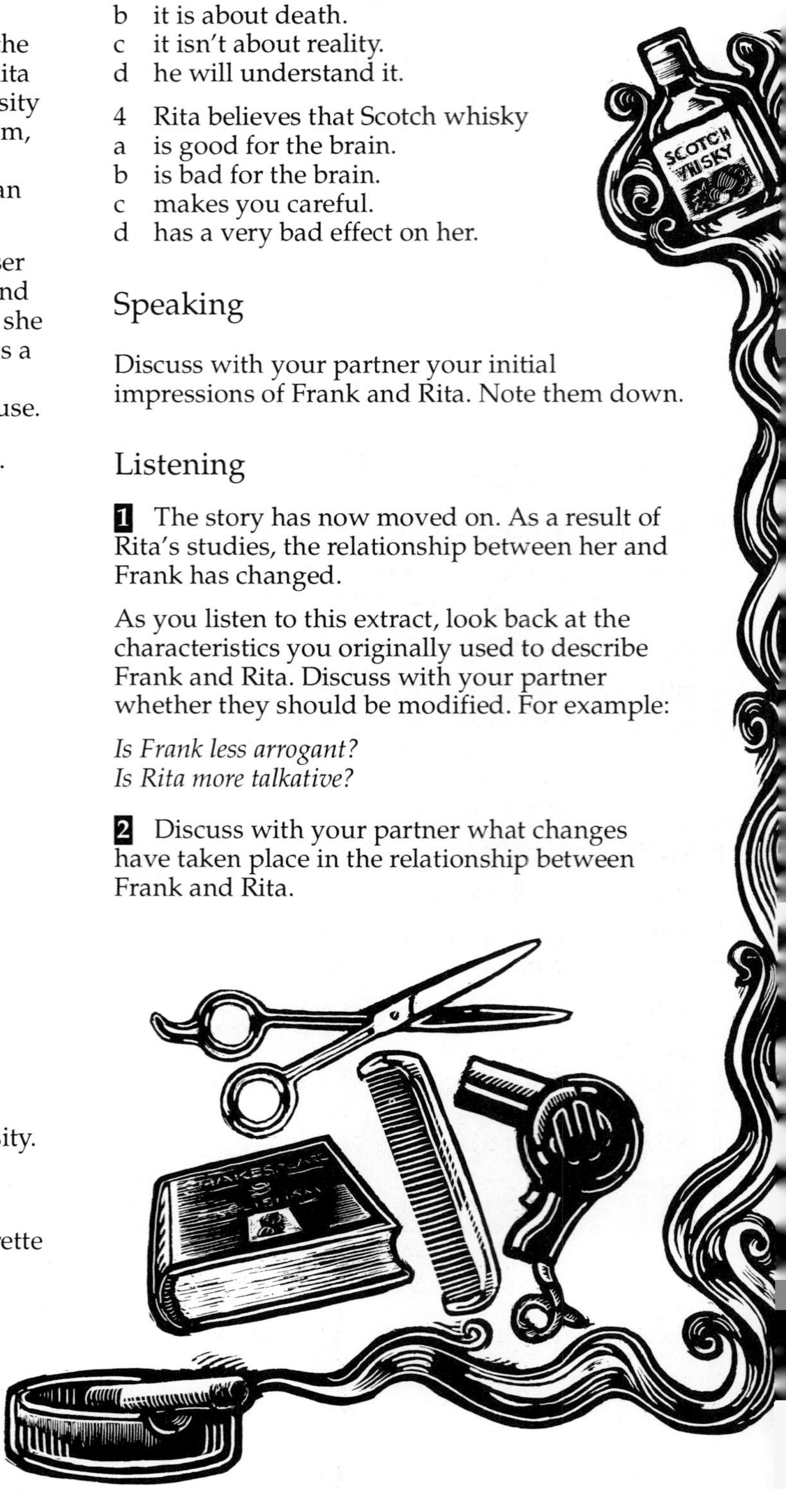

RITA I was dead surprised when they took me. I don't suppose they would have done if it'd been a proper university. The Open University's different though, isn't it?

FRANK I've – erm – not had much more experience of it than you. This is the first O.U. work I've done.

RITA D'y' need the money?

FRANK I do as a matter of fact.

RITA It's terrible these days, the money, isn't it? With the inflation an' that. You work for the ordinary university, don't y'? With the real students. The Open University's different, isn't it?

FRANK It's supposed to embrace a more comprehensive studentship, yes.

RITA (Inspecting a bookcase.) Degrees for dishwashers.

FRANK Would you – erm – like to sit down?

RITA No! Can I smoke? (She goes to her bag and rummages in it.)

FRANK Tobacco?

RITA Yeh. (She half-laughs.) Was that a joke? (She takes out a packet of cigarettes and a lighter.) Here – d' y' want one? (She takes out two cigarettes and dumps the packet on the desk.)

FRANK (After a pause.) Ah – I'd love one.

RITA Well, have one.

FRANK (After a pause.) I – don't smoke – I made a promise not to smoke.

RITA Well, I won't tell anyone.

FRANK Promise?
(As Frank goes to take the cigarette Rita whips it from his reach.)

RITA (Doing a Brownie salute.) On my oath as an ex-Brownie. (She gives him the cigarette.) I hate smokin' on me own. An' everyone seems to have packed up these days. (She lights the cigarettes.) They're all afraid of gettin' cancer.

FRANK (Looks dubiously at his cigarette.)

RITA But they're all cowards.

FRANK Are they?

RITA You've got to challenge death an' disease. I read this poem about fightin' death ...

FRANK Ah – Dylan Thomas ...

RITA No. Roger McGough. It was about this old man who runs away from hospital an' goes out on the ale. He gets pissed an' stands in the street shoutin' an' challengin' death to come out an' fight. It's dead good.

FRANK Yes. I don't think I know the actual piece you mean ...

RITA I'll bring y' the book – it's great.

FRANK Thank you.

RITA You probably won't think it's any good.

FRANK Why?

RITA It's the sort of poetry you can understand.

FRANK Ah. I see.

RITA (Begins looking idly round the room.)

FRANK Can I offer you a drink?

RITA What of?

FRANK Scotch?

RITA (Going to the bookcase.) Y'wanna be careful with that stuff, it kills y' brain cells.

FRANK But you'll have one? (He gets up and goes to the small table.)

RITA All right. It'll probably have a job findin' my brain.

FRANK (Pouring the drinks.) Water?

RITA (Looking at the bookcase.) Yeh, all right. (She takes a copy of 'Howards End' from the shelf.) What's this like? (Frank goes over to Rita, looks at the title of the book and then goes back to the drinks.)

FRANK 'Howards End'?

RITA Yeh. It sounds filthy, doesn't it? E. M.-Foster.

FRANK Forster.

RITA Oh. Yeh. What's it like?

FRANK Borrow it. Read it.

RITA Ta. I'll look after it. (She moves back towards the desk.) If I pack the course in I'll post it to y'.

3 As Frank's grip on his professional and domestic life is loosened by the effects of alcohol (his girlfriend walks out and his university superiors begin to question his behaviour) Rita's awareness and confidence grows. Frank has given her some of his own poems to read.

Listen to this final extract and complete each statement below.

1 An *allusion* is an
a idea based on fantasy.
b overt or implied reference to literature.

2 Mary Shelley
a had a child called Frankenstein.
b wrote a book about a scientist called Frankenstein.

3 Frank believes his poetry is so
a profound that Rita still cannot understand it.
b empty and shallow that nobody would want to read it.

4 Rita is angry with Frank because she feels that he
a hasn't taught her anything of value.
b can't accept that they are now equals.

5 Frank believes that Rita's new-found culture will make her a
a better person.
b different person, but no better.

Speaking

1 Rita says: *I've got a room full of books. I know what clothes to wear, what wines to buy, what plays to see, what papers to read.* Does this mean that she is cultured?

2 Discuss with your partner where you would place Frank and Rita on the scale of success and failure at the beginning of this Unit.

3 Comment on the relevance of *Educating Rita* to the quotation at the beginning of this Unit.

Use of English

Frankenstein is often alluded to when we want to say that something we have created is out of control. (In the original story, however, Frankenstein was the scientist, not the monster.) For example:

Nuclear power has become one of the Frankensteins of the twentieth century.

1 Look at the following literary figures and discuss in what contexts you would allude to them.

1 James Bond
2 Oedipus
3 Count Dracula
4 Cleopatra
5 Faust
6 Pinocchio
7 Casanova
8 The Godfather
9 Alice in Wonderland

2 Complete the following sentences by alluding to the most appropriate figure from the list above. Add any other words you think are necessary to make the sentences sound natural. For example:

The fact that he never married and lived at home until his mother died suggested he might have *had an Oedipus complex / been an Oedipus at heart.*

1 His sallow complexion, nocturnal habits and pointed teeth made me wonder whether … was the ideal landlord or not.
2 She may not be beautiful in the classical sense but her effect on men is … .
3 Just because he has some influence over local politicians doesn't make him … .
4 Suave, sophisticated, charming he may be but don't be taken in by … . He's actually a real coward.
5 She is so scatter-brained and illogical I am sure she would be happier living in … .
6 Don't believe a word he says, he tells more tall stories than … .
7 He may think he's … but how many of the girls listed in his address book has he actually gone out with?
8 I'm not prepared to … and sell my soul just to get a degree.

3 Choose three of the figures below and write sentences alluding to them. Compare your sentences with your partner's. Then think up allusions of your own.

Macchiavelli
Pythagoras
Sherlock Holmes
Joan of Arc
Einstein
Hercules
Robin Hood
Charlie Chaplin
Marilyn Monroe

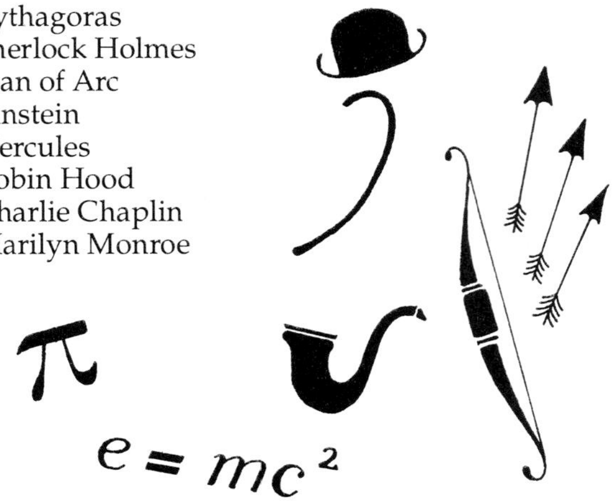

Reading

1 Read the poem *Musée des Beaux Arts* (Museum of Fine Arts) by W. H. Auden. In it he alludes to various paintings he has seen in an art gallery, all of which reflect an aspect of human behaviour.

2 Identify the parts of the poem that refer to different paintings. Discuss how many paintings are mentioned.

3 Read the poem again and decide which of the following statements best summarises it. Tick (✓) the appropriate box.

- ☐ The pleasures of visiting art galleries.
- ☐ The pain endured by human beings when they are suffering.
- ☐ The enjoyment of other people's suffering.
- ☐ The indifference to other people's suffering.
- ☐ The indifference of famous painters to suffering.

MUSÉE DES BEAUX ARTS

About suffering they were never wrong.
The Old Masters: how well they understood
Its human position; how it takes place
While someone else is eating or opening a window or just walking dully along;
How, when the aged are reverently, passionately waiting
For the miraculous birth, there always must be
Children who did not specially want it to happen, skating
On a pond at the edge of the wood:
They never forgot
That even the dreadful martyrdom must run its course
Anyhow in a corner, some untidy spot
Where the dogs go on with their doggy life and the torturer's horse
Scratches its innocent behind on a tree.

In Breughel's Icarus, for instance: how everything turns away
Quite leisurely from the disaster; the ploughman may
Have heard the splash, the forsaken cry,
But for him it was not an important failure; the sun shone
As it had to on the white legs disappearing into the green
Water; and the expensive delicate ship that must have seen
Something amazing, a boy falling out of the sky,
Had somewhere to get to and sailed calmly on.

4 According to legend, Icarus, the son of Daedalus, attempted to fly by attaching wings made of feathers to his arms with wax. As he flew near the sun, the wax melted and he fell into the sea and drowned.

Breughel's picture shows him disappearing into the water head first. In what other contexts would you allude to Icarus? Discuss with your partner where you would place Icarus on the success or failure scale at the beginning of this Unit.

5 Allusions do not necessarily have to refer to aspects of literature. They can also refer to other things which the writer assumes the reader will know.

Read the poem by a more modern writer, Wendy Cope.

6 Discuss the questions below with a partner.

1 What pictures do the allusions create in your minds?
2 Who are *they* in the last line?
3 Why is the poem called *Advertisement*?
4 How would you summarise the poem?

ADVERTISEMENT

The lady takes The Times and Vogue.
Wears Dior dresses. Gucci shoes.
Puts fresh-cut flowers round her room
And lots of carrots in her stews
A moss-green Volvo, morning walks.
And holidays in Guadeloupe;
Long winter evenings by the fire
With Proust and cream of carrot soup.
Raw carrots on a summer lawn.
Champagne, a Gioconda smile;
Glazed carrots in a silver dish
For Sunday lunch. They call it style.

Speaking

1 Look at the photographs of the two people. Discuss with your partner what they might have achieved and how they may have done so.

2 Read the passages below. Each relates to one of the photographs. Match the passage to the photograph and decide whether what you have read affects your opinion of the level of that person's success.

1 Life's been good to me so far. I've been on the road a long time, but it's what I like best – playing to my fans. My hearing is not what it was, but I'm certainly not going deaf and for a critic to remark that I've got Van Gogh's ear for music is absolutely out of order. I admit that I might have over-indulged on occasions, so I'm not as rich as some people think I am, but at the end of the day my rewards are in the creative field and not the material.

2 Glamorous, exotic, easy? You must be joking. You try posing at six o'clock in the morning when it's freezing cold just because the photographer wants the right light, and having to smile. It makes it even worse when he says my face has the Mona Lisa look. A Giaconda smile? Who is he trying to kid? Still, I've made enough money not to have to worry about whether or not I look enigmatic.

3 OK, so I'm no William Shakespeare. So what? When was the last time you saw a copy of *Hamlet* at the railway bookstall? My last book, what was it called now? I forget. Never mind, it's practically sold out all over the world. What with my refusal to pay taxes and generous donations to charity, I'm more like that other guy, you know the one. He lived in some big forest … .

Reading and writing

Some people measure success in terms of intellectual achievement. Other people measure it in terms of material possessions and will often go to any lengths to acquire what they desire.

In this extract from *Doctor Fischer in Geneva* by Graham Greene, Dr Fischer, who has become extremely rich by developing a special kind of toothpaste, invites people he knows to a party. He likes to give his guests expensive presents in return for their taking part in games. He has also invited Jones, who has recently married his estranged daughter.

1 Read this longer text as fast as you can, so that you follow the story even if you do not appreciate the detail at this stage. Then explain briefly what the story tells us about material success.

'Come in, Jones,' Doctor Fischer said. 'You can serve dinner as soon as it's ready, Albert.'

The table was laid with crystal glasses which caught the lights of a chandelier overhead: even the soup plates looked expensive. I wondered a little at seeing them there: it was hardly the season for cold soup. 'This is Jones, my son-in-law,' Doctor Fischer said. 'You must excuse his glove. It covers a deformity. Mrs Montgomery, Mr Kips, Monsieur Belmont, Mr Richard Deane, Divisionnaire Krueger.' I could feel the fumes of their hostility projected at me like tear-gas.

'I have met Monsieur Jones,' Belmont said as though he were a prosecution witness identifying the accused.

'Jones is a great linguist,' Doctor Fischer said. 'He translates letters about chocolates,' and I realized he must have made inquiries about me from my employers. 'Here, Jones, at our little parties we use English as our common language because Richard Deane, great star though he may be, speaks no other.'

Everyone laughed as though on cue except Deane who gave a mirthless smile. 'He has the qualities after a drink or two to play Falstaff except a lack of humour and a lack of weight.

'I always insist,' Doctor Fischer said, 'at my little parties that everybody enjoys himself.'

'They are a riot.' Mrs Montgomery said, 'a riot.'

'Doctor Fischer is invariably a very good host,' Divisionnaire Krueger informed me with condescension.

'And so generous,' Mrs Montgomery said. 'This necklace I'm wearing – it was a prize at our last party. There the prizes are,' Mrs Montgomery said. 'I helped him choose.' She went over to a side-table where I noticed now a pile of gift-wrapped parcels.

'Prizes for what?' I asked.

'Certainly not for intelligence,' Doctor Fischer said, 'or the Divisionnaire would never win anything.'

'All we have to do is just to put up with his little whims,' Mrs Montgomery explained, 'and then he distributes the prizes. There was one evening – can you believe it? – he served up live lobsters with bowls of boiling water. We had to catch and cook our own. One lobster nipped the General's finger.'

'I bear the scar still,' Divisionnaire Krueger complained.

'The only wound in action which he has ever received,' Doctor Fischer said.

'To the table then,' Doctor Fischer said, 'and I will explain to our new guest the purpose of my little parties, while Albert brings in the dinner.'

Albert entered carrying a silver tray on which there was a large pot of caviare and little silver dishes of egg and onion and sliced lemons.

'You will excuse Albert for serving me first,' Doctor Fischer said.

'I adore caviare,' Mrs Montgomery said. 'I could live on it.'

'You could afford to live on it if you were prepared to spend your own money.'

'I'm not such a rich woman as all that.'

'Why bother to lie to me? If you weren't as rich as you are, you would not be sitting at this table. I invite only the very rich.'

'What about Mr Jones?'

'He is here as an observer rather than as a guest, but of course, as he is my son-in-law, he may imagine he has great expectations. Expectations too are a form of wealth. Albert, the bibs.'

For the first time I noticed that there were no napkins by our places. Albert was fastening a bib round Mrs Montgomery's neck. She gave a squeal of pleasure. 'Ecrevisses! I love écrevisses.'

'Ah, here is your dinner, so I can now begin my own.'

Mrs Montgomery gave a high shriek. ▸

◂ 'Why, this is porridge, cold porridge.'
'Real Scotch porridge. You should appreciate it, with your Scotch name.' Doctor Fischer gave himself a helping of caviare and poured himself out a glass of vodka.
'It will destroy all our appetite,' Deane said.
'Don't be afraid of that. There is nothing to follow.'
'This is going too far, Doctor Fischer,' Mrs Montgomery said. 'Cold porridge. Why, it's totally inedible.'
'Don't eat it then. Don't eat it, Mrs Montgomery. By the rules you will only lose your little present. To tell you the truth I ordered porridge especially for Jones. I had thought of some partridges, but how could he manage with one hand?'
To my astonishment I saw that the Divisionnaire and Richard Deane had begun to eat and Mr Kips had at least picked up his spoon.
'If we could have a little sugar,' Belmont said, 'it might perhaps help.'
'I understand that the Welsh – no, no, I remember, Jones, I mean the Scots – consider it a blasphemy to spoil their porridge with sugar. They even eat it, I am told, with salt. Offer the gentlemen salt, Albert. Mrs Montgomery has decided to go hungry.'
'Oh no, I won't ruin your little joke, Doctor Fischer. Give me the salt. It can't make the porridge any worse than it is.'
Within a minute or two to my wonder they were all eating in silence and with a grim intensity. Perhaps the porridge clogged their tongues. 'You don't attempt yours, Jones?' Doctor Fischer asked me and he helped himself to a little more caviare.
'I'm not hungry enough.'
'Nor rich enough,' Doctor Fischer said. 'For several years now I have been studying the greediness of the rich. The presents I hand out when the dinner is over they could easily afford to give themselves, but then they would have earned them if only by signing a cheque. The rich hate signing cheques. Hence the success of credit cards. One card takes the place of a hundred cheques. They'll do anything to get their presents for nothing. This is one of the hardest tests I've submitted them to yet, and look how quickly they are eating up their cold porridge, so that the time for the presents will arrive. You, I am afraid, will get nothing, if you don't eat.'
'I have something of more value than your present waiting for me at home.'
'Very gallantly put,' Doctor Fischer said, 'but don't be too confident. Women don't always wait. I doubt if a missing hand aids romance.
'Why do you do it?' I asked.
'Why should I tell you? You are not one of us. You never will be. Don't count on your expectations from me.'
'I don't.'
'You have a poor man's pride, I see. After all, why shouldn't I tell you? You are a sort of son. I want to discover, Jones, if the greed of our rich friends has any limit. If there's a "Thus far and no further." If a day will come when they'll refuse to earn their presents. Their greed certainly isn't limited by pride.'

2 Read the passage again. Then decide whether each statement 1 – 9 is true or false.

1 Jones wears a glove because he has something wrong with his hand.
2 Falstaff is a character who is neither fat nor funny.
3 Mrs Montgomery obviously does not enjoy Dr Fischer's parties.
4 The phrase *little whims* means unusual behaviour.
5 *Porridge* is a filling Scottish dish that is eaten hot and is unpleasant to eat when cold.
6 Dr Fischer really wanted to serve partridges but felt that Jones would be unable to eat them.
7 Dr Fischer believes that rich people are rarely greedy.
8 Graham Greene wants to show how corrupting materialism can be.
9 Jones is a frequent guest at Dr Fischer's parties.

3 In the passage the writer does not always express his ideas in an explicit way, so that the meaning is immediately obvious. The reader must infer the meaning from the context. For example:

It was hardly the season for cold soup implies that the weather was cold.
As though he were a prosecution witness identifying the accused suggests that Belmont had a low opinion of Jones.

Complete the following sentences in the same way.

1 *Jones is a great linguist, … he translates letters about chocolates* implies that Dr Fischer …
2 *The Divisionnaire would never win anything* implies that …
3 *The only wound in action he ever received* suggests that …
4 *As he is my son-in-law he may imagine he has great expectations* implies that …
5 *I'm not hungry enough* implies that Jones …
6 *I have something of more value than your present waiting for me at home* implies that Jones …

4 Which of the following comments is relevant to this passage? Tick (✓) the appropriate boxes. Discuss the reasons for your choice with a partner.

☐ It exposes a truth about human nature.
☐ It tests the reader's credulity.
☐ Dr Fischer acts like a crazy puppet master.
☐ It is cynical rather than satirical.
☐ Nobody would behave like that.

Use of English

1 Read the extract again and complete each of the following sentences in an appropriate way. You will need to use more than one word.

1 When Jones arrived, he … to the other guests.
2 Mr Belmont said that … Monsieur Jones.
3 Mrs Montgomery … briefly.
4 Dr Fischer insisted that everyone … at his little parties.
5 On one occasion the general's finger … by a lobster.
6 When Albert entered carrying a large pot of caviare, Mrs Montgomery … be served some.
7 Belmont asked … little sugar.
8 Dr Fischer claimed that the success of credit cards … signing cheques.
9 He also believed that he … a harder test.

2 Summarise (in 70 – 100 words) the events leading up to the guests eating the porridge.

Listening and speaking

1 It is often very difficult to express true feelings after achieving success or when coming to terms with failure. Because of this, people tend to rely on received expressions, words they have heard used frequently in similar situations. These often become clichés. Examples of this are two expressions which have been used so often by sports personalities when asked on TV how they felt after winning or losing a match that they are now treated as a joke. They are:

I was over the moon.
I was as sick as a parrot.

There is, however, a wide range of language available. It is just not always easy to recall it on the spur of the moment or to choose the appropriate phrase.

Listen to different people talking about their success. Match expressions a – h with speakers 1 – 8.

1 an actress
2 a learner driver
3 a politician
4 a tennis player
5 a violinist
6 a person accused of a crime
7 a TV game show winner
8 a person who has just sold his house at a profit

a I was ecstatic.
b I was so glad – and not just for me.
c It was a magnificent triumph.
d I was shattered but well pleased.
e I can't believe it.
f It was OK – well that's a bit of an understatement.
g I was absolutely delighted.
h I was quite thrilled.

2 Listen to the extracts again. Note down other expressions which are used to describe feelings of success.

3 Work with a partner. Look at the two photographs and take it in turns to describe the event, the setting and the people. Then discuss what each of the successful people might say in that situation.

4 Continue to work with your partner and look at the symbols of success. Decide which you think are the most and the least significant. Discuss what other symbols of success you would like to acquire.

Reading

Read the extract opposite from *When Greek meets Greek* by Graham Greene. Complete each statement 1 – 5 in the most appropriate way.

1 Miss Fennick thinks that Mr Priskett is
a very clever.
b cleverer than her uncle.
c very surprising.
d not very clever.

2 A *swindle* is
a a type of college.
b an advertising slogan.
c a way of making money illegally.
d a statement checked by a lawyer.

3 The examinations have to be simple because
a the tutors have no time to mark the papers.
b the students are not intelligent.
c subjects like economics and classics are very difficult.
d students who fail get their money back.

4 To get a degree, the students will have to study
a at Oxford.
b for three years.
c in a public library.
d for a shorter time than is normal.

5 The main purpose of St Ambrose's College is to
a make money.
b provide an education for soldiers.
c carry out research.
d carry on the traditions of Oxford University.

Vocabulary development

Complete the sentences by choosing the most appropriate item a – d.

1 Martin Kingsley's latest novel has been … as a masterpiece.
a claimed b acclaimed c merited
d criticised

2 As a high-powered executive, Sophie Roddick sometimes finds her job … .
a ambitious b achieving c stressful
d distressed

3 My main … for going to university is that it will improve my employment prospects.
a function b opportunity c decision
d motive

4 Although Frank can be … at times, he is also very sarcastic.
a irony b sceptic c witty d septic

5 Doctors warned him that alcohol was seriously … his judgement.
a affecting b effecting c preventing
d enhancing

6 Only through reading can students become more culturally … .
a knowing b taught c capable
d aware

7 The icy weather gradually … its grip as the temperature started to rise.
a tautened b undid c loosened
d tightened

8 The Captain gives the impression he is well-educated, but really it is just an … .
a allusion b imagination c affection
d illusion

9 John Keats often … to Greek mythology in his poetry.
a alluded b elided c dreamed
d related

10 Sam was strangely lacking in emotions and felt … to the suffering of other people.
a different b indifferent c unaware
d sympathy

11 Wendy Cope … that you did not necessarily acquire style just by wearing Gucci shoes.
a inferred b implied c induced
d expressed

12 Oscar Wilde received an … reception when a huge crowd waited to greet him on his arrival in New York.
a erratic b erotic c exotic
d ecstatic

13 Thoughts of failure … on Dylan's mind.
a prayed b preyed c probed
d pried

14 To say that Einstein was good at maths somewhat … his abilities.
a portrays b describes c understates
d undergoes

15 The reader may not … understand what Dr Fischer's motives are.
a rather b quiet c quite d hardly

'And what do you think of the college, Miss Fennick?'
'I think it's a good idea. I'm surprised my uncle thought of it.'
'In a way it was partly my idea.'
'I'm more surprised still,' the girl said firmly.
Mr Priskett, folding his hands in front of his white coat as though he were pleading before a tribunal, went on: 'You see, I said to your uncle that with all these colleges being taken over by the military and the tutors having nothing to do they ought to start teaching by correspondence.'
'Of course,' Mr Priskett pleaded, 'I hadn't thought of all this – the common-room, I mean, and St Ambrose's.'
'My niece,' Mr Fennick said, 'knows very little of the set-up.' He began to move restlessly around the room touching things with his hand. The girl said briskly, 'As I see it, Uncle is running a swindle called St Ambrose's College, Oxford.'
'Not a swindle, my dear. The advertisement was very carefully worded.' He knew it by heart: every phrase had been carefully checked with his copy of *Every Man His Own Lawyer* open on the table. He repeated it now.
'Degree-diplomas will be granted at the end of three terms instead of the usual three years.' He explained, 'That gives a quick turnover. One can't wait for money these days. *Gain a real Oxford education at Tom Brown's old college. For full particulars of tuition fees, battels etc., write to the Bursar.'*
'And do you mean to say the University can't stop that?'
'Anybody,' Mr Fennick said with a kind of pride, 'can start a college anywhere. I've never said it was part of the University.'
'But *battels* mean board and lodgings.'
'In this case,' Mr Fennick said, 'it's quite a normal fee to keep your name in perpetuity on the books of the old firm – I mean the college.'
'And the tuition ...'
'Priskett here is the science tutor. I take history and classics. I thought that you, my dear, might tackle economics?'
'I don't know anything about them.'
'The examinations, of course, have to be rather simple – within the capacity of the tutors. (There is an excellent public library here.) And another thing the fees are returnable if the degree-diploma is not granted. Nobody will ever fail,' Mr Priskett brought breathlessly out with scared excitement.

Writing

In the Proficiency examination you may be asked to write a description of a person, either real or imaginary, who has particular qualities. You will be assessed on how well you communicate to the examiner what this person is really like and how well you bring the character to life.

1 Look back through the Unit and choose a person from the texts (such as Frank, Rita or Dr Fischer). Who do you think has been successfully brought to life? Discuss with your partner the reasons for your choice.

2 Describe a person, either real or imaginary, who you consider to be a success. (Use about 350 words.)

When you write your description, you need to consider the following points:

1 Choose a person who you know you have enough material on before you start writing. Remember that the suggested number of words, either 300 or 350, should be thought of as the minimum not the maximum.

2 Organise your composition. Think carefully about paragraphing: start a new paragraph when you start to describe a different aspect of the person. For example:

Paragraph 1: introduction – a general description of physical and personal characteristics.
Paragraph 2: an objective description of what makes this person special when compared to other people.
Paragraph 3: a subjective description of what particularly appeals to you about this person.
Paragraph 4: a more critical look at these aspects of this person.
Paragraph 5: a conclusion and final assessment summarising the points that have been made.

3 Make sure that the type of language you use is consistent. Do not begin the composition in a formal way and then switch to an informal style.

4 Always read through what you have written in a positive but critical way, not only checking for language errors but also thinking about the composition as a whole. Make sure that your ideas link up and that you have connected them appropriately.

5 Check very carefully that there are no basic errors in the opening sentences as these are likely to make the strongest impression on the examiner.

STARRING .....

A good book is the best of friends.

Martin Tupper

Speaking

1 Discuss with a partner your attitude towards books. Use the questionnaire to help you.

2 What conclusions can you draw about your partner's attitude towards books and reading?

1 Why do you read?

☐ For pleasure.
☐ For information.
☐ To improve your level of education.
☐ For any other reason. Please give details. ....

2 Given the choice, which would you read?

☐ A novel.
☐ A non-fiction book.
☐ A magazine.
☐ A newspaper.
☐ A technical journal.
☐ Another type of reading material. Please give details. ....

3 When are you most likely to read?

☐ Early morning.
☐ Morning.
☐ Lunchtime.
☐ Afternoon.
☐ Evening.
☐ Night.
☐ Weekend.
☐ On holiday.

4 During your leisure time which of these activities are you most likely (✓) or least likely (✗) to do?

☐ Reading.
☐ Watching TV.
☐ Going out to the cinema or theatre.
☐ Eating in a restaurant.
☐ Going to a disco.
☐ Taking exercise/doing some sporting activity.
☐ Playing a game such as chess or Trivial Pursuits.

3 Evaluating a novel entails thinking about both the form (the way it is written) and the substance (what it is about).

Look at the list of literary features below and discuss with your partner which factors relate to:

a substance.
b form.
c a combination of the two.

- ☐ a well thought-out plot
- ☐ believable characters
- ☐ colourful description
- ☐ an underlying message or moral
- ☐ a happy ending
- ☐ clearly sequenced prose
- ☐ density: easy or difficult to understand when read only once
- ☐ sophisticated vocabulary
- ☐ complex use of language
- ☐ innovation: different from other books within the same genre
- ☐ interesting setting: enables the reader to identify with different times, people and places
- ☐ human interest: related to personal experience
- ☐ universal relevance both for the present and future
- ☐ appeal: appeals to different age groups

4 Look at the list again. Discuss which factors you consider important when analysing whether or not a text is well written. Give each a number according to the scale below.

Not important	←→				Important
0	1	2	3	4	5

5 We often say that a book was 'a good read' if it contained some or all of the features you have just considered, but what makes a good film? List the criteria you use when evaluating a film, video or TV programme. Compare your list with a partner's.

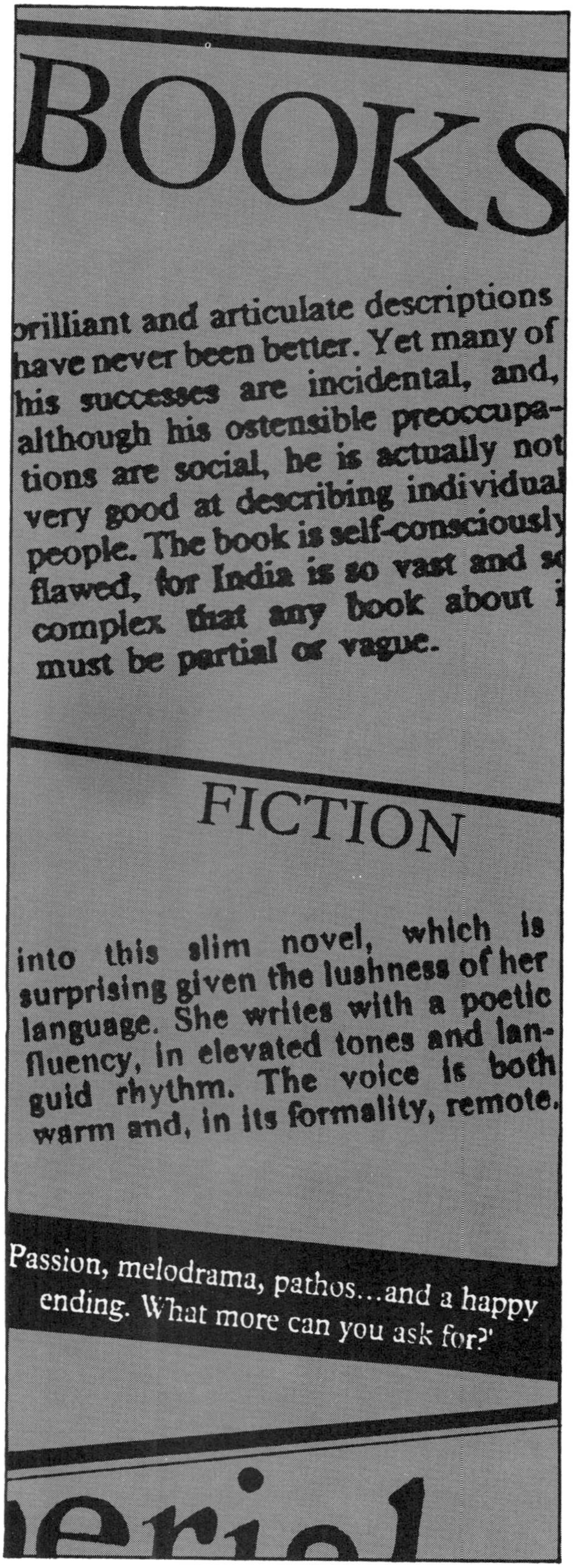

Reading and speaking

You are now going to compare and evaluate two extracts written in very different styles: The first from the novel *Brideshead Revisited* by Evelyn Waugh; the second from an American short story by the Nobel Prize for Literature winner, Saul Bellow. To prepare for this, read and check your comprehension of each text by completing the exercise that goes with it.

1 First, read and check your understanding of the vocabulary in the extract from *Brideshead Revisited*.

Find the words in the text that mean the same as each of the items below.

1 not to be entered or interfered with
2 strange or unusual behaviour
3 brave because there is an element of risk
4 walking without lifting your feet
5 how something is done so as not to be seen
6 how something is said so as to sound sulky and childish
7 not careful
8 happy, probably because of someone else's misfortune
9 not straight or at an odd angle
10 inappropriate in the circumstances

2 Now check your understanding of the text. Read the following statements and decide if they are true or false.

1 Charles receives no money from his father when he is studying at university.
2 His father is an archaeologist.
3 His father refuses to lend him any money because he cannot afford to.
4 Charles's relationship with his father could be described as respectful but lacking in affection.
5 Charles wants to smoke a cigar in order to annoy his father.
6 Charles's father tries very hard to persuade him to stay at home.
7 Cousin Melchior was not a very successful businessman.
8 The book his father was reading during dinner was a humorous one.
9 Charles's financial difficulties seem to amuse his father.

I returned home for the Long Vacation without plans and without money. My last cheque overdrew my account, and I had been told that, without my father's authority, I must draw no more. My next allowance was not due until October. I was thus faced with a bleak prospect and, turning the matter over in my mind, I felt something not far off remorse for the prodigality of the preceding weeks.

My father, I knew, was in the house, but his library was inviolable, and it was not until just before dinner that he appeared to greet me. He was then in his late fifties, but it was his idiosyncrasy to seem much older than his years; to see him one might have put him at seventy, to hear him speak at nearly eighty. He came to me now, with the shuffling, mandarin-tread which he affected, and a shy smile of welcome. When he dined at home – and he seldom dined elsewhere – he wore a frogged velvet smoking suit of the kind which had been fashionable many years before and was to be so again, but, at that time, was a deliberate archaism.

'My dear boy, they never told me you were here. Did you have a very exhausting journey? They gave you tea? You are well? I have just made a somewhat audacious purchase from Sonerschein's – a terracotta bull of the fifth century. I was examining it and forgot your arrival. Was the carriage very full? You had a corner seat?' (He travelled so rarely himself that to hear of others doing so always excited his solicitude.) 'Hayter brought you the evening paper? There is no news, of course – such a lot of nonsense.'

Dinner was announced. My father from long habit took a book with him to the table and then, remembering my presence, furtively dropped it under his chair. 'What do you like to drink? Hayter, what have we for Mr Charles to drink?'

'There's some whisky.'

'There's whisky. Perhaps you like something else? What else have we?'

'There isn't anything else in the house, sir.'

'There's nothing else. You must tell Hayter what you would like and he will get it in. You are here for long?'

'I'm not quite sure, Father.'

'It's a very long vacation,' he said wistfully. 'In my day we used to go on what were called reading parties, always in mountainous areas. Why? Why,' he repeated petulantly, 'should alpine scenery be thought conducive to study?'

'I thought of putting in some time at an art school – in the life class.'

'My dear boy, you'll find them all shut. The students go to Barbizon or such places and paint in the open air. There was an institution in my day called a "sketching club" – mixed sexes' (snuffle), 'bicycles' (snuffle), 'pepper-and-salt knickerbockers, holland umbrellas, and, it was popularly thought, free love' (snuffle), 'such a lot of nonsense. I expect they still go on. You might try that.'

'One of the problems of the vacation is money, Father.'

'Oh, I shouldn't worry about a thing like that at your age.'

'You see, I've run rather short.'

'Yes?' said my father without any sound of interest.

'In fact I don't quite know how I'm going to get through the next two months.'

'Well, I'm the worst person to come to for advice. I've never been 'short' as you so painfully call it. And yet what else could you say? Hard up? Penurious? Distressed? Embarrassed? Stoney-broke?' (snuffle). 'On the rocks? In Queer Street? Let us say you are in Queer Street and leave it at that.'

'Then what do you suggest my doing?'

'Your cousin Melchior was imprudent with his investments and got into a very queer street. He went to Australia.'

I had not seen my father so gleeful since he found two pages of second-century papyrus between the leaves of a Lombardic breviary.

'Hayter, I've dropped my book.'

It was recovered for him from under his feet and propped against the épergne. For the rest of the dinner he was silent save for an occasional snuffle of merriment which could not, I thought, be provoked by the work he read.

Presently we left the table and sat in the garden-room; and there, plainly, he put me out of his mind; his thoughts, I knew, were far away, in those distant ages where he moved at ease, where time passed in centuries and all the figures were defaced and the names of his companions were corrupt readings of words of quite other meaning. He sat in an attitude which to anyone else would have been one of extreme discomfort, askew in his upright armchair, with his book held high and obliquely to the light. Now and then he took a gold pencil-case from his watch-chain and made an entry in the margin. The windows were open to the summer night; the ticking of the clocks, the distant murmur of traffic on the Bayswater Road, and my father's regular turning of the pages were the only sounds. I had thought it impolitic to smoke a cigar while pleading poverty; now in desperation I went to my room and fetched one. My father did not look up. I pierced it, lit it, and with renewed confidence said, 'Father, you surely don't want me to spend the whole vacation here with you?'

'Eh?'

'Won't you find it rather a bore having me at home for so long?'

'I trust I should not betray such an emotion even if I felt it,' said my father mildly and turned back to his book.

3 Now read the extract from *The Old System* by Saul Bellow. Complete the statements in the most appropriate way.

1 Dr Braun lay in bed because
a it was dark and cold.
b his thoughts depressed him.
c he was deep in thought.
d he had nothing special to do.

2 While washing and eating, he was
a lost in thought.
b absorbed in what he was doing.
c overcome by sensuality.
d self-aware.

3 He … contemporary attitudes towards life.
a was critical of
b deeply disliked
c was amused by
d had learnt a lot from

4 While Isaac was alive, Dr Braun
a had an affair with Tina.
b refused to talk to him about his work.
c did not realise that he loved him.
d relied on him for stability.

5 Dr Braun was
a rational and unfeeling.
b modest but rather unstable.
c loving but unfaithful.
d emotional and irrational.

4 Read both texts again. Consider the style and quality of each text by finding two similarities and two differences between them.

Speaking

1 With a partner, come to some conclusions about the ways both texts were written, using the criteria for judging literature that you have already discussed. Explain which text you prefer and why.

2 Discuss the reasons why you would or would not wish to continue reading the books in which these passages appear.

It was a thoughtful day for Dr Braun. Winter. Saturday. The short end of December. He was alone in his apartment and woke late, lying in bed until noon, in the room kept very dark, working with a thought – a feeling: Now you see it, now you don't. Now a content, now a vacancy. Now an important individual, a force, a necessary existence; suddenly nothing. A frame without a picture, a mirror with missing glass. The feeling of necessary existence might be the agressive, instinctive vitality we share with a dog or an ape. The difference being in the power of the mind or spirit to declare *I am*. Plus the inevitable inference *I am not*. Dr Braun was no more pleased with being than with its opposite. For him an age of equilibrium seemed to be coming in. How nice! Anyway, he had no project for putting the world in rational order, and for no special reason he got up. Washed his wrinkled but not elderly face with freezing tap water, which changed the nighttime white to a more agreeable color. He brushed his teeth. Standing upright, scrubbing the teeth as if he were looking after an idol. He then ran the big old-fashioned tub to sponge himself, backing into the thick stream of the Roman faucet, soaping beneath with the same cake of soap he would apply later to his beard. Under the swell of his belly, the tip of his parts, somewhere between his heels. His heels needed scrubbing. He dried himself with yesterday's shirt, an economy. It was going to the laundry anyway. Yes, with the self-respecting expression human beings inherit from ancestors for whom bathing was a solemnity. A sadness.

But every civilized man today cultivated an unhealthy self-detachment. Had learned from art the art of amusing self-observation and objectivity. Which, since there had to be something amusing to watch, required art in one's conduct. Existence for the sake of such practices did not seem worth while. Mankind was in a confusing, uncomfortable, disagreeable stage in the evolution of its consciousness.

He opened a fresh can of coffee, much enjoyed the fragrance from the punctured can. Only an instant, but not to be missed. Next he sliced bread for the toaster, got out the butter, chewed an orange; and he was admiring long icicles on the huge red, circular roof tank of the laundry across the alley, the clear sky, when he discovered that a sentiment was approaching. It was said of him, occasionally, that he did not love anyone. This was not true. He did not love anyone steadily. But unsteadily he loved, he guessed, at an average rate.

The sentiment, as he drank his coffee, was for two cousins in upstate New York, the Mohawk Valley. They were dead. Isaac Braun and his sister Tina. Tina was first to go. Two years later, Isaac died. Braun now discovered that he and Cousin Isaac had loved each other. For whatever use or meaning this fact might have within the peculiar system of light, movement, contact, and perishing in which he tried to find stability. Toward Tina, Dr Braun's feelings were less clear. More passionate once, but at present more detached.

Isaac's wife, after he died, had told Braun, 'He was proud of you. He said, "Sammy has been written up in *Time*, in all the papers, for his research. But he never says a word about his scientific reputation!"'

'I see. Well, computers do the work, actually.'

'But you have to know what to put into these computers.'

This was more or less the case. But Braun had not continued the conversation. He did not care much for being *first* in his field. People were boastful in America. Matthew Arnold, a not entirely appetizing figure himself, had correctly observed this in the US. Dr Braun thought this native American boastfulness had aggravated a certain weakness in Jewish immigrants. But a proportionate reaction of self-effacement was not praiseworthy. Dr Braun did not want to be interested in this question at all. However, his cousin Isaac's opinions had some value for him.

Use of English

1 Look at the structures below which are taken from the texts you have just read.

I thought of putting in some time at an art school.
Then what do you suggest my doing?
Bathing was a solemnity.
Tina was first to go.
To see him one might have put him at about seventy.

In each of these examples, the main verb is followed by another verb in either the *-ing* form or the infinitive. In order to make the correct choice between these two forms, it is important to understand what basic functions within a sentence these verb forms perform. There are some general rules to guide you.

1 *He gave up studying medicine.*
He got out of working for Mr Gradgrind.
She put up with him (his) complaining constantly.

In these examples, the *-ing* form has the same quality as and could be replaced by a noun which forms the object of the main verb:

He gave up his medical studies.
He got out of his job for Mr Gradgrind.
She put up with his constant complaints.

If a verb acts as the object of a two- or three-word verb it will always be in the *-ing* form.

2 *Everyone dreads meeting the tax inspector.*
Ken Dodd avoided paying tax, which is legal.
Lester Piggott evaded paying tax, which is illegal.

In these examples, the *-ing* form can be replaced by a noun.

Everyone dreads a meeting with the tax inspector.
Ken Dodd avoided the payment of tax.
Lester Piggott evaded the payment of tax.

Certain verbs are always followed by the *-ing* form of the verb. For a list of these verbs and further practice, see the back of this book.

2 Replace the words in italics with an appropriate verb form and any other words that may be necessary.

1 Imelda denied *the theft of* the shoes.
2 I consider *your sudden departure* to be of the utmost concern.
3 Donald risked *his life* when saving his child.
4 Gabrielle finished *her interrogation of* the suspect.
5 Gerald avoided *the judge's stare* by looking at the ground.

3 When the *-ing* form of the verb acts as a noun it can also be used as the subject of the sentence. For example:

Paying tax is a legal requirement.
Going abroad is the only way to escape the long arm of the law.

Rewrite each sentence below replacing the noun that is the subject with an *-ing* form or vice versa.

1 Disposal of nuclear waste is a critical factor in this cost analysis.
2 Condemning the President's actions was dangerous but unavoidable.
3 Deciding what action to take caused George considerable stress.
4 The admission that a gross error has been made will be the only way to satisfy the electorate.
5 Resigning gracefully was the only option open to Ken in the circumstances.

4 When the *-ing* form is the subject of a sentence, it often can be replaced by the infinitive form without any significant change in meaning. For example:

To retire was Ken Dodd's only solution. To pay tax is a legal requirement.

Alternatively the sentence can be transformed so that a verb form no longer acts as the subject of the sentence. For example:

All Ken Dodd could do in the circumstances was to retire. There is a legal requirement to pay tax.

Reading

1 Complete each of the sayings below with the most appropriate ending.

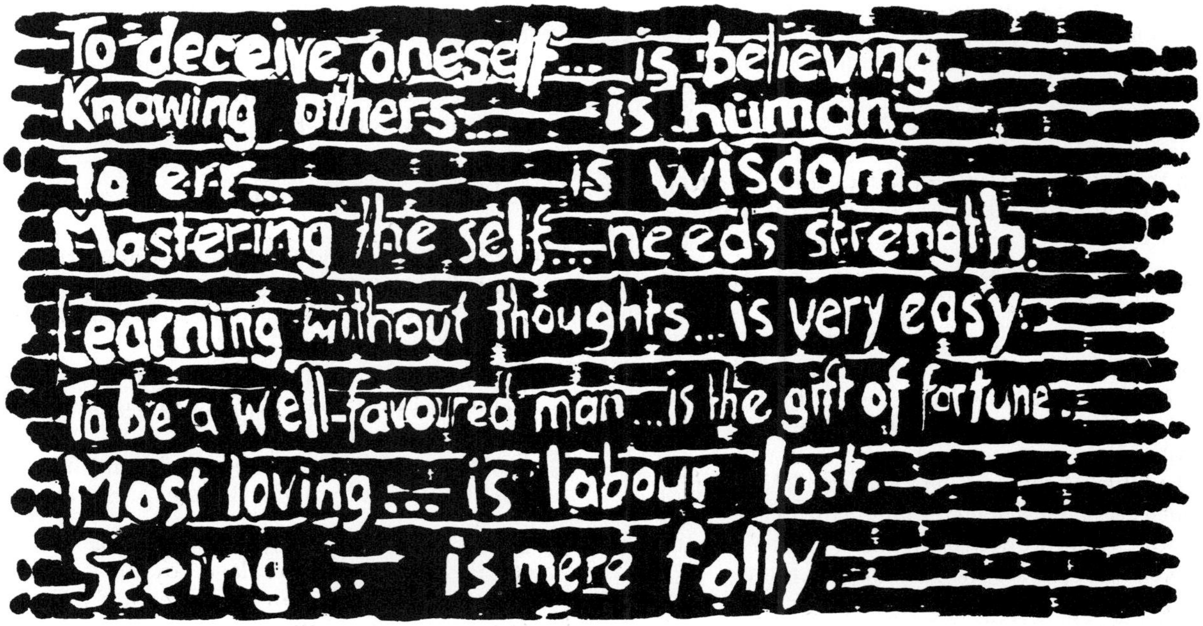

2 Compare your completed sayings with your partner and discuss what point is being made in each of them.

3 Each of the sayings contains either a gerund or an infinitive. If the gerund was changed into an infinitive or the infinitive into a gerund:

1 would the sentence still be grammatically correct?
2 if correct, would the meaning change?

Discuss your conclusions with your partner.

Use of English

1 The *-ing* form also performs the function of describing an action which is linked to or follows the main verb. In this case it cannot be replaced by a noun because it does not form the object of the main verb. For example:

He wrote me this note saying he could come.

In this example, the objects of the verb are *me* and *note*. *Saying* introduces what *he wrote.*

2 When there is a distinct separation between two actions, however, the verb which follows the main verb will usually be in the infinitive. In this structure, the main verb often refers to a state of mind or an action involving a decision. For a list and further practice, see the back of this book.

You were supposed to commit suicide.
Frank refused to publish his poems.
Rita hoped to graduate.
Dr Fischer threatened not to give his guests a present.

3 In other instances, the second action is, conceptually, either linked to or separate from the first action. In these cases, the choice of whether to use the *-ing* form or the infinitive will depend on the meaning.

She stopped to read the map.
(First she stopped, then she read.)
She stopped reading the map.
(The actions are simultaneous.)

Alice tried to protest but the Queen interrupted her.
(She made an attempt to protest but was prevented from doing so. The action was started but not completed.)
Alice tried protesting but the Queen wouldn't listen.
(Alice protested. The actions were completed although their aim was not fulfilled.)

The Governors regret to inform you that your son has been expelled from the school.
(They are sorry that they have to give this information. When used in this sense, the verb is usually in the present tense.)
He regretted leaving / having left the fencing equipment on the train.
(He felt sorry later about the mistake he had made.)
You may not think so now, but you will regret not completing your education.
(In the future you will look back and feel sorry about something that you failed to do in the past.)

Nick remembered to invite Jay to the party but he decided not to come.
(Jay received the invitation but declined it.)
Nick didn't remember inviting Miss Baker to the party despite her being there.
(Miss Baker came to the party even though she probably hadn't received an invitation.)
When Cooper regained consciousness, he couldn't remember being shot by the long-haired man.
(Cooper's mind had gone blank and as a result he could not recall the shooting incident.)

4 There are instances where the verb describing the action which occurs in relation to the main verb can be either in the *-ing* form or in the infinitive.The actions, conceptually, can either be linked using the *-ing* form or separated using the infinitive and there is little or no difference in meaning.

He wrote saying he could come.
He wrote to say he could come.

Gatsby began throwing a pile of shirts.
Gatsby began to throw a pile of shirts.

Daisy began to cry.
Daisy began crying.

5 Complete the following sentences with an appropriate verb form.

1 Donna regretted ... Laura's diary when she realised how personal the entries were.
2 Tom would not have been so ill if only he had stopped ... .
3 Mr Wilson recognised Daisy because he remembered ... her at his garage the previous week.
4 Sisyphus tried ... the stone up to the top of the hill but as soon as he got to the steepest part it rolled down again.
5 I regret ... that I find your conduct absolutely deplorable.
6 Lucy stopped ... the letter her boss had dictated and re-read the advertisement which would transport her to the island of dreams.
7 In desperation, Sophie tried ... every doorbell in the block but not one person bothered to answer.
8 Although she was chronically absent-minded, Aunt Agatha always remembered ... a present for Bertie on his birthday.

Vocabulary development

Charles Ryder's father uses many different expressions to describe being short of money. Some of them are more formal than others and some are very rarely used nowadays.

hard up, penurious, distressed, embarrassed, stoney-broke, on the rocks, in Queer Street.

1 Discuss with your partner what point he was making to his son by using these expressions.

2 Discuss which of them you would use in a personal conversation.

3 Decide which of them can be used formally.

4 Look at the groups of expressions about people below. In each group, one of the expressions is different in meaning. Decide which is the odd one out.

1 *short of money:*
in the red, skint, in hock, cashiered, strapped for cash.
2 *wealthy:*
rolling in it, loaded, well-heeled, well-off, cashed up.
3 *emotional:*
touchy, highly strung, sensitive, nervy, eclectic.
4 *unemotional:*
dispassionate, detached, disinterested, unmoved, poker-faced.
5 *hypocritical:*
two-faced, full of cant, fork-tongued, unequivocal, Machiavellian.
6 *unusual* or *abnormal:*
assymetric, off-the-wall, freaky, unique, eccentric.
7 *immoral:*
unethical, depraved, despicable, destitute, unprincipled.
8 *shy:*
retiring, private, hermit-like, inanimate, solitary.
9 *ignored* or *rejected:*
ostracised, blackballed, given the cold shoulder, cut dead, prescribed.
10 *highly intelligent:*
more than half-bright, brilliant, not stupid, swollen-headed, quick(-thinking).
11 *unintelligent:*
dense, moronic, thick, feather-brained, dim-witted, bland.

Speaking

1 We often use synonyms when we partly agree with what someone has said but feel it should be modified in some way, because the language is either too intense or not intense enough. For example:

Andrew Lloyd Webber is absolutely rolling in it.
I wouldn't say that exactly, but he's certainly pretty well-off.
Greta Garbo was supposed to have been rather retiring.
I'd have said she was absolutely hermit-like.

Remember that *quite* can be used as an intensifier or as a modifier, depending on the word it collocates with.

If this word has an absolute sense, *quite* intensifies its meaning: *quite appalling, quite right, quite ridiculous.*

If the word can be used to differing degrees, *quite* modifies its meaning:
quite intelligent, quite friendly, quite nasty.

Complete conversations 1 – 5 in a similar way. Choose appropriate modifiers and intensifiers from the lists below.

modifiers	intensifiers
pretty	*intensely*
somewhat	*highly*
rather	*absolutely*
slightly	*totally*
almost	*incredibly*
quite	*amazingly*
	quite

1 Bingo Little's behaviour in the Drones Club was unbelievably emotional.
Oh come on. It wasn't that bad. He was just … .

2 Henry Wilcox's attitude to women was somewhat hypocritical.
That's an understatement. He was … .

3 Eunice Parchman struck me as being totally off-the-wall.
That's a bit harsh. She was …

4 I admit that the speech was quite badly written but the presentation was superb.
Don't be so charitable! You know as well as I do that … .

5 I know it was supposed to be a comedy but I thought the film was extremely harrowing.
What a sensitive soul you are! It was …

2 Choose words from the vocabulary exercise you have just done. With a partner, create similar conversations of your own about a film or a TV programme you have just seen.

Listening

1 Look at the list of words below. They all describe the style in which a book is written. Some of them will be used in the extract you are about to hear. Mark those that are positive in meaning with a tick (✓) and those that are negative in meaning with a cross (✗).

☐ elegant	☐ pretentious
☐ seamless	☐ evocative
☐ contrived	☐ imaginative
☐ lyrical	☐ self-conscious
☐ well-crafted	☐ formless
☐ turgid	☐ slushy

2 You will now hear an extract from a radio programme in which literary critics discuss new publications. Listen and complete the notes.

	T.T.	P.P.	J.W.	C.E.
The Unfair Vanity				
General opinion				
Reasons given				
Opinion of content				
Opinion of language				
The Able Citizen				
General opinion				
Reasons given				
Opinion of content				
Opinion of language				
Some Rob You with a Six-gun				
General opinion				
Reasons given				
Opinion of content				
Opinion of language				

Speaking

Written by the famous nineteenth-century writer, Charles Dickens, the extract on the right provides a classic example of how to begin a novel.

1 Read the beginning of *David Copperfield* on the right. Discuss with your partner how effectively it attracts the reader's attention. Compare it with the beginning of *The Old System* on page 27.

2 Look at these examples of first lines and decide:

1 how effective they are in grabbing the reader's attention.
2 what techniques each of the writers uses, in both form and substance, to make the opening sentence arresting.

It was a bright cold day in April and the clocks were striking 13.
1984 by George Orwell

I am a camera with its shutter open, quite passive, recording, not thinking.
Goodbye to Berlin by Christopher Isherwood

It is a truth universally acknowledged that a single man in possession of a good fortune must be in want of a wife.
Pride and Prejudice by Jane Austen

The scene and smoke and sweat in a casino are nauseating at three in the morning.
Casino Royale by Ian Fleming

Call me Ishmael!
Moby Dick by Herman Melville

Whether I shall turn out to be the hero of my own life, or whether that station will be held by anybody else, these pages must show. To begin my life with the beginning of my life, I record that I was born (as I have been informed and believe) on Friday, at twelve o'clock at night. It was remarked that the clock began to strike, and I began to cry, simultaneously.

In consideration of the day and hour of my birth, it was declared by the nurse, and by some sage women in the neighbourhood who had taken a lively interest in me several months before there was any possibility of our becoming personally acquainted, first, that I was destined to be unlucky in life; and secondly, that I was privileged to see ghosts and spirits; both these gifts inevitably attaching, as they believed, to all unlucky infants of either gender, born towards the small hours on a Friday night.

Use of English

There is a view that education is too book-centred and academic and has little to do with real life. This is often described as the ivory tower approach. However, attitudes are changing.

Complete the following passage, adapted from an article in *The Times*, by filling in each of the blanks with one word.

PETER Williamson, the newly appointed dean of London Business School's Master of Business Administration programmes is fond of ... (1) the apocryphal story of the Hong Kong entrepreneur who hires an expensive MBA-educated graduate ... (2) design a new strategy for his business. After watching his new recruit ... (3) his thumbs for weeks, the businessman asks when he can benefit from some new insight. 'Oh,' the young man replies, 'I need a case study first.'

The joke sums ... (4) what a growing army of critics feel about traditional business school education – academic, over-analytical and out of ... (5) with day-to-day problems. The London School has decided to tackle the critics. It is redesigning the MBA ... (6) the ivory tower approach. The new course is just one of the measures intended to ... (7) the school's academic, elitist image. It also intends to create a career management centre, ... (8) students wider information about ... (9) employers in all the developed countries. In ... (10) the criteria for selecting students are ... (11) review. The findings are likely to recommend a change in the way the General Matriculation Test is used, ... (12) that more account is taken of applicants' practical experience. The reforms will require considerable negotiation skills. The School is still smarting from criticisms levelled ... (13) it by members of the business community in a previous report. Many said it was too research-orientated and that the MBA programme lacked focus and was conservative, boring, narrow, staid, old-fashioned and even entrenched. This unexpected ... (14) in the face provided the opportunity to introduce the new approach. Yet Professor Williamson ... (15) that the reforms of academic working methods will not happen overnight.

Speaking

1 Work with a partner and discuss these different approaches to studying. Decide which appeals most to you.

2 Look at the list of techniques that are needed to study effectively below. Discuss with your partner how you might apply them in your own studies.

1. evaluating
2. memorising
3. researching
4. collating
5. criticising
6. classifying
7. enumerating
8. ordering
9. analysing
10. coordinating

Writing

Using about 350 words, discuss the statement:

In the modern world, reading is no longer the most effective way of acquiring knowledge.

Before starting to write your composition consider the following points.

1 Read the title of the composition very carefully so that you are aware of all its implications.

2 Think about the structure of the composition. When you are asked to discuss a statement, it is essential to put both sides of the argument.

3 Plan the composition by assembling your ideas in a logical sequence of paragraphs.

4 Think about the style you are going to use. Decide what kind of English is appropriate for this task and why. Consider how your choice of style will help the reader to follow your argument.

5 Decide on how the composition is going to begin and end before you start writing.

6 Remember that the 350 words should be considered as the minimum not the maximum.

7 Check your work. First make sure that your argument is clear. Then check your use of English.

To travel hopefully is a better thing than to arrive.

Robert Louis Stevenson

Listening

In this quotation the writer suggests that if we achieve our aims, we often experience a sense of anti-climax because the reality is not quite what we expected it to be.

1 Listen to a number of people talking about achieving their aspirations and whether or not they turned out to be what they had expected.

Identify them and number them in the order in which they speak.

- ☐ engineer
- ☐ poet
- ☐ university student
- ☐ courier at a holiday resort
- ☐ business executive
- ☐ foreign language learner

2 For each speaker, note down:

1. their aspirations.
2. what really happened to them.
3. how accurate their expectations proved to be.

3 What about you? Describe past aspirations of yours and what actually happened. Then describe your present aspirations and how likely you are to achieve them.

4 Discuss the quotation at the beginning of this Unit.

Speaking

What aspirations do you have in learning English?

1 Look at the reasons for learning English listed below. Discuss with a partner which are appropriate to each of you.

- ☐ I need to pass an exam.
- ☐ It's for my job.
- ☐ It will help me get a better job.
- ☐ I just love the language.
- ☐ English is the international language.
- ☐ I can't get enough of those phrasal verbs.
- ☐ I want to read English literature in the original.
- ☐ I travel a lot, so I need it.
- ☐ I don't know why but I find it very beautiful.
- ☐ It's not my choice, my parents/my bosses think I should learn to speak it.
- ☐ It will improve my education.

2 Come to some conclusions about why you and your partner are learning the language.

Reading

Read the following extract from *Jude the Obscure* by Thomas Hardy. Jude comes from a poor farming background and lives in a village not far from Christminster, Hardy's name for Oxford. When the old schoolmaster leaves to go and study at the university, Jude, despite lacking a formal education, is determined to follow in his footsteps.

1 Answer the following questions.

1 When do you think the story was set?
a Fifty years ago.
b A hundred years ago.
c Three hundred years ago.

2 What aspects of the text helped you to make up your mind?

2 What impression do you get from the text of the attitudes towards education and towards medicine at the time it was written?

3 Complete the following statements in the most appropriate way.

1 Physician Vilbert
a was interested in Jude's education.
b sold medicine in Christminster.
c had a low opinion of himself.
d had no wish to take advantage of Jude.

2 Jude
a felt let down by Physician Vilbert.
b was influenced by supernatural forces.
c did not follow Physician Vilbert's instructions.
d showed little emotion.

3 Jude's ideas about learning languages
a were based on a misconception.
b came from Physician Vilbert.
c did not change.
d came to him in a dream.

Walking somewhat slowly by reason of his concentration, the boy – an ancient man in some phases of thought, much younger than his years in others – was overtaken by a light-footed pedestrian, whom, not withstanding the gloom, he could perceive to be wearing an extraordinarily tall hat, a swallow-tailed coat, and a watch chain that danced madly and threw around scintillations of sky-light as its owner swung along upon a pair of thin legs and noiseless boots. Jude, beginning to feel lonely, endeavoured to keep up with him.

'Well, my man! I'm in a hurry, so you'll have to walk pretty fast if you keep alongside of me. Do you know who I am?'

'Yes, I think. Physician Vilbert?'

'Ah I'm known everywhere, I see. That comes of being a public benefactor.'

Vilbert was an itinerant quack-doctor, well known to the rustic population, and absolutely unknown to anybody else, as he, indeed, took care to be, to avoid inconvenient investigations. Cottagers formed his only patients, and his Wessex-wide repute was among them alone. His position was humbler and his field more obscure than those of the quacks with capital and an organized system of advertising. He was, in fact, a survivor. The distances he traversed on foot were enormous, and extended nearly the whole length and breadth of Wessex. Jude had one day seen him selling a pot of coloured lard to an old woman as a certain cure for a bad leg, the woman arranging to pay a guinea, in instalments of a shilling a fortnight, for the precious salve, which, according to the physician, could only be obtained from a particular animal which grazed on Mount Sinai, and was to be captured only at great risk to life and limb. Jude, though he already had his doubts about this gentleman's medicines, felt him to be unquestionably a travelled personage, and one who might be a trustworthy source of information on matters not strictly professional.

'I s'pose you've been to Christminster, Physician?'

'I have – many times,' replied the long thin man. 'That's one of my centres.'

'It's a wonderful city for scholarship and religion?'

'You'd say so, my boy, if you'd seen it. Why, the very sons of the old women who do the washing of the colleges can talk in Latin – not good Latin, that I admit, as a critic: dog-Latin cat-Latin, as we used to call it in my undergraduate days.'

'And Greek?'

'Well that's more for the men who are in training for bishops, that they may be able to read the New Testament in the original.'

'I want to learn Latin and Greek myself.'

'A lofty desire. You must get a grammar of each tongue.'

'I mean to go to Christminster some day.'

'Whenever you do, you say that Physician Vilbert is the only proprietor of those celebrated pills that infallibly cure all disorders of the alimentary system, as well as asthma and shortness of breath. Two and threepence a box, specially licensed by the government stamp.'

'Can you get me the grammars if I promise to say it hereabout?'

'I'll sell you mine with pleasure; those I used as a student.'

'O, thank you, sir!' said Jude gratefully, but in gasps, for the amazing speed of the physician's walk kept him in a dogtrot which was giving him a stitch in the side.

'I think you'd better drop behind, my young man. Now I'll tell you what I'll do. I'll get you the grammars, and give you a first lesson, if you'll remember, at every house in the village, to recommend Physician Vilbert's golden ointment, life-drops, and female pills.'

'Where will you be with the grammars?'

'I shall be passing here this day fortnight at precisely this hour of five-and-twenty minutes past seven. My movements are as truely timed as those of the planets in their courses.'

'Here I'll be to meet you,' said Jude.

'With orders for my medicines?'

'Yes, Physician.'

Jude then dropped behind, waited a few minutes to recover breath, and went home with a consciousness of having struck a blow for Christminster.

4 The most appropriate title for this extract is
a *Alternative Medicine.*
b *Friends, Romans and Countrymen.*
c *Thwarted Aspirations.*
d *The Grammar Doctor.*

5 Jude could best be described as
a indolent but inquisitive.
b intelligent but lazy.
c weak and gullible.
d sensitive but determined.

4 Why do you think it was so important to study Latin and Ancient Greek at that time? What relevance do you think these so-called 'dead' languages have today?

5 Later in the story, Jude finally achieves his aim of going to Christminster. However, he does not achieve the qualifications necessary to enter the university but goes there to find work as a stonemason, which is now his trade.

Read the text on the right and answer the questions.

1 Why did Jude find Christminster so impressive?
2 What does he mean by *the true goal of all of us*?
3 Did the fact that Jude saw the city at night make a difference to his first impressions?

It was a windy, whispering, moonless night. To guide himself he opened under a lamp a map he had brought. The breeze ruffled and fluttered it, but he could see enough to decide on the direction he should take to reach the heart of the place.

After many turnings he came up to the first ancient mediaeval pile that he had encountered. It was a college, as he could see by the gateway. He entered it, walked round, and penetrated to dark corners which no lamplight reached. Close to this college was another; and a little further on another; and then he began to be encircled as it were with the breath and sentiment of the venerable city. When he passed objects out of harmony with its generalexpression he allowed his eyes to slip over them as if he did not see them.

He rambled under the walls and doorways, feeling with his fingers the contours of their mouldings and carving. The minutes passed, fewer and fewer people were visible, and still he serpentined among the shadows, for had he not imagined these scenes through ten bygone years, and what mattered a night's rest for once? High against the black sky the flash of a lamp would show crocketed pinnacles and indented battlements. Down obscure alleys, apparently never trodden now by the foot of man, and whose very existence seemed to be forgotten, there would jut into the path porticoes, oriels, doorways of enriched and florid middle-aged design, their extinct air being accentuated by the rottenness of the stones. It seemed impossible that modern thought could house itself in such decrepit and superseded chambers.

'Beautiful city! So venerable, so lovely, so unravaged by the fierce intellectual life of our century, so serene! ... Her ineffable charm keeps ever calling us to the true goal of all of us, to the ideal, to perfection.'

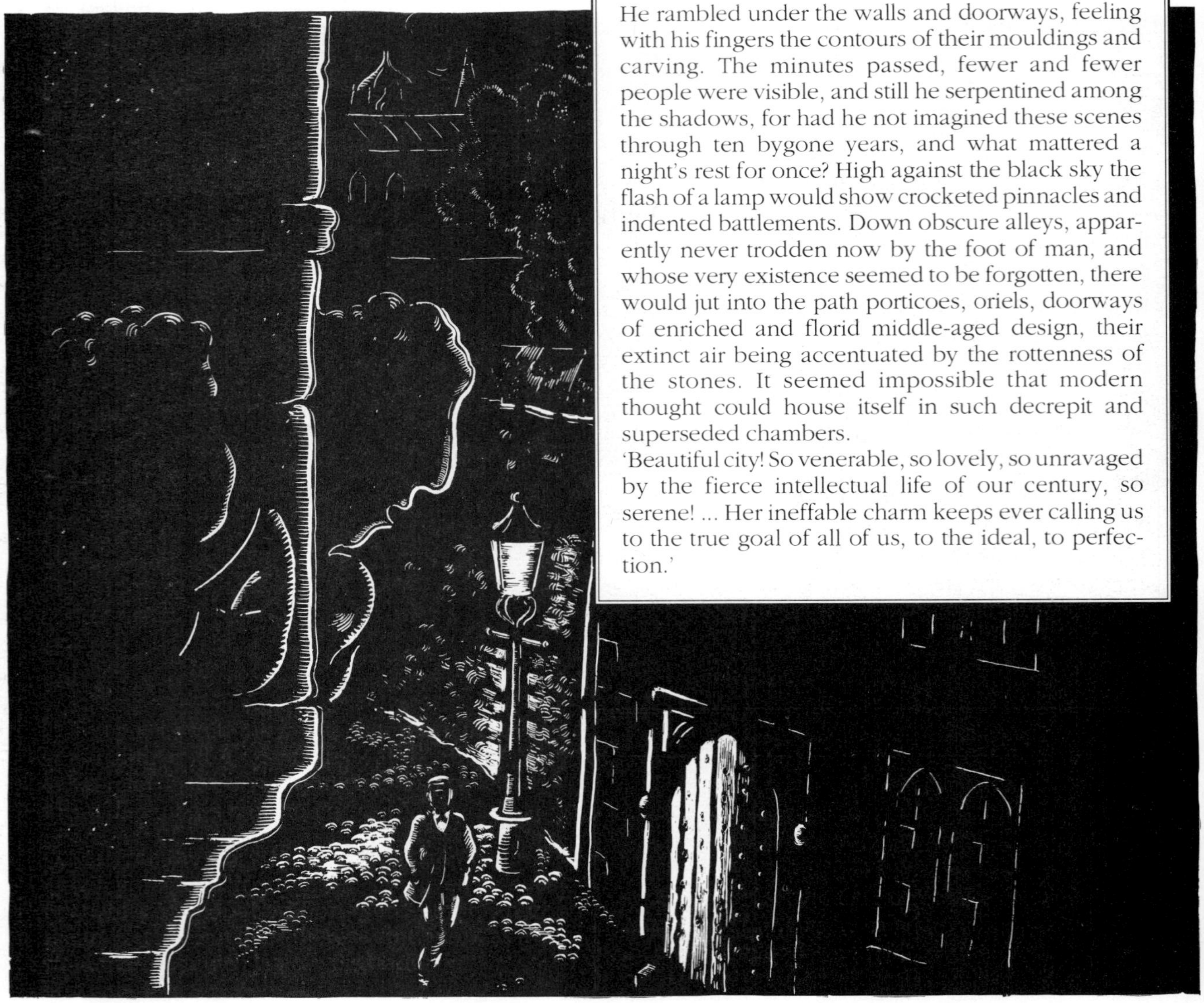

6 Now read on.

1 What causes Jude to change his mind about Christminster?
2 According to Jude, how has the appearance of the buildings changed since the night before?
3 Who were *those happy young contemporaries?*
4 What do you think Jude means by *a wall*?

Necessary meditations on the actual, including the mean bread-and-cheese question, dissipated the phantasmal for a while, and compelled Jude to smother high thinkings under immediate needs. He had to get up, and seek for work, manual work; the only kind deemed by many of its professors to be work at all.

Passing out into the streets on this errand he found the colleges had treacherously changed their sympathetic countenances: something barbaric loomed in the masonaries of all. The spirits of the great men had disappeared.

What at night had been perfect and ideal was by day the more or less defective – real. Cruelties, insults, had, he perceived, been inflicted on the aged erections. The condition of several moved him as he would have been moved by maimed sentient beings. They were wounded, broken, sloughing off their outer shape in the deadly struggle against years, weather, and man.

The rottenness of these historical documents reminded him that he was not, after all, hastening on to begin the morning practically as he had intended. He had come to work, and to live by work, and the morning had nearly gone. It was, in one sense, encouraging to think that in a place of crumbling stones there must be plenty for one of his trade to do in the business of renovation.

It was not till now, when he found himself actually on the spot of his enthusiasm, that Jude perceived how far away from the object of the enthusiasm he really was. Only a wall divided him from those happy young contemporaries of his with whom he shared a common mental life; men who had nothing to do from morning till night but to read, mark, learn, and inwardly digest. Only a wall but what a wall!

Speaking

1 Look at the photographs and discuss with your partner what impressions you have of each of them.

2 Read the passages below and discuss with your partner how they relate to the photographs and what your opinions are of the views expressed.

1 I'm a real night owl and only really come alive after the stroke of midnight. Clubs and discos are my natural habitat. I feel free and relaxed, meeting my friends, chatting, being part of a crowd. I love music, the louder the better and I love dancing all night long but come the dawn I do my Count Dracula routine and hide under the bedclothes as soon and as long as I can.

2 'Come to the big city,' they said, 'the streets are paved with gold and everyone is happy.' It's a myth. People rush around in circles going nowhere, the streets are piled high with rubbish and you can end up living rough in a cardboard box. Talk about feeling lonely in a crowd! I'm going back to my little village. I don't care if it is in the back of beyond because the people who live there are real.

3 It looks beautiful on a box of chocolates or from a train window but the reality is completely different. I left my office job to come out here but I wish I hadn't. As far as I'm concerned, farming is all hard work, no free time and awful smells. Anyone who believes that the idyllic get-away-from-it-all country life is real has obviously never worked on a farm.

3 Discuss with your partner any personal experiences you have had where the actual circumstances were not what you had imagined them to be.

Reading and writing

1 Read the extract from *The Bell Jar* by Sylvia Plath on this and the next page. Answer the following questions.

1 Although the book was written over thirty years ago, is there anything in the text to indicate that the story was not set in the present day?
2 What do you think might have occurred before the events described in the text?

2 As quickly as you can, find words or phrases in the text that mean the same as the following. They do not necessarily appear in the same order as in the text.

1 ordinary and unimportant
2 unusual and largely unknown
3 had not found time for
4 looking pale and feeling unconfident
5 act in an obstinate way
6 I was sure to do it
7 strongly supporting
8 shouting loudly
9 close tightly
10 get down to work

3 How would you describe (a) Esther's (b) Jay Cee's attitude towards learning languages?

4 Why do you think that Esther has difficulty in reconciling her attitudes to studying, as shown in the following quote?

All my life I'd told myself studying and reading and writing and working like mad was what I wanted to do ... and what did I do but balk and balk ... ?

6 Summarise, in about 60 words each, the attitudes of Esther and Jay Cee.

When I made my wan entrance into the office at about ten o'clock, Jay Cee stood up and came round her desk to shut the door, and I sat in the swivel chair in front of my typewriter table facing her, and she sat in the swivel chair behind her desk facing me, with the window full of potted plants, shelf after shelf of them, springing up at her back like a tropical garden.

'Doesn't your work interest you, Esther?'

'Oh, it does, it does,' I said. 'It interests me very much.'

I felt like yelling the words, as if that might make them more convincing, but I controlled myself.

All my life I'd told myself studying and reading and writing and working like mad was what I wanted to do, and it actually seemed to be true. I did everything well enough and got all A's, and by the time I made it to college nobody could stop me.

I was college correspondent for the town Gazette and editor of the literary magazine and secretary of the Honour Board, which deals with academic and social offences and punishments, a popular office, and I had a well-known woman poet and professor on the faculty championing me for graduate school at the biggest universities in the east, and promises of full scholarships all the way, and now I was apprenticed to the best editor on any intellectual fashion magazine, and what did I do but balk and balk like a dull cart horse?

'I'm very interested in everything.' The words fell with a hollow flatness on to Jay Cee's desk, like so many wooden nickles.

'I'm glad of that,' Jay Cee said a bit waspishly. 'You can learn a lot in this month on the magazine, you know, if you just roll up your shirt-cuffs. The girl who was here before you didn't bother with any of the fashion show stuff. She went straight from this office on to Time.'

'My!' I said, in the same sepulchral tone. 'That was quick!'

'Of course, you have another year at college yet,' Jay Cee went on a little more mildly. 'What do you have in mind after you graduate?'

What I always thought I had in mind was getting some big scholarship to graduate school or a grant to study all over Europe, and then I thought I'd be a professor and write books of poems or write books of poems and be an editor of some sort.

Usually I had these plans on the tip of my tongue.

'I don't really know,' I heard myself say. I felt a deep shock, hearing myself say that, because the minute I said it, I knew it was true. ▸

◂ It sounded true, and I recognized it, the way you recognize some nondescript person that's been hanging around your door for ages and then suddenly comes up and introduces himself as your real father and looks exactly like you, so you know he really is your father, and the person you thought all your life was your father is a sham.

'I don't really know.'

'You'll never get anywhere like that.' Jay Cee paused. 'What languages do you have?'

'Oh, I can read a bit of French, I guess, and I've always wanted to learn German.' I'd been telling people I'd always wanted to learn German for about five years. What I didn't say was that each time I picked up a German dictionary or a German book, the very sight of those dense, black, barbed-wire letters made my mind shut like a clam.

'I've always thought I'd like to go into publishing.' I tried to recover a thread that might lead me back to my old, bright salesmanship. 'I guess what I'll do is apply at some publishing house.'

'You ought to read French and German,' Jay Cee said mercilessly, 'and probably several other languages as well, Spanish and Italian – better still, Russian. Hundreds of girls flood into New York every June thinking they'll be editors. You need to offer something more than the run-of-the-mill person. You better learn some languages.'

I hadn't the heart to tell Jay Cee there wasn't one scrap of space on my senior year schedule to learn languages in. I was taking one of those honours programmes that teaches you to think independently, and except for a course in Tolstoy and Dostoevsky and a seminar in advanced poetry-composition, I would spend my whole time writing on some obscure theme in the works of James Joyce. I hadn't got round to reading Finnegan's Wake, but my professor was very excited about my thesis and had promised to give me some leads on images about twins.

'I'll see what I can do,' I told Jay Cee. 'I probably might just fit in one of those double-barrelled, accelerated courses in elementary German they've rigged up.' I thought at the time I might actually do this. I had a way of persuading my Class Dean to let me do irregular things. She regarded me as an interesting experiment.

Use of English

1 The phrases below, which are from the text, indicate different ways of speaking.

the words fell with hollow flatness
a bit waspishly
in the same sepulchral tone

Listen to the recording. Each sentence 1 – 3 is said in three different ways but only once in the way given in italics. Choose the one that sounds appropriate.

1 *with hollow flatness*
I'm very interested in everything.
2 *waspishly*
I'm glad of that.
3 *in a sepulchral tone*
My! That was quick!

2 In these examples, both adverbs and adverbial phrases are used. It is usually possible to change an adverb into an adverbial phrase and vice versa with little or no change in meaning.
For example:

waspishly: *in a waspish manner.*
with hollow flatness: *flatly* (except in *he flatly denied it* where it means *totally.)*
in a sepulchral tone: *sepulchrally.*

However, in the following sentence no adverb can be formed from the adjective, so an alternative adjectival form can be used.

I can't come tonight, said Josephine in a bored way.
I can't come tonight, said Josephine, sounding bored.

Keeping the same meaning, change the adverbial phrases in italics into adverbs. Not all the adjectives or nouns can be made into equivalent adverbs, so you may need to use appropriate synonyms.

1 Marlowe answered the detective's questions *in a nonchalant manner.*
2 'I will do all I can, within my limited powers to help you, sir,' said Mr Micawber *with respect.*
3 'Rules are rules; they cannot be ignored at your whim,' reiterated Skullion *in that tedious way of his.*
4 'We're going to win the match,' yelled the Borchester United fans *in confident mood.*
5 'Stick with me and you'll see the best places in New York,' Ritzo said *in a confiding whisper.*
6 'Tea will be served *in a short time,'* Jeeves announced.
7 'What an outrageous suggestion,' retorted Wooster *sounding short.*
8 'You will never replace the real lady of the house,' said Mrs Danvers *with contempt.*
9 'So this is what you call home,' said Dorothy, *with a supercilious edge* to her voice.
10 'Bring me the handbag,' demanded Lady Bracknell *in her strident way.*

3 Listen to the way each of the recorded sentences is spoken and match it with an appropriate adverb from the list below. Number the boxes in the appropriate order.

☐ condescendingly
☐ sarcastically
☐ adoringly
☐ meditatively
☐ defiantly
☐ sternly
☐ politely
☐ confidingly
☐ triumphantly
☐ stridently

Speaking

Work with a partner. Take it in turns to say a sentence below in a way you think reflects the meaning of one of the adverbs from the list in Use of English 3. Let your partner tell you how you said it each time. Say the sentence again if your partner is in doubt or chooses the wrong adverb.

1 I think English food is absolutely delicious.
2 Close the door behind you.
3 When will it all end?
4 How on earth did you do that?
5 There's no time like the present.
6 It's a funny old world.
7 I hope you get whatever you deserve.
8 Money isn't everything, you know.
9 I didn't get where I am today by going to university.
10 Absence makes the heart grow fonder.

Reading, listening and writing

Adverbs and adverbial phrases are often very important in stage directions in a play.
In this extract from *The Importance of Being Earnest* by Oscar Wilde, Gwendolen and Cecily both believe they are engaged to be married to Mr Ernest Worthing. In fact there are, for a number of reasons, two men using that name.

1 Read the extract, paying particular attention to the stage directions.

2 Decide whether each of these statements about the text is true or false.

1 Cecily speaks to Gwendolen confidingly because she does not want anyone else to hear.
2 An *entanglement* is something that is not easy to escape from.
3 *When I see a spade I call it a spade* means that Cecily is trying to be polite.
4 Gwendolen says that she has never seen a spade because it is a tool associated with the working classes.
5 *Common* is used by Cecily to mean both usual and uncultured.
6 She uses *agricultural depression* to mean simply a decline in the rural economy.
7 Gwendolen's attitude towards Cecily is caused by jealousy.
8 *I am trespassing on your valuable time* is usually said by the guest rather than the host.

3 Listen to the extract. Discuss what you think is meant by *the shallow mask of manners*. Base your discussion on the way that both Cecily and Gwendolen make derogatory but polite remarks to each other.

CECILY (Rather shy and confidingly)
Dearest Gwendolen, there is no reason why I should make a secret of it to you. Our little country newspaper is sure to chronicle the fact next week. Mr Ernest Worthing and I are engaged to be married.

GWENDOLEN (Quite politely, rising)
My darling Cecily, I think there must be some slight error. Mr Ernest Worthing is engaged to me. The announcement will appear in the Morning Post on Saturday at the latest.

CECILY (Very politely, rising)
I am afraid you must be under some misconception. Ernest proposed to me exactly ten minutes ago. (Shows diary)

GWENDOLEN (Examines diary through her lorgnette carefully)
It is certainly very curious, for he asked me to be his wife yesterday afternoon at 5.30. If you would care to verify the incident, pray do so. (Produces diary of her own) I never travel without my diary. One should always have something sensational to read in the train. I am sorry, dear Cecily, if it is any disappointment to you, but I am afraid I have the prior claim.

CECILY
It would distress me more than I can tell you, dear Gwendolen, if it caused you any mental or physical anguish, but I feel bound to point out that since Ernest proposed to you he clearly has changed his mind.

GWENDOLEN (Meditatively)
If the poor fellow has been entrapped into any foolish promise I shall consider it my duty to rescue him at once, and with a firm hand.

CECILY (Thoughtfully and sadly)
Whatever unfortunate entanglement my dear boy may have got into, I will never reproach him with it after we are married.

GWENDOLEN
Do you allude to me, Miss Cardew, as an entanglement? You are presumptuous. On an occasion of this kind it becomes more than a moral duty to speak one's mind. It becomes a pleasure.

CECILY
Do you suggest, Miss Fairfax, that I entrapped Ernest into an engagement? How dare you? This is no time for wearing the shallow mask of manners. When I see a spade I call it a spade. ▸

◂ GWENDOLEN (Satirically)
I am glad to say that I have never seen a spade. It is obvious that our social spheres have been widely different.

(Enter MERRIMAN, followed by the FOOTMAN. He carries a salver, table cloth, and plate stand. CECILY is about to retort. The presence of the servants exercises a restraining influence, under which both girls chafe.)

MERRIMAN
Shall I lay tea here as usual, miss?

CECILY (Sternly, in a calm voice)
Yes, as usual.

(MERRIMAN begins to clear the table and lay the cloth. A long pause. CECILY and GWENDOLEN glare at each other.)

GWENDOLEN
Are there many interesting walks in the vicinity, Miss Cardew?

CECILY
Oh! Yes! a great many. From the top of one of the hills quite close one can see five counties.

GWENDOLEN
Five counties! I don't think I should like that. I hate crowds.

CECILY (Sweetly)
I suppose that is why you live in town?

(GWENDOLEN bites her lip, and beats her food nervously with her parasol.)

GWENDOLEN (Looking round)
Quite a well-kept garden this is, Miss Cardew.

CECILY
So glad you like it, Miss Fairfax.

GWENDOLEN
I had no idea there were any flowers in the country.

CECILY
Oh, flowers are as common here, Miss Fairfax, as people are in London.

GWENDOLEN
Personally I cannot understand how anybody manages to exist in the country, if anybody who is anybody does. The country always bores me to death.

CECILY
Ah! This is what the newspapers call agricultural depression, is it not? I believe the aristocracy are suffering very much from it just at present. It is almost an epidemic amongst them, I have been told. May I offer you some tea, Miss Fairfax?

GWENDOLEN (With elaborate politeness)
Thank you. (Aside) Detestable girl! I require tea!

CECILY (Sweetly)
Sugar?

GWENDOLEN (Superciliously)
No, thank you. Sugar is not fashionable any more.

(CECILY looks angrily at her, takes up the tongs, and puts four lumps of sugar into the cup.)

CECILY (Severely)
Cake or bread and butter?

GWENDOLEN (In a bored manner)
Bread and butter, please. Cake is rarely seen at the best houses nowadays.

CECILY (Cuts a very large slice of cake, and puts it on the tray)
Hand that to Miss Fairfax.

(MERRIMAN does so, and goes out with FOOTMAN. GWENDOLEN drinks the tea and makes a grimace. Puts down cup at once, reaches out her hand to the bread and butter, looks at it, and finds it is cake. Rises in indignation.)

GWENDOLEN
You have filled my tea with lumps of sugar, and though I asked most distinctly for bread and butter, you have given me cake. I am known for the gentleness of my disposition, and the extraordinary sweetness of my nature, but I warn you, Miss Cardew, you may go too far.

CECILY (Rising)
To save my poor, innocent, trusting boy from the machinations of any other girl there are no lengths to which I would not go.

GWENDOLEN
From the moment I saw you I distrusted you. I felt that you were false and deceitful. I am never deceived in such matters. My first impressions of people are invitably right.

CECILY
It seems to me, Miss Fairfax, that I am trespassing on your valuable time. No doubt you have many other calls of a similar character to make in the neighbourhood.

Speaking

Goneril and Regan used to be friends but they have not seen each other for a long time. Goneril unexpectedly comes to visit Regan who, though not wishing to appear impolite, feels that these days they have little in common and would like Goneril to leave. Goneril realises this but rather maliciously tries to prolong the visit. Work with a partner. Taking the parts of Goneril and Regan, develop a conversation along these lines.

Reading and writing

I never travel without my diary. One should always have something sensational to read in the train.

This very well-known quotation is an excellent example of literary overstatement, containing both irony and humour. The underlying assumption is, of course, that it is other people's diaries which are sensational rather than one's own.

1 Why do you think people keep diaries? Think of any diary extracts you have read and what the appeal of them might be. Do you think they were written for the writer's or the reader's benefit?

2 Look at the two extracts from other diaries on this and the next page. One was written in the nineteenth century the other in the twentieth. Decide which you think is the more modern.

3 What are the similarities in style in these extracts? Why do you think they are written in a similar way?

4 Keeping the same meaning, rewrite each of the following sentences so that it includes the word in brackets. You may make any changes that are necessary to the sentence but do not change the form of the word.

1 Don't forget to come and see me next time you're in town. (pay)
2 Having just arrived from Brazil, Angel Clare went straight to Tess's cottage. (fresh)
3 It is very discourteous to arrive late for a meeting. (manners)
4 Professor Connery lectured us on the legends of King Arthur for over two hours. (forth)
5 Orsino was totally oblivious of what Viola was planning. (idea)
6 'It is utter folly to proceed in this way,' Michael warned. (making)
7 Cora was in such a deep sleep that Steerpike was unable to rouse her. (up)
8 Despite all your careful explanations, I still do not understand. (none)

MONDAY, 18 SEPTEMBER

At 2.30 we all drove to Llan Thomas with Mrs Hilton, meeting Major Thomas, Lechmere and Charlie at the Brecon turnpike coming into Hay on foot to pay calls. Mrs Thomas and Mary came into the drawing room first. I was very nervous when Mrs Thomas came in, but she received me very kindly and cordially just as usual. The croquet things were got out, two sets playing on the same ground across from either peg. The girls gradually came out onto the lawn. I began to fear Daisy was not coming. She was the last of all, I was horribly afraid she had been advised not to appear, because I was there. Presently I turned and there she was in a black velvet jacket and light dress, with a white feather in her hat and her bright golden hair tied up with blue riband. How bright and fresh and happy and pretty she looked.
She stood by me all the game watching us. I talked to her a good deal and she was so nice and sweet.
I love her more and more each time I see her. I think she loves me a little. I hope so. God grant it. I am sure she does not dislike me, and I believe, I do believe, she likes me and cares for me. I fancy I can see it in her clear loving deep grey eyes, so true and fearless and honest, those beautiful Welsh eyes that seem to like to meet mine. I think she likes to be with me and talk with me, or why did she come back to me again and again and stand by me and talk to no one else? I wish I could tell her how dearly I love her but I dare not. Perhaps I am deceiving myself and mistaken after all. Perhaps what I think is love is only her innocent childlike affectionate way with all, and she might be the same with anyone else. I cannot believe it. I will not believe it. How proud and glad I felt every time she came and stood by me. And I thought she seemed proud and fond too. How fond we should be of each other.

MONDAY, 22 MAY

To-day I went to Oxford by the 1 o'clock train to pay a visit to my dear old college friend Anthony Lawson Mayhew at his new home St Margaret's, Bradmore Road. I had not been to Oxford for two years. The first sight of the old University from the railway, and the noble cluster of famous towers and spires always rouse in me an indescribable thrill of pride and love and enthusiasm. There is nothing like Oxford.

Mayhew met me at the station at 3 o'clock. He came straight from the Taylor Buildings where he had been attending a lecture given by a Dane named Thomassen fresh from Copenhagen. The lecture was on the Slavonic languages and as the lecturer had a severe cold and a 'Slavonic cough' and spoke in a very low voice. Mayhew was not much wiser. We walked up into the dear old streets. As a heavy shower came on we went into the Radcliffe library where I became engrossed by a life of Heine. When the shower had passed we wandered towards St Margaret's. In the Parks we met Griffiths, the present Warden of Wadham, a kind pleasant courteous old gentleman, and Spurling whom I remembered as a very junior scholar when I took my degree and went down. He is now Dean of Keble College. We also met a short stout gentleman with a double chin and large umbrella, a kindly face and a merry eye, who buttonholed Mayhew and began to inveigh in an aggrieved tone against the folly, perversity and bad taste of the University residents and visitors in rushing in crowds of 1200 to hear the Bishop of Derry (Alexander) give an ornamental rhetorical flourish by way of a Bampton Lecture in the morning and leaving himself (Professor Pritchard, Professor of Astronomy and Select Preacher) to hold forth to empty benches in the afternoon. He thought it was a sin and a shame. He declared the Bishop's Bampton Lectures to be growing worse week by week and to be an insult to the understanding of the University. 'Sir,' he said, 'they are barren, there is nothing in them at all. They neither satisfy the intellect nor touch the heart. I have in my pocket,' he continued, 'a letter from a Manchester gentleman who is steeped to the eyes in cotton. He says that he was spending Sunday in Oxford and he heard in the University Church what he will never forget as long as he lives.' At this point the Professor's merry eye twinkled and he smiled broadly. Thinking that the Manchester gentleman's remark applied to the balderdash which the Professor represented the Bishop's Bampton Lecture to have been and taking my cue from the Professor's smile I here laughed loud and long. The Professor eyed me oddly and went on with his story, from which I was horrified to learn that the remark in the Manchester gentleman's letter applied not to the Bishop of Derry's Bampton Lecture but to Professor Pritchard's own select sermon which had touched the cotton lord to the heart and done him much spiritual good. And I had received the recital of this interesting, touching and solemn episode with a loud and derisive laugh. Meantime my dear old absent-minded friend had become oblivious of dinner and we arrived an hour too late, to find the ladies, his wife and mother, had waited half an hour and then had given us up for lost.

After dinner we went down to the river and saw the boat races very well from the Queen's Barge.

Reading

In the age of fast food and fast living, responses to requests are changing. Read the article.

Answer the following questions.

1 What is the main point being made?
2 What is implied in the last sentence of the text?
3 Some people might describe this article as *witty*, others might say it was *pretentious* or *pointless*. What adjectives would you use to describe it?
4 What reasons would you give when saying whether you did or did not enjoy this article?

Use of English

The more questions we are asked , the less likely we are to be offered any choice at all.

This structure is often used to emphasise balance or contrast, especially between what is expected to happen and what actually happens. For example:

The more closely I read the play, the more interesting it became.
The more I looked at the painting, the less I liked it.

The comparative forms may be used without a noun if the noun which is omitted can easily be deduced from the context. For example:

The more (food) he eats, the thinner he gets.
The more (language) we are taught, the less we seem to understand.

In the second part of the sentence, the verb is inverted if the comparative form agrees with the subject. For example:

The more hardship the Government inflicted, the greater was the people's resolve to overthrow their leaders.

The structure can be used to express a contrast so strong and seemingly illogical that it may be called a paradox. For example:

The more successful you are, the harder you fall.
The more she was surrounded by people, the lonelier she felt.

It is also often used in shortened form to express approval or preference with *the better (...)* as the second part of the sentence.

A *Shall we leave now?*
B *Yes. The sooner the better, as far as I'm concerned.*

1 Complete each of the sentences 1 – 8 with the most appropriate ending a – h. There may be more than one alternative.

1 The higher our insurance premiums are,
2 The more we spend,
3 The greater the police presence is,
4 The smaller the fish are,
5 The more instructions we are given,
6 The less that is known about them,
7 The more intelligent we are,
8 The more violent a film is,

a the more difficult it is to feel satisfied.
b the more complicated it becomes.
c the less likely we are to have an accident.
d the greater the chances are of being caught.
e the longer are the queues to see it.
f the less efficiently the system works.
g the higher is the likelihood of trouble.
h the better we shall feel.

2 Complete each of the sentences below so that it expresses a contrast or a paradox.

1 The hotter the weather gets, ...
2 The worse off Dimkins became, ...
3 The more leisure time we have, ...
4 The less Jane drives, ...
5 The older the President became, ...

3 Write similar sentences using each of the endings below.

1 ..., the less likely you are to be appreciated.
2 ..., the more irate the dealer became.
3 ..., the sooner you will be able to leave.
4 ..., the greater are the chances of being discovered.
5 ..., the less beautiful was Dorian's face.

Multiple Choice Conversation

IS it my imagination or has there been a strange development in the way we talk in the 1980s? Have we all become multiple choice speakers? Here, for instance, is an exchange I sometimes hear in my local pub.

'Bitter, please.'
'Right – pint or half?'
'Half, please.'
'Best or ordinary?'
'Best, please.'
'Straight glass or handle?

It's more like filling in a form than having a conversation. It happens in the buffet of my local station, too.

'Coffee, please.'
'Drink here or take away?'
'Take away, please.'
'Black or white?'
'Black, please.'
'Large or small?'
'Large, please.'
'Sugar or no sugar?'

And that's without the milk vs. cream battle, the hot vs. cold milk, or even brown vs. white sugar controversy. The same quasi-bureaucratic process can take place when buying rail tickets, getting a glass of wine, booking a hotel room or even trying to get hold of a drink of water.

'Sparkling or still, sir?'
'Oh, sparkling, please.'
'A large or small bottle?'
'Small, please.'
'Ice and lemon, or plain?'

I seem to remember that when amoeba breed, they simply split into two and carry on. Our sentences are getting like that. Every statement can immediately be subdivided into two further possibilties. At a recent wedding, when the vicar asked the groom if he would take his bride for richer or for poorer, I am sure I heard the groom reply: *'For richer, please.'*

You can always try to circumvent this self-perpetuating process by putting all the answers in your very first request. I have tried it. It doesn't work. Here is a conversation I had at the local station buffet recently.

'A large black coffee to take away, please.'
'Right, sir,' ... pause to find fresh supply of mugs under counter ...
'Sorry, was that black, sir?'
'Yes.'
'Right. Did you say large?'
'Yes, I did.'

And so on. You cannot win. I thought I had won last week when I said to the lad at the buffet:

'One black coffee. In a LARGE mug. No sugar. Repeat, black coffee in a large mug to take away, no sugar. All right?'
But he merely looked at me and said:
'Do you want the lid on or not?'

One of the reasons I gave up smoking was that I couldn't simply buy a packet of cigarettes any more. I had to undergo interrogation.

'Plain or filter?'
'Filter, please.'
'King-size or ordinary?'
'Ordinary.'
'Flip-top or standard pack?'

The thing that worries me about all this is the illusion it creates that we are getting more choice than ever before that each question represents a true option for the customer, created by a loving producer. Almost the opposite is true. The more questions we are asked, the less likely we are to be offered any choice at all. My local station buffet offers one kind of coffee, and that's it. Whether the water comes sparkling or still, in a large or small bottle, it's the same.

Even when the waiter asks you if your steak is to be well done or rare, you know in your heart of hearts that most British restaurants do it medium well done, whatever you ask for. Even when the hotel asks you if you want a twin, double or single room, you know that every hotel today will give you a twin room even if you want a double or single; they will just charge you differently, that's all.

Even in my local pub, the publican's information-gathering technique (*'Half or pint? Straight or handle?'*) cannot disguise the fact that he sells only Courage's beers. It is not his fault. Courage, which owns the pub, will not let him sell any other kind of local beer unless he signs a different and much more hard-hearted agreement. It's a spurious choice, like buying sausages.

'A pound of sausages, please.'
'Pork or beef, sir?'
'Pork, please.'
'Ordinary or chipolatas?'
'Chips, please.'
'Herby or plain?'

But whatever the introduction, you are about to eat the same old bready, cereal-filled, flavourless British sausage. Because there are lots of questions, we fail to notice that there are only a few different answers. Multiple choice conversation is a conjuring trick in which the conjuror goes on about the size of the mug or chatters about the label in order to distract you from the central lack of choice.

Which brings me to the American presidential election ...

Speaking

Look at the pictures and discuss with your partner what the paradox might be in each of them.

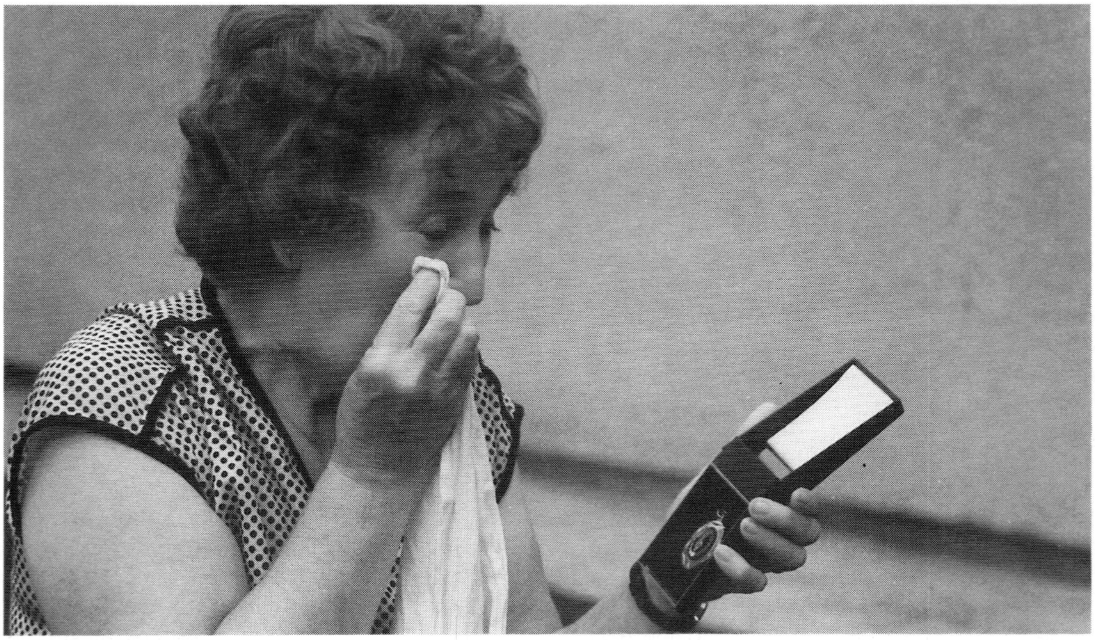

A homeless child playing in the street

Reading

Travelling hopefully can be the subject of our dreams as well as an approach to real life.

Read *Through Nightmare* by Robert Graves. Decide whether each of the following statements is true or false.

1 You should worry about the settings in which your dreams take place.
2 Dreamers themselves rarely appear in their own dreams.
3 People who appear in dreams are usually just like ordinary people.
4 The dream in the poem involved a difficult journey.
5 The poet did not understand what the dream was all about.
6 *A lost and moated land* suggests that the dreamer was happy to arrive there.

Writing

Describe, in about 350 words, a place you always wanted to visit, which, when you arrived there, was very different from what you had expected.

THROUGH NIGHTMARE

Never be disenchanted of
That place you sometimes dream yourself into,
Lying at large remove beyond all dream,
Or those you find there, though but seldom
In their company seated
The untameable, the live, the gentle.
Have you not known them? Whom? They carry
Time looped so river-wise about their house
There's no way in by history's road
To name or number them.
In your sleepy eyes I read the journey
Of which disjointedly you tell; which stirs
My loving admiration, that you should travel
Through nightmare to a lost and moated land,
Who are timorous by nature.

A thing of beauty is a joy for ever.

John Keats

Speaking

1 What things come to mind when you think about beauty? Note them down and compare your list with those of other students.

2 Look at the photographs and discuss with your partner which you consider to be beautiful.

If you think that *beautiful* is not the most appropriate word to describe a particular photograph, what other adjectives would you choose from the list below to describe it?

bizarre
dull
exquisite
controversial
extraordinary
ostentatious
surprising
classical
breath-taking
functional
strange
ordinary

3 Which of the adjectives listed above could also be used adverbially with *beautiful*? For example:

Strangely beautiful collocates appropriately.
Ordinarily beautiful makes no sense.

4 Discuss how you think our opinions on what is beautiful might be influenced by fashion and contemporary culture. Consider the effects of items 1 – 5 below.

1 Advertising.
2 Nostalgia: the periods in the past such as the 1920s or the 1960s that it is fashionable to remember at present.
3 The state of the economy.
4 The taste of famous and influential people.
5 The cinema, TV, newspapers and magazines.

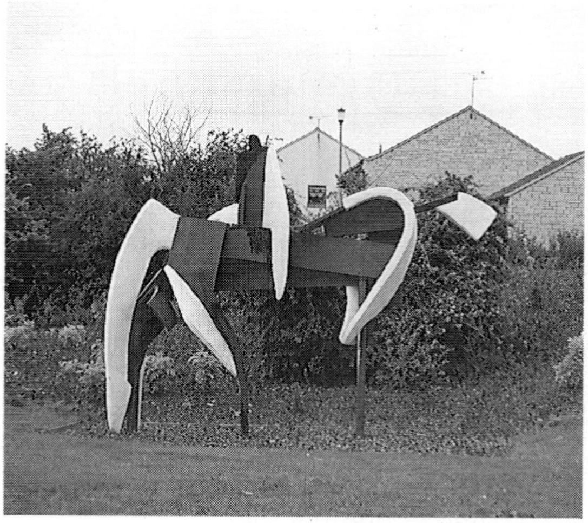

Reading

The text below was written by John Ruskin, a nineteenth-century writer and critic whose ideas were originally thought of as highly controversial but later became widely accepted.

1 Decide whether each of statements 1 – 5 is true or false.

1 According to Ruskin the main purpose of art is to entertain.
2 True art provides long-lasting pleasure.
3 A child's love of toys is often short-lived.
4 For artistic ideas to thrive and develop they must be constantly changing.
5 That a work of art is new does not necessarily mean that it is good.

◊

POPULAR ART The first great principle we have to hold by in dealing with the matter is that the end of Art is NOT to amuse; and that all Art which proposes amusement as its end, or which is sought for that end, must be of an inferior, and is probably of a harmful, class.

The end of Art is as serious as that of all other beautiful things – of the blue sky and the green grass, and the clouds and the dew. They are either useless, or they are of much deeper function than giving amusement. Whatever delight we take in them, be it less or more, is not the delight we take in play, or receive from momentary surprise. It might be a matter of some metaphysical difficulty to define the two kinds of pleasure, but it is perfectly easy for any of us to feel that there is generic difference between the delight we have in seeing a comedy and in watching a sunrise. Not but that there is a kind of Divina Commedia, a dramatic change and power, in all beautiful things: the joy of surprise and incident mingles in music, painting, architecture, and natural beauty itself, in an ennobled and enduring manner, with the perfectness of eternal hue and form. But whenever the desire of change becomes principal; whenever we care only for new tunes, and new pictures, and new scenes, all power of enjoying Nature or Art is so far perished from us; and a child's love of toys has taken its place. The continual advertisement of new music (as if novelty were its virtue) signifies, in the inner fact of it, that no one now cares for music. The continual desire for new exhibitions means that we do not care for pictures; the continual 'demand for new books means that nobody cares to read.

Not that it would necessarily, and at all times, mean this; for in a living School of Art there will always be an exceeding thirst for, and eager watching of, freshly-developed thought. But it specially and sternly means this, when the interest is merely in the novelty; and great work in our possession is forgotten, while mean work, because strange and of some personal interest, is annually made the subject of eager observation and discussion. *Cestus of Aglaia, VIII. (O.R., I., page 388, 389).*

2 A *novelty* is something that is appealing because it is new. Look at the following items. Decide which are just novelties and which are still likely to be popular in a few years' time.

1 a portable telephone
2 a Rubik cube
3 a Filofax
4 a personal cassette player
5 inflatable trainers
6 a video camera
7 a skateboard
8 Mickey Mouse slippers

3 Art is generally thought of as referring to paintings, drawings and sculptures, but this is not necessarily the case. Modern art, especially, appears in many different forms. Artists are experimenting with a wide range of techniques, often using the latest developments in technology. One such artist is Jenny Holzer, who has used the technology needed to produce electronic advertising displays.

Read the article on the next page and answer the questions.

Choose the word or phrase, a or b, that is closest in meaning to each item 1 – 7.

1 *live off*
a rely on
b derive income from

2 *subvert*
a change
b undermine

3 *hazard of notoriety*
a conflict of ideas
b danger of being well-known

4 *truisms*
a statements of the obvious
b negative expressions

5 *till slips*
a articles of clothing
b payment receipts

6 *hanker for*
a want to have again
b want to forget about

7 *gizmo*
a social analysis
b novel invention

4 Answer the following questions, as far as possible using your own words.

1 What is ironic about the banks and corporations buying Jenny Holzer's work?
2 Why is it doubtful that she has reformed any bankers?
3 What does *this* (paragraph 4) refer to?
4 Why has public display of her work become increasingly difficult?
5 What is Jenny Holzer's main artistic aim?
6 Give reasons why you think her work should or should not be classified as art.

The Message Is The Message

'Art is meant to disturb.' Georges Braque

Oh, the rich: they're so smart!

Targetted by artist and populist propagandist Jenny Holzer in slogans like PRIVATE PROPERTY CREATED CRIME, INHERITANCE MUST BE ABOLISHED and IT'S NOT GOOD TO LIVE OFF CREDIT, the capitalist corporations and collectors, the art élite and art-buying banks respond simply and swiftly: they simply buy the stuff.

KNOW YOUR ENEMY is one thing, INVEST IN HER is altogether more effective. It not only challenges art's ability to disturb or subvert, it derides the substance of her work and questions whether Holzer – one of art's most fêted subversives – has made any genuine impact at all.

'Have I reformed any bankers you mean?' she considers. 'It's a good question. I doubt it. The first hazard of notoriety is that they just think, "Oh, maybe I can make some money off this." You question if you're just helping someone make money who probably has a lot of it already.'

For one as earnest and politically over-sensitive as Holzer, this is not something to be taken lightly. What's more, her dilemmas are mounting. Much like Warhol, Hockney, Gilbert and George, Holzer is best known for what is probably her weakest work, the provocative, high-impact 'Truisms' which made her name: PROTECT ME FROM WHAT I WANT, MONEY CREATES TASTE.

Having forged a reputation for displaying her work on T-shirts and baseball caps, on electronic signboards in Piccadilly Circus and Times Square, on New York payphones, parking meters and the Virgin Megastore's till slips, Holzer's work has progressed in such a way that public display has become increasingly difficult. Not only has she learnt to excel at huge museum installations, but the cost of them has soared into hundreds of thousands of dollars.

Jenny Holzer's anti-capitalist slogans used to unsettle passers-by for free; now her works sell for thousands.

You might wonder if she doesn't hanker for the days of 1979's 'Inflammatory Essays', displayed anonymously but effectively on plain posters scattered around New York (apparently inspired by a Manhattan crazy who filled the Times Square area with warnings against leprosy): DON'T RELAX. I'LL CUT THE SMILE OFF YOUR FACE ... raged one essay. THE GAME IS ALMOST OVER SO IT'S TIME YOU ACKNOWLEDGE ME. DO YOU WANT TO FALL NOT EVER KNOWING WHO TOOK YOU?

'The work has the most impact anonymously on the street, when they're not thinking about whether it's 'art' or not. They confront the content. I try to hit the issues which people actually live or die by.'

The point of her work has not changed. 'This sounds completely pretentious and unrealistic, but, hey, why stop now,' she says with a harsh laugh. 'To keep everybody from dying horribly. That's the stakes to me ... You could always be dead in a second, simply through good old-fashioned political means.'

Her subjects, by and large, are death (fear of death, nuclear death, sexual death, deliberate death); survival; power and control political and personal. Fear, pain, anger, uncertainty ensue. Anything except art. Holzer is, mercifully, uninterested in self-referential cleverness. Despite the resonance of her slogans in the LED form she has made her own, she dismisses the notion of making statements on 'the power of modern-day mass communications' or 'mass-media consciousness'; statements critics read into her work nonetheless.

'It's only in the art world that it's seen as "a comment on". It's just a good gizmo,' she shrugs. 'I like the LEDs' efficiency and shock value, their hypnotic quality.'

Use of English

Not only has she learnt to excel at huge museum installations, but the cost of them has soared into hundreds of thousands of dollars.

In this structure the subject (*she*) and the auxiliary have been inverted in order to emphasise the point that her work has progressed.

Inversion, when used sparingly, can highlight a point very effectively. It is usually found in written, not spoken, English.

The subject and verb are inverted when the sentence begins with any of the words or phrases taken from the categories below.

Adverbs of frequency
Never
Rarely
Seldom
Once in a …
Many a time

Time expressions
No sooner … than
Hardly
Scarcely

Negative expressions
Not only … but (also) … (as well).
In (Under) no circumstances
Nowhere

1 Rewrite the sentences below so that each one starts with an appropriate expression from the list above. For example:

John has often climbed that hill.
Many a time has John climbed that hill.

1 That was the worst accident I had ever seen.
2 Holmes examined the suitcase and a moment later he identified the thief.
3 It is absolutely forbidden for unauthorised personnel to enter the power station.
4 It was not clear until Hawking had published his ideas how controversial his theory was.
5 The tax has to be paid by the husband and wife and all children aged eighteen and over.

2 Complete the following sentences in an appropriate way.

1 Hardly … when I noticed the keys were inside.
2 Nowhere … that was as beautiful as that sunlit shore.
3 Once in a lifetime … a performance like that.
4 Rarely … such an extraordinary talent.
5 Seldom … a hostile reception.

Reading

Certain types of behaviour can be described as art forms in themselves, especially when they have a calculated effect on other people. For example:

He has turned his methods of eliciting sympathy into a fine art.

In the passage opposite, the writer describes the art of irritating people and how to improve it. Read it through. Complete each statement appropriately with one of the items a – d.

1 The style of the passage is
a formal.
b tongue-in-cheek.
c serious.
d straightforward.

2 The main purpose of the article is to
a entertain.
b criticise.
c educate.
d inform.

3 The satire is mainly directed at people
a who give parties.
b who do not give parties.
c who run finishing schools.
d with irritating habits.

4 The writer suggests that nowadays at the end of a party
a the room is left very untidy.
b people rearrange the furniture in a strange way.
c vases are broken.
d there is very little mess to tidy up.

5 The passage implies that the writer is irritated by people who
a shake hands.
b knock before entering a room.
c are well-mannered.
d noisily play with coins in their pockets.

6 The writer suggests that you can ruin another person's anecdotes by
a drinking while the person is telling the story.
b constantly looking at your watch.
c clapping at regular intervals.
d appearing to miss the point of the story.

... AND *moreover*

Craig Brown

MORE AND MORE I am finding that people simply don't know how to misbehave at parties. You arrive at a party, an attentive host leads you to a room of pleasant people, they engage you in interesting, amusing conversation, talking a little bit about themselves, a little bit about you and a little bit about topics of mutual interest; nobody drinks too much, nobody picks a quarrel, at the allotted time, you all leave, waving merrily (but not too merrily) and vowing to keep in touch.

Of course, in the old days they really knew how to lay on a perfectly dreadful evening, but nowadays people just don't seem to go to the trouble. They'd rather leave a room spick and span, carpets unstained, vases intact, with only the odd cushion slightly out of place.

It seems ages since a halfway-decent havoc has been wreaked. The Johnny-Come-Latelies have all gone, too, to be replaced by the Johnny-Come-Bang-On-Time, the Johnny-Leave-Early, Johnny-Send-Prompt-Thank-you-Letters. The young these days just do not show the faintest lack of consideration for their hosts.

I trust that all this will change with the opening of a new finishing school, Wink 'n' Feel Place, where school-leavers will be given a first-class grounding in Disgraceful Manners, Applied Slouching, Resentful Stares and Self, Self, Self.

This one-year Diploma Course formally starts in September and goes through until July, but candidates will be expected to turn up late without so much as a word of warning sometime halfway through November and to push off again around late August, leaving the ashtrays overflowing, the plates unwashed and the lavatories in a terrible state.

Working through the following curriculum, students will gain a basic knowledge of thoughtless behaviour and will be fluent in 20 different areas of standard irritation.

Month 2: if the student bothers to show up at all, he should saunter any-old-how into the principal's office, first taking care not to knock. Over a cup of coffee, into which he will be expected to dunk his cigarette stub, he will be given a full timetable to enable him to turn up precisely halfway through lectures. A variety of fresher parties will be thrown in the first month, but don't worry if you start by shaking hands, listening attentively and offering thanks: old habits are hard to shake off in these early stages.

Months 3 – 4: with the aid of dummies, the student will be tutored in staring over shoulders in search of someone rather more interesting. Before the end of the first week he will have reached a state of proficiency whereby he can spend anything up to 15 minutes looking at other people in the room without a frontward glance at the person who is talking to him.

Month 5: the candidate will be expected to disappear without leaving any excuse whatsoever, at no point alerting the schools as to his whereabouts. Towards the end of the month advanced students may consider getting a drunken friend to phone the principal with an excuse so far-fetched as to be insulting.

Month 6: the Visiting Reader in Coin-Jangling will be giving a series of lectures on the 'Role of the Coin-Jangler as a social irritant'. Pupils will be instructed in clinking pound coins together while simultaneously jogging from one foot to the other. This will be in preparation for the Car Showroom Party, where such behaviour is obligatory.

Month 7: Musical Instruction. Students are expected to pick one course from the following:

(a) mouthing the words of songs while dancing with an exaggerated look of angst on the face;

(b) playing dummy guitar to old Led Zeppelin numbers;

(c) bringing the party to a standstill by placing a Monty Python record on the turntable and joining in with the funny voices.

Month 8: Ruining Others' Anecdotes. Timing your 'So what happened then?' to coincide with the end of an anecdote; saying 'Can I get you another drink?' five seconds before the punch line; saying, 'Actually, that once happened to me' at the conclusion of a riotous story.

You are cordially requested to settle the term's fees far too late, after much quibbling, and preferably with a stolen credit card.

Vocabulary development

1 As quickly as you can, find a word or phrase in the passage which means the same as each of the following:

1 when something is supposed to happen
2 a person giving a party
3 a humorous story involving oneself
4 very clean and tidy
5 act in a kind and polite way
6 standing in a lazy way
7 a person who is very punctual
8 arguing over something trivial
9 to walk without rushing
10 to put into liquid

2 *Havoc has been wreaked.*

The verb *to wreak* is rarely used except with the word *havoc*. Although it is synonymous with *to cause*, it cannot replace it. You cannot, for example, *wreak* an explosion.

There are a number of expressions containing words that can only be found in that expression. Some are listed below.

a dab hand
a figment of one's imagination
with bated breath
short shrift
to stand one in good stead
to lend/give credence to
to batten down the hatches
a foregone conclusion
to scotch the rumour
to run amuck

Complete each sentence 1 – 10 with an appropriate expression from the list above.

1 The celebrity audience waited … as the envelope giving the Oscar winner's name was slowly opened.
2 The discovery that the forensic tests were inaccurate will … to the argument that the men are innocent.
3 May I take the opportunity, through the columns of this newspaper, to … that my relationship with Mr Chuck Windsor is anything other than that of two colleagues working closely together.
4 Although I believe the present ill wind blowing through the economy will be short-lived, we must still … and ride it out.
5 You may well believe that you saw Frank with another woman, but as far as he is concerned it was … .
6 Bernard may not be good academically but he is … at mending cars.
7 Despite the huge difference in abilities between the two teams, the result is certainly not … .
8 If the police do not intervene soon, the demonstrators are bound to get out of control and … through the streets.
9 All this excellent work will … with any prospective employer.
10 Although Tom is good-looking and charming, he was given … when he asked Margot to go out with him.

Listening

Listen to the following conversation, in which Brian and Jenny are discussing what really gets on their nerves.

1 Listen to the recording. Decide whether each statement below is true or false.

1 Brian is annoyed when he bangs his head.
2 Brian used to work in Australia.
3 Jenny hates strangers listening to her personal conversations.
4 Steve pretends to be a famous person when strangers overhear conversations.
5 Jenny experiments by talking about James Bond.
6 Steve is easily bored when discussing car journeys.

2 Listen to the recording again. Select the appropriate meaning a – c for each of these words or phrases.

1 *gets my goat*
a annoys me
b amuses me
c surprises me

2 *to duck*
a to dive
b to stoop
c to avoid

3 *stumbled*
a fell over
b tripped
c was clumsy

4 *a bête noire*
a a favourite
b a brick
c a dislike

5 *earwigging*
a listening sympathetically
b listening inquisitively
c listening absent-mindedly

6 *prime*
a warn
b ignore
c test

7 *eavesdroppers*
a nextdoor neighbours
b listeners
c guests

8 *it's on the tip of my tongue*
a I'm about to say it
b I'll remember it soon
c it's hard for me to pronounce

9 *a blow-by-blow account*
a the story of a fight
b a surprising story
c a detailed story

Speaking

Discuss with a partner aspects of behaviour you find irritating and any strategies you have developed for coming to terms with them.

Reading, writing and speaking

The desire to make beautiful things is a very strong motivation and as such should be treated with caution.

The following extract is taken from the original story of *Frankenstein* written by Mary Shelley in 1816. Victor Frankenstein, having discovered that he possessed the ability to animate lifeless things, decides to create a person who is both beautiful and powerful.

1 Read the passage on the next page. Some of the language is more appropriate to the time in which it was written than it is to the present day. For example:

beheld the accomplishment of my toils: saw what my work had achieved.

Look at each of the following sentences and phrases from the passage and decide which definition, a or b, is closest in meaning to it.

1 *A convulsive motion agitated its limbs.*
a A sudden jerk caused its arms and legs to move.
b Its body shook violently.

2 *His yellow skin scarcely covered the work of arteries and muscles beneath.*
a You could see his insides through his yellow skin
b The arteries and muscles were invisible beneath his yellow skin.

3 *The different accidents of life are not so changeable as the feelings of human nature.*
a The accidents brought about by human nature can often change our lives.
b People's natural feelings change even more than life, with all its ups and downs.

4 *I had desired it with an ardour that far exceeded moderation.*
a I wanted it more than I can say.
b I felt rather indifferent towards it.

5 *No mortal could support the horror of that countenance.*
a Nobody, however ugly, could turn his back on that face.
b Nobody could possibly look at a face as ugly as that.

2 The language used creates a sense of despair and depression. Read through the passage again and note how the following items are used to enhance this feeling.

It was on a dreary night
With an anxiety that almost amounted to agony
the rain pattered dismally against the panes
the wretch
shrivelled complexion
breathless horror and disgust
the dim and yellow light of the moon
wrinkled his cheeks

With an anxiety that almost amounted to agony is also an example of alliteration. The first letter of a number of words in close proximity to each other is the same. This makes the reader aware of the sounds the words make, which in turn focuses attention on the meaning. This can be a very effective technique in descriptive writing but must not be over-used.

3 Bearing this vocabulary in mind, write a composition entitled *Night Fright*. (Use about 200 words.)

4 The idea of Frankenstein has been used over and over again in films, comics, TV adaptations and advertising campaigns. Discuss why it has lasted for so long and why it still appeals to people today.

It was on a dreary night of November that I beheld the accomplishment of my toils. With an anxiety that almost amounted to agony, I collected the instruments of life around me, that I might infuse a spark of being into the lifeless thing that lay at my feet. It was already one in the morning; the rain pattered dismally against the panes, and my candle was nearly burnt out, when, by the glimmer of the half-extingushed light, I saw the dull yellow eye of the creature open; it breathed hard, and a convulsive motion agitated its limbs.

How can I describe my emotions at this catastrophe, or how delineate the wretch whom with such infinite pains and care I had endeavoured to form? His limbs were in proportion, and I had selected his features as beautiful. Beautiful! Great God! His yellow skin scarcely covered the work of muscles and arteries beneath; his hair was of a lustrous black, and flowing; his teeth of a pearly whiteness; but these luxuriances only formed a more horrid contrast with his watery eyes, that seemed almost of the same colour as the dun-white sockets in which they were set, his shrivelled complexion and straight black lips.

The different accidents of life are not so changeable as the feelings of human nature. I had worked hard for nearly two years, for the sole purpose of infusing life into an inanimate body. For this I had deprived myself of rest and health. I had desired it with an ardour that far exceeded moderation; but now that I had finished, the beauty of the dream vanished, and breathless horror and disgust filled my heart. Unable to endure the aspect of the being I had created, I rushed out of the room and continued a long time traversing my bed-chamber, unable to compose my mind to sleep. At length lassitude succeeded to the tumult I had before endured, and I threw myself on the bed in my clothes, endeavouring to seek a few moments of forgetfulness. But it was in vain; I slept, indeed, but I was disturbed by the wildest dreams and every limb was convulsed; when, by the dim and yellow light of the moon, as it forced its way through the window shutters, I beheld the wretch – the miserable monster whom I had created. He held up the curtain of the bed; and his eyes, if eyes they may be called, were fixed on me. His jaws opened, and he muttered some inarticulate sounds, while a grin wrinkled his cheeks. He might have spoken, but I did not hear; one hand was stretched out, seemingly to detain me, but I escaped and rushed downstairs. I took refuge in the courtyard, belonging to the greatest agitation, listening attentively, catching and fearing each sound as if it were to announce the approach of the demoniacal corpse to which I had so miserably given life.

Oh! No mortal could support the horror of that countenance. A mummy again endued with animation could not be so hideous as that wretch. I had gazed on him while unfinished; he was ugly then, but when those muscles and joints were rendered capable of motion, it became a thing such as even Dante could not have conceived.

I passed the night wretchedly. Sometimes my pulse beat so quickly and hardly that I felt the palpitation of every artery; at others, I nearly sank to the ground through langour and extreme weakness.

Mingled with this horror, I felt the bitterness of disappointment; dreams that had been my food and pleasant rest for so long a space were now become a hell to me; and the change was so rapid, the overthrow so complete!

Listening

Another example of one person trying to create a thing of beauty in another occurs in *Pygmalion* by George Bernard Shaw. Professor Henry Higgins, an authority on the spoken language, attempts to change the way a flower seller called Eliza Doolittle speaks so that the sound of her voice becomes beautiful.

1 Listen to the passage and answer the questions.

1 How does Eliza feel at the start of her first lesson? Why?
2 Why does Eliza have to say the alphabet?
3 How does Higgins help Eliza to say 'cup'?
4 Why does Eliza burst into tears although Higgins is pleased with her?
5 What has Eliza got to do for the rest of the day?

2 Describe any sounds that you find hard to pronounce in English. Discuss how you can improve your pronunciation.

3 English is spoken correctly in an almost infinite variety of ways. Listen to these examples.

1 Match each speaker with one of the countries below. Number the countries in the order in which they are relevant to the recording.

- ☐ Scotland
- ☐ Ireland
- ☐ Australia
- ☐ The West Indies
- ☐ The USA
- ☐ England

2 List the accents in order (a) of difficulty and (b) of appeal to you. Compare your lists with a partner.

Use of English

Complete the passage about the famous film star Greta Garbo with one appropriate word for each blank.

The Last Mysterious Lady

TO several generations of film-goers Greta Garbo was only the world's most famous recluse. Wasn't she the star who in the 1932 film Grand Hotel had murmured 'I want to be alone' and then played out that ... (1) for the rest of her life? What else could make people ... (2) her with awe? After all she stopped making movies over half a century ... (3) she never won an Oscar and made fewer films than any other star of ... (4) magnitude. Even in the distant era of silent films her hypnotic style of acting was considered an odd anachronism, but for many she was the ... (5) haunting beauty and the finest actress in movie history. Garbo used her gorgeousness to suggest that the characters she ... (6) were creatures from a nobler, alien world doomed to exile among the puny men and cramped conventions of earth. She was typecast as the siren who lures men to hell only to get there first. Cinema would never see the ... (7) of her again.

The Garbo charisma was a creation ... (8) mysterious in its beginning as in its impact. She was ... (9) Greta Gustafsson to a poor Swedish family and gave little ... (10) of her unique hold on the camera. In her early publicity films she giggles, models dresses and gorges herself on cakes. ... (11) is no beauty here, no acting ability. What could Mauritz Stiller, the pioneer director, have ... (12) in her? Maybe the future of movies. He ... (13) her name to Garbo and brought her to Hollywood. She was signed to the studios of MGM and at their ... (14) slimmed down, had her teeth capped and adjusted her hairline. In these improbable circumstances she went on to create the ... (15) for which she became famous. Many of these films testify... (16) her acute, intuitive knowledge and use of screen ... (17). In 1941 she made Two-Faced Woman which ... (18) out to be her last film. For years she was reported to be mulling over other beguiling projects but eventually the vacation became permanent. Still her withdrawal was a good and gracious career ... (19). By refusing to make a comeback film, star in a soap opera or do a TV commercial she ... (20) her image and achievement indelible. She became the discreet curator of her own museum.

Reading and writing

In descriptive writing, the choice of words is of the utmost importance in conveying not only meaning but also sense and feeling.
Read this extract from the beginning of *The Picture of Dorian Gray* by Oscar Wilde, in which the language is particularly rich and evocative.

1 In the first paragraph there are three words which have a similar meaning, but when collocated with different adjectives create a very powerful impression in the reader's mind. *Rich odour, heavy scent and delicate perfume* all convey a sense of smell, but the language triggers the imagination so that the distinctions between them is immediately apparent even if someone has no personal experience of exactly what rose, thorn and lilac smell of.

Find examples in the text where you think the language is designed to appeal to our other senses: sight, sound, touch and taste.

The studio was filled with the rich odour of roses, and when the light summer wind stirred amidst the trees of the garden, there came through the open door the heavy scent of the lilac, of the more delicate perfume of the pink-flowering thorn.
From the corner of the divan of Persian saddle-bags on which he was lying, smoking, as was his custom, innumerable cigarettes, Lord Henry Wotton could just catch the gleam of the honey-sweet and honey-coloured blossoms of a laburnum, whose tremulous branches seemed hardly able to bear the burden of a beauty so flamelike as theirs; and now and then the fantastic shadows of birds in flight flitted across the long tussore-silk curtains that were stretched in front of the huge window, producing a kind of momentary Japanese effect, and making him think of those pallid, jade-faced painters of Tokyo who, through the medium of an art that is necessarily immobile, seek to convey the sense of swiftness and motion. The sullen murmur of the bees shouldering their way through the long unmown grass, or circling with monotonous insistence round the dusty gilt horns of the straggling woodbine, seemed to make the stillness more oppressive. The dim roar of London was like the note of a distant organ.
In the centre of the room, clamped to an upright easel, stood the full-length portrait of a young man of extraordinary personal beauty, and in front of it, some little distance away, was sitting the artist himself, Basil Hallward, whose sudden disappearance some years ago caused, at the time, such excitement and gave rise to so many strange conjectures.
As the painter looked at the gracious and comely form he had so skilfully mirrored in his art, a smile of pleasure passed across his face, and seemed about to linger there. But he suddenly started up, and closing his eyes, placed his fingers upon the lids, as though he sought to imprison within his brain some curious dream from which he feared he might awake.
'It is your best work, Basil, the best thing you have ever done,' said Lord Henry languidly. 'You must certainly send it next year to the Grosvenor. The Academy is too large and too vulgar. Whenever I have gone there, there have been either so many people that I have not been able to see pictures, which was dreadful, or so many pictures that I have not been able to see the people, which was worse. The Grosvenor is really the only place.'
'I don't think I shall send it anywhere,' he answered, tossing his head in that odd way that used to make his friends laugh at him at Oxford. 'No, I won't send it anywhere.'
Lord Henry elevated his eyebrows and looked at him in amazement through the thin blue wreaths of smoke that curled up in such fanciful whorls from his heavy, opium-tainted cigarette. 'Not send it anywhere? My dear fellow, why? Have you any reason? What odd chaps you painters are! You do anything in the world to gain a reputation. As soon as you have one, you seem to want to throw it away. It is silly of you, for there is only one thing in the world worse than being talked about, and that is not being talked about.'

2 Complete each of sentences 1 – 8 with one word from the list below.

stirred	*gleam*	*flitted*	*murmur*
straggling	*linger*	*languidly*	*stillness*

1 The … of voices in the audience died away as the curtain rose at the beginning of the play.
2 Octavia … amongst her admirers pausing only to acknowledge their congratulations.
3 From the air the … lines of retreating soldiers could be observed stretching out as far as the eye could see.
4 At the end of a meal in my favourite restaurant I just love to … over a cup of coffee and soak up the atmosphere.
5 Lord Emsworth … tossed his coat around his shoulders and sauntered off in the direction of the welcoming warmth of the Savoy Hotel.
6 When the survivors emerged from the wreckage they were astounded by the awesome … of their immediate surroundings.
7 The pale shaft of moonlight cast a ghostly … on the grotesque statue seemingly guarding the entrance to the vaults.
8 As Raffles deftly sprang the safe open, the sleeping guard … briefly but then resumed his slumbers.

3 What can you infer from the two sentences below?

Whenever I have gone there, there have either been so many people that I have not been able to see the pictures, which was dreadful, or so many pictures I have not been able to see the people which was worse.

There is only one thing in the world worse than being talked about and that is not being talked about.

4 Find examples of alliteration in the text on the previous page or in any other books, magazines or advertisements that you can find. Discuss the effects achieved.

Reading

1 Read the poem *Splendid Girls*. How would you describe the style in which it was written?

2 What is implied in the last line of the poem?

3 What do you think is the message of the poem?

SPLENDID GIRLS

Those splendid girls at the wheels of powerful cars,
Sheer mechanism setting of slender charms.
I glimpse daredevil smiles as they whip past.
What are they all eager for, driving so fast
That I see them only momentarily? They are
Wholly desirable for half a heart-beat.
They have such style, such red nails! They are so neat!
But though they appear to drive at a dangerous speed
They do not do anything at random, that's for sure.
So keep your shirt on, they are spoken for.
They are as bright and lively as advertisements
For cigarettes or petrol or soap.
But there is no danger, and there is no hope.
Those reckless smiles have been carefully painted.
They are that sort of doll.
Everything, but everything, is under control.

Writing

Describe an object or place that you consider to be beautiful. Use about 350 words.

Before starting to write think very carefully about your choice, as in a composition of this type it is very easy to 'dry up' and run out of things to say. Think about what to include in each paragraph.

Paragraph 1: A general introduction to what is considered to be beautiful with some universally accepted examples. What you consider to be beautiful in general terms.

Paragraph 2: An objective description of your chosen place or object with as much detail as you can. If you have chosen an object, do not attempt anything too technical unless you are sure you have the necessary range of vocabulary.

Paragraph 3: A subjective response describing why you think it is beautiful. Describe what appeal it has to the different senses, not just sight. Here it is important to use enhancing language in comparison to the more straightforward language you would use in the previous paragraph.

Paragraph 4: Reasons why other people may or may not find it beautiful. Refer back to your opening paragraph by saying how the object or place fits in with other examples of beauty.

Paragraph 5: Conclusion. Make a comparison between your subjective opinion and other people's views and conclude by saying whether or not you think they would coincide.

The wheel has come full circle. Let it rest.

William Shakespeare

Speaking

1 The invention of the wheel is considered to be the most significant scientific breakthrough in the whole of human history. The expression *You cannot reinvent the wheel* is used to convey the idea that the ultimate point of progress has been reached. How do you think progress should be measured?

2 It now takes the same length of time to cross London by car as it did a hundred years ago in a horse-drawn carriage. Below is a list of measures that could be taken to solve this problem. To what extent do you agree with each of them? Write a number in each box that reflects your opinion according to the scale below.

Totally disagree ⟷					Absolutely agree
0	1	2	3	4	5

- ☐ All cars should be banned from entering the city.
- ☐ People should be encouraged to share their cars.
- ☐ The Government should invest more in public transport.
- ☐ Horse riding lessons should be made compulsory.
- ☐ Car production should be drastically reduced.
- ☐ No one under the age of twenty-five or over sixty should be able to hold a driving licence.
- ☐ Travelling in comfort and style is much more important than the time a journey takes.

3 Consider the following problems. Discuss with a partner what measures should be taken to solve them.

1 On average, a letter takes twice as long to be delivered today as it did a hundred years ago.
2 Four times more people went to the cinema sixty years ago.

Listening

The twentieth century is considered to be a golden age of scientific progress, where all kinds of technological wizardry have become commonplace. What effects has this had on the quality of life?

Listen to a group of people expressing different opinions on this question.

Note down for each speaker:

1 whether they think that the effect of scientific progress on the quality of life has been positive, negative or both positive and negative.
2 any examples they give to support their view.

Reading

The passage opposite is taken from the novel *Island* by Aldous Huxley. In it, he describes a Utopian existence where a kind and happy people live together in harmony, and where science and art work together in parallel.

1 Answer questions 1 – 7.

1 What is meant by *a training of the whole mind-body*?
2 Why was it surprising that Mr Menon *broke into a loud long peal of laughter*?
3 What is meant by *extremely eminent*?
4 What point is being made by describing the two men at Cambridge?
5 *No specialization, no civilization*. Keeping the same meaning, rewrite this statement, beginning the sentence with *without*.
6 Who were *all those pathetic and repulsive creatures* that Mr Menon met on his first trip abroad?
7 What is the connection between playing roulette and understanding mathematics?

2 Summarise, in between 60 and 70 words, what Mr Menon considered were the *sciences of life*.

'What's the relevance,' Will asked, 'of all this elaborate training of the mind-body to formal education? Does it help a child to do sums, or write grammatically, or understand elementary physics?'

'It helps a lot,' said Mr Menon. 'A trained mind-body learns more quickly and more thoroughly than an untrained one. It's also more capable of relating facts to ideas and both of them to its own on-going life.' Suddenly and surprisingly – for that long melancholy face gave one the impression of being incompatible with any expression of mirth more emphatic than a rather weary smile – he broke into a loud long peal of laughter.

'What's the joke?'

'I was thinking of two people I met last time I was in England. At Cambridge. One of them was an atomic physicist, the other was a philosopher. Both extremely eminent. But one had a mental age, outside the laboratory, of about eleven and the other was a compulsive eater with a weight problem that he refused to face. Two extreme examples of what happens when you take a clever boy, give him fifteen years of the most intensive formal education and totally neglect to do anything for the mind-body which has to do the learning and the living.'

'And your system, I take it, doesn't produce that kind of academic monster?'

The Under-Secretary shook his head. 'Until I went to Europe, I'd never seen anything of the kind. They're grotesquely funny,' he added. 'But, goodness, how pathetic! And, poor things, how curiously repulsive!'

'Being pathetically and curiously repulsive – that's the price we pay for specialization.'

'For specialization,' Mr Menon agreed, 'but not in the sense you people ordinarily use the word. Specialization in that sense is necessary and inevitable. No specialization, no civilization. And if one educates the whole mind-body along with the symbol-using intellect, that kind of necessary specialization won't do much harm. But you people don't educate the mind-body. Your cure for too much scientific specialization is a few more courses in the humanities. Excellent! Every education ought to include courses in the humanities. But don't let's be fooled by the name. Hence all those pathetic and repulsive creatures that so astonished me on my first trip abroad.'

'What about formal education?' Will now asked. 'What about indispensable information and the necessary intellectual skills? Do you teach the way we do?'

'We teach the way you're probably going to teach in another ten or fifteen years. Take mathematics, for example. Historically mathematics began with the elaboration of useful tricks, soared up into metaphysics and finally explained itself in terms of structure and logical transformations. In our schools we reverse the historical process. We begin with structure and logic; then, skipping the metaphysics, we go on from general principles to particular applications.'

'And the children understand?'

'Far better than they understand when one starts with utilitarian tricks. From about five onwards practically any intelligent child can learn practically anything, provided always that you present it to him in the right way. Logic and structure in the form of games and puzzles. The children play and, incredibly quickly, they catch the point. After which you can go onto practical applications. Taught in this way, most children can learn at least three times as much, four times as thoroughly, in half the time. Or consider another field where one can use games to implant an understanding of basic principles. All scientific thinking is in terms of probability. The old eternal verities are merely a high degree of likeliness; the immutable laws of nature are just statistical averages. How does one get these profoundly unobvious notions into children's heads? By playing roulette with them, by spinning coins and drawing lots. By teaching them all kinds of games with cards and boards and dice.'

'Evolutionary Snakes and Ladders – that's the most popular game with the little ones,' said Mrs Narayan. 'Another great favourite is Mendelian Happy Families.'

'And a little later,' Mr Menon added, 'we introduce them to a rather complicated game played by four people with a pack of sixty specially designed cards divided into three suits. Psychological bridge, we call it. Chance deals you your hand, but the way you play it is a matter of skill, bluff, and co-operation with your partner.'

'Psychology, Mendelism, Evolution – your education seems to be heavily biological,' said Will.

'It is,' Mr Menon agreed. 'Our primary emphasis isn't on physics and chemistry; it's on the sciences of life.'

Use of English

Revise the use of continuous forms in English.

1 Read the examples below of the past continuous. Say why the past continuous is used. Then compare your explanation with the explanation given.

What's so funny?
Oh, nothing really. I was thinking about two people I met when I was last in England.

The past continuous is used because the thought process was interrupted by the question.

Hello. Sorry to keep you waiting. I'm rushed off my feet today.
Oh dear. I was hoping we could have lunch together.

The visitor may well be disappointed. His or her hopes have been interrupted by unforeseen circumstances, so the past continuous is used.

How nice to see you. What can I do for you?
Well, I was hoping you'd be free to have lunch.

The past continuous is used here as a polite, tentative form. It assumes that the speaker's hopes may well be dashed and so frees the other person to explain why something is not possible.

2 Match sentences 1 – 4 with explanations a – d.

1 I'm hoping to go sailing this weekend.
2 I was hoping to go sailing this weekend.
3 I hoped to go sailing this weekend.
4 I had hoped to go sailing this weekend.

a I changed my mind, so it isn't going to happen.
b There may be a storm, so it's unlikely to happen.
c I found out I had to work, so it can't happen.
d The forecast is good, so it's likely to happen.

3 Look at the example below. Complete conversations 1 – 3 appropriately. Include the verbs: *think, expect* and *look forward to*.

John Self: I'd like a word with Rosemary Massi.
Secretary: Miss Massi is in a conference at the moment. Would you care to leave a message?
John Self: *I was hoping to* have lunch with her.
Secretary: I don't think that will be possible. She's likely to be tied up all afternoon.

1 A: Are there any messages for me?
B: I don't think so, madam.
A: Oh. … a call from New York.
B: I'll just check, madam.

2 A: You aren't leaving, are you? …
B: … Why?
A: … of doing some more work.
B: …
A: Oh, all right. I'll do it tomorrow.

3 A: So, are we …?
B: …
A: What a shame. …
B: …

4 Now look at this conversation. Identify the continuous form and explain its use.

James Bond: Come on. I know a little place where we can eat the best lasagne in the world, undisturbed.
Miss Moneypenny: But James, I should be writing my report.
James Bond: There's plenty of time for that later.
Miss Moneypenny: Oh, very well. How did you know I can never resist lasagne?

I should be writing my report suggests that Miss Moneypenny feels guilty because she is not doing something during the time she has allocated for it. Compare this with *I should write my report*, a general statement with no implicit link to a particular point in time.

5 Complete the following dialogues in an appropriate way.

1 A: What do you think of the course?
B: It looks pretty interesting, but there's an awful lot to do. I know I … all the books on the reading list, but I doubt if I'll manage to.
A: Don't worry. I didn't last year and I did OK.

2 A: I saw that video last week. It's really scary.
B: Yea. I've been glued to it for the last hour. I … a letter to my mother but it'll just have to wait.

3 A: I don't know why I'm here, you know.
B: But we haven't seen each other for ages.
A: I know, but it's nearly half-time and I … the match. After all, I am the manager.

6 A continuous form is also used when making logical deductions about what is happening now or about something which has happened in the past. Look at these examples.

Tess:	I haven't had anything to eat for three days.
Angel:	*You must be starving.*
Brian:	I've beaten the deadline.
Lisa:	*You must have been working hard.*
Inspector:	I reckon Tommy Denning's alibi is false.
Sergeant:	*He can't be telling the truth.* It just doesn't add up.
Deirdre:	I'm sure I saw Reginald in the supermarket just now.
Ken:	I doubt it. He's meant to be in Australia by now.
Deirdre:	*I may have been dreaming then.*

7 Complete conversations 1 – 5 in an appropriate way.

1 A: She had all these travel brochures on her desk and spent a lot of time on the phone this morning. But Des, her boyfriend, doesn't know anything about it. What's she up to?
B: She … him.

2 A: Speaking of engagements, rumour has it that Edith Hope and Geoffrey Long are about to tie the knot.
B: They … . Edith doesn't even like him.

3 A: What a prize! First class travel, luxury hotels, sightseeing trips, loads of spending money – and they are not due back for another week.
B: I really envy them. …

4 A: He says he has spent the whole of this afternoon at the football stadium.
B: He … the match. It has been postponed until next Saturday because the pitch is in such bad condition.

5 A: A guy was saying on TV just now that in a few years the whole of London will be under water, there will be hurricanes all the time, even in summer, and intensely cold winters.
B: He … . As far as I know, the climate may change, but only very gradually.

Reading

1 Read the extract opposite from *The Dark* by James Herbert. Then decide whether each of these statements is true or false.

1 Bishop has little understanding of scientific theories.
2 Bishop states that it is very rare for people actually to see ghosts.
3 The audience was not totally convinced by Bishop's arguments.
4 A telepathic image is something that always appears on a screen.
5 The paranormal can be defined as phenomena which cannot be explained in conventional scientific terms.

Speaking

If you had been in the audience during Bishop's lecture how would you have responded?

Discuss your reactions with your partner. The following language may be useful.

Negative

I'm very sceptical.
I find it hard to swallow.
There is little concrete evidence.
It all sounds a load of nonsense.
Scientific explanations – my foot!
What a lot of mumbo-jumbo!

Positive

I thought his ideas were plausible.
The arguments are certainly convincing.
Just because it seems strange doesn't mean it isn't true.
Look at the evidence.
You can't dispute the logic.

Bishop glanced discreetly at his watch and was relieved that the two-hour lecture was nearly up.
'So you can see by my list of equipment on the blackboard, parapsychology – the study of paraphysical phenomena – uses technology rather than the more unreliable and, if I may say so, the dubious spiritualistic methods. Graph paper will usually tell you more about strange disturbances in a house than self-imposed mental trances.'
A nervous hand fluttered in the air from the second row. Bishop noticed the man wore a clerical collar. 'May I, er, ask a question?' the equally nervous voice said.
'Please do,' Bishop encouraged. 'In fact, we'll spend the last ten minutes discussing any points you might want to raise.'
'Well, it was just that for someone whose profession is the investigation of the paranormal or paraphysical ...'
'Call it ghost-hunting – it's simpler,' said Bishop.
'Yes, ghost-hunting. Well, it hasn't really been made clear by you whether or not you actually believe in ghosts.'
Bishop smiled. 'The truth of the matter is, having been involved in the study of parapsychology for some years, I'm still unsure. Certainly I've come up against the inexplicable time and time again, but everyday science is uncovering new facts about our own powers. Somebody once said that mysticism is just tomorrow's science dreamed today. I think I'd go along with that. For instance, we know concentrated thought, or often unconscious thought, can physically move objects. Scientists throughout the world, particularly Russia, are now studying psychokinetic power. Years ago it would have been called witchcraft.'
'But how does that explain spirit sightings?' A middle-aged woman, plump and pleasant looking, had asked the question. 'There are so many cases of hauntings you hear about practically every day.'
'Perhaps not every day, but there are between two and three hundred sightings each year, and probably just as many not publicised. One of the many theories is that ghosts are caused by someone under stress, their minds giving out electrical impulses in the way the heart does, and these impulses are picked up later in particular circumstances.'
'What about places that have been haunted for centuries, then?' said a young, bearded man in the front row, who was leaning forward antagonistically. 'Why haven't they just faded away?'
'It could be explained by regeneration: the transmission, or apparition, draws on energy from electrical impulses that surround us all. This could account for the appearance of a ghost. A spirit can "live" on indefinitely as long as its image can be seen by others: the ghost is actually telepathic waves, the image created in the mind of a living person – years, days, perhaps centuries before and transmitted into the mind or minds of others living today.'
'You're putting it down to electricity, then?' The bearded man in the front row sat back and folded his arms, the slightest indication of smugness in his smile.
'No, not exactly. But an electrical charge given to the nerve tissues of the brain can make a subject see flashes or hear noises. It would seem that a charge given to the appropriate receptive area of the brain can create a phantom image. Remember, the brain functions through electrical impulses and we're also surrounded by them. Impulses picked out of the air by our senses – that's us acting as receivers – isn't a difficult concept to understand. You may have heard of crisis apparitions, where someone sees an image of a friend or relative who is going through some traumatic experience, perhaps dying, many miles away. A voice may even be heard at the same time.'
A few heads nodded appreciatively.

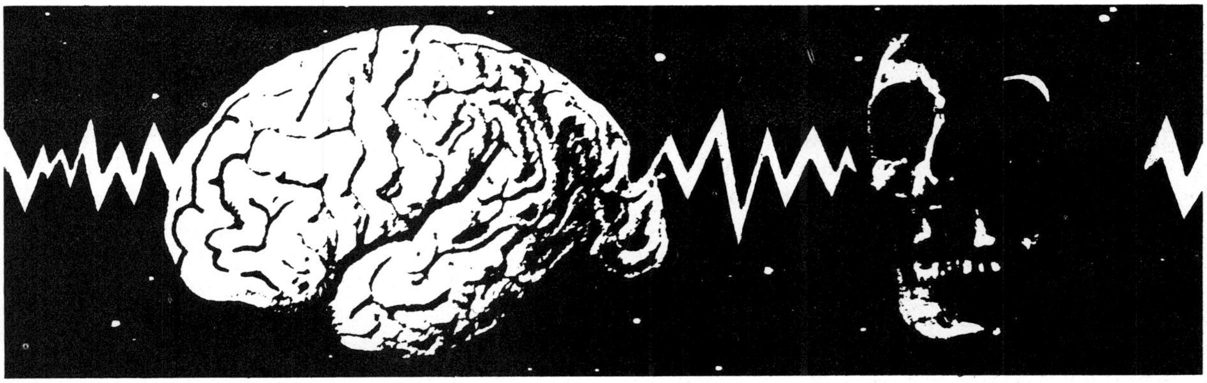

Vocabulary development

Each of the two- and three-word verbs numbered 1 – 9 is used in the text. Decide on its meaning in this context. Then match it with the verb or phrase a – i that is closest to it in meaning.

1 come up against
2 go along with
3 give out
4 be picked up
5 fade away
6 put down to
7 draw on
8 account for
9 go through

a encounter
b disappear from view
c emit
d establish the cause as
e experience
f accept the idea of
g use
h be the reason for
i be heard

2 Complete the following sentences with an appropriate verb from the previous exercise. Make sure the verbs are used in the correct form.

1 The Government's refusal to allow the experiments to continue ... the hostile opinions expressed in the press.
2 Being imprisoned for a crime you have not committed is obviously something nobody would wish ... .
3 Much to Captain Kirk's dismay, the signal he ... inexplicably started ... and eventually disappeared altogether.
4 Although sympathetic to some of these esoteric ideas, I cannot ... the concept that the Earth is, in fact, hollow.
5 The more radical your ideas are, the greater the scepticism you ... .
6 Jane seemed to ... some inner strength as she listened impassively to the news.
7 The moment Meryl enters the room, her very presence seems ... the message that she is in control.
8 Surely the destruction of the rain forests alone ... these sudden climatic changes?

Speaking and reading

1 Each of the passages below relates to one of the photographs. Work with a partner and discuss:

1 the link between the passage and the photograph.
2 the context from which each of the passages was taken.
3 how each passage relates to the theme of scientific progress.

1 Who's going to use it? Can you imagine sitting on a crowded train watching a programme with the person sitting next to you craning his neck to get a better look? Don't people get enough of it at home? I suppose it might have some business applications, but for the life of me I can't think what. Surely advances in technology can be put to better use than this?

2 With the growing concerns about changes in climate and the increasing likelihood of droughts affecting even the British Isles, where wet weather is taken for granted, the search for sources of that precious commodity, water, is being stepped up. The authorities, despite the wealth of sophisticated equipment at their disposal, are relying on the ancient art of water-divining to track down supplies. How it works remains a mystery, but its practitioners can point to considerable success at a fraction of the cost of conventional geological analysis.

3 Spills may be a thing of the past, but thrills are here to stay. As you hurtle through the lovely landscape, you can enjoy your meal safe in the knowledge that it will stay on the plate, not fall into your lap. Revolutionary technology keeps the train so stable that the only way you can find out if it is moving is to look out of the window. When you have to move fast, there is no need to hit the road. Going by car is history. You are always on the right lines when travelling courtesy of The Hi-Speed train.

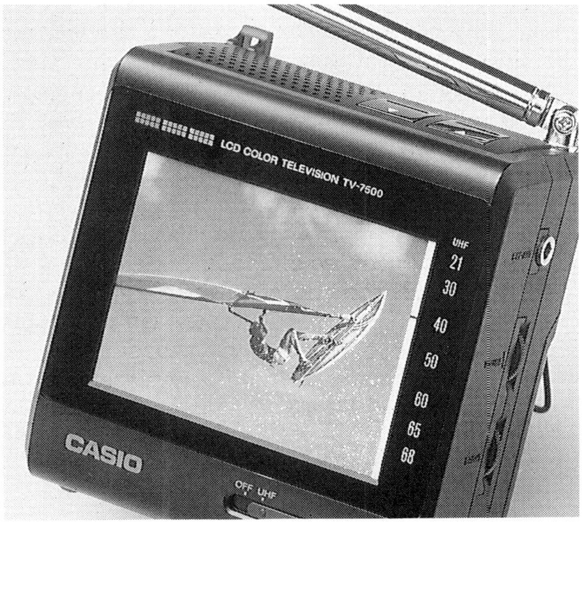

2 Read through these three newspaper articles. They all appeared around 1 April, April Fool's Day, when newspapers traditionally publish stories which seem to be genuine but in fact are not. Only one of these articles is a hoax. Discuss with your partner which you think it is. Decide which parts of the text led you to this conclusion.

3 *Truth is sometimes stranger than fiction.* How far would you agree with this statement?

Hairdresser's Application May Aid Spaceship

A former hairdresser from Hartlepool has developed a novel material that NASA, the American space agency, is considering as a heat shield for shuttles and spaceships. The material owes much to home-spun chemistry learnt over 20 years doing perms and dyeing hair in Middlesbrough.

Tests carried out at the Atomic Weapons Establishment, at Shoeburyness, Essex, indicate that the substance can withstand a simulated nuclear flash.

A human hand coated with the material remains cool and unscathed when subjected to the intense heat of a blowtorch. Eggs, similarily coated, stay uncooked after four minutes under the torch's 1,200°C flame.

The material, called Ultra High Tech Starlite, has been devised by Maurice Ward, an inventor with an affection for bow-ties, who gave up hairdressing in 1976 after runing a salon for 20 years and went on to found a plastics business making damp-proof membranes for buildings.

A few years ago, Mr Ward decided that there was a desperate need for a very lightweight, fire-resistant material for protecting airliners and passengers in an accident, and Ultra High Tech Starlite was born.

Precise details of the substance are being kept secret until Mr Ward is fully protected by patents. Nevertheless, his invention has already attracted the interest of the Defence Ministry and of NASA. Officials at the space agency's base at Huntsville, Alabama, have asked Mr Ward to submit a detailed proposal on the material in return for development funding. They are keen to find an alternative for the shuttle's ceramic thermal tiles, which tend to fall off.

Charles Martin, a retired former chief engineer with British Aerospace Space Systems, who was responsible for the company's role in America's Strategic Defence Initiative (SDI), confirmed the interest of the space agency.

'A lot of people are interested in the material,' Mr Martin said. 'The tests at Shoeburyness were done by the establishment people themselves. The material does seems to work, though goodness knows why.'

Mr Martin said that the difficulty was that the interested parties were keen to analyse the remarkable material, adding: 'He (Mr Ward) is in trouble then, because they will find out his secret, and I do not blame him for wanting to hang on to it.'

The inventor himself is busy forming a marketing company for the material, for which he sees many potential applications. Ultra High Tech Starlite comes in a variety of formulations and Mr Ward has concocted one that, he believes, could be used to fight the Gulf oil-well fires far more cheaply than conventional techniques.

Traditional methods require huge volumes of water, scarce in the desert. Mr Ward's formulation, it is claimed, can be mixed with oil, turning the crude into a material that could be sprayed over surrounding areas to cool the sand and pipes.

Gold Traces Reported In Daffodil Pigments

Botanical scientists in Amsterdam say they have found trace elements of rare metals in the pigments of some flowers, and are hoping to prove that gold exists in daffodils. That could lead to a sharp upturn in business for the Dutch bulb industry.

Dr Jan Auhad, of the Department of Molecular Studies at the city's municipal university, told a conference of international biologists in Durban yesterday that examination by electron microscopy of the flower part of the pseudo-narcissus (common daffodil) showed minute traces of the metal in some varieties. The most reactive were flowers grown in coastal parts of the Netherlands and on the Isles of Scilly.

He said the amounts of gold present were so small as to be unrecoverable by present-day commercial chemistry techniques but it should be possible, through selective propagation, to intensify the colour density of the flowers. It is expected that this would deepen the gold trace sufficiently to make extraction a viable proposition. Dr Auhad said several million flowers would be needed to produce an ounce of gold. Marketable by-products from the mass of fibrous leavings would be required to offset the costs of metal extraction.

The Amsterdam researchers continue the work of Professor Richard Wilstatter, the German organic chemist whose studies on the structure of chlorophyll brought him the Nobel Prize in 1915. His later work resulted in the granting of patents for extracting gold from sea water.

Lack Of Exercise As Damaging To The Human Heart As Smoking

People who take little or no exercise may put themselves almost as much at risk of heart disease as those who smoke 20 cigarettes a day, according to a group of medical experts.

Lack of exercise is as dangerous to the heart as high blood pressure or high levels of blood cholesterol, if the results of research recently completed by the group prove to be reliable.

The comparative risks have been assessed on the basis of research studies over the past 40 years of physically active men and their sedentary counterparts, such as London bus drivers and conductors, and postmen and clerks. Of particular concern is the other conclusion that the group have come to: fewer than twenty per cent of the people working in Britain today take sufficient exercise.

Parts of the report make sobering reading: 'Physical inactivity is seldom regarded as an important risk factor for coronary heart disease and as a result, prevention policies tend to emphasise other aspects of lifestyle change,' it says. 'There is now sufficient research evidence to suggest that this view should be reconsidered. It must be concluded that the risk attributable to physical inactivity in the British population is sufficient to give cause for concern.'

Doctors are being urged to set the pace, by walking briskly, swimming and cycling themselves as an example to their patients. It remains to be seen how successful this campaign will be. It is arguable that the majority of the population neither know nor care what their doctor does in his or her free time.

In the meantime, on your bikes until you are puffing gently!

Use of English

Read the following extract from *The Ascent of Man* by Dr J. Bronowski, the highly acclaimed book based on a television series which outlined the history of human progress. Answer questions 1 – 10.

1 What does *that* refer to in line 8?
2 Why is the metaphor of *the wheeled chariot* used to describe the sun?
3 What is meant by *irrigation systems*?
4 Why are the words *punctuation marks* appropriate in this context?
5 What is the purpose of a bow-lathe?
6 What point is being made by saying *but I … in England in 1945*?
7 What is the threat that modern machines pose?
8 How do machines increase the surplus won from nature?
9 What is meant by a *draught animal*?
10 What would be another good example from your experience of *a maverick source of energy*?

The wheel is found for the first time before 3000 BC in what is now southern Russia. These early finds are solid wooden wheels attached to an older raft or sledge for drawing loads, which thereby is converted into a cart. From then on the wheel and axle becomes the double root from which invention grows. For example, it is turned into an instrument for grinding wheat and using the forces of nature to do that: the animal forces first, and later the forces of wind and water. The wheel becomes a model for all motions of rotation, a norm of explanation and a heavenly symbol of more than human power in science and in art alike. The sun is a wheeled chariot, and the sky itself is a wheel, from the time that the Babylonians and the Greeks mapped the turning of the starry heavens. In modern science natural motion (that is, undisturbed motion) goes in a straight line; but for Greek science, the form of motion that seemed natural (that is, inherent in nature) and in fact perfect was motion in a circle.

About the time that Joshua stormed Jericho, say 1400 BC, the mechanical engineers of Sumer and Assyria turned the wheel into a pulley to draw water. At the same time they designed large-scale irrigation systems, the maintenance shafts still survive like punctuation marks across the Persian landscape.

By now the village artisan has become an inventor in his own right. He combines the basic mechanical principles in sophisticated tools which are, in effect, early machines. They are traditional in the Middle East: the bow-lathe, for example, which is one of the classical schemes for turning linear into rotary motion. Here the scheme depends, ingeniously, on winding a string round a drum and fastening the ends of the string to the two ends of a sort of violin bow. The piece of wood to be worked is fixed to the drum; it is turned by moving the bow to and fro, so that the string rotates the drum that holds the piece of wood, which is scored by a chisel. The combination is several thousand years old, but I saw it used by gypsies making chair-legs in a wood in England in 1945.

Yet as the machine has tapped larger sources of power, it has come more and more to outdistance its natural use. How is it that the machine in its modern form now seems to us a threat?

The question as it strikes us hinges on the scale of power that a machine can develop. We can put it in the form of alternatives: is the power within the scale of the work for which the machine was devised, or is it so disproportionate that it can dominate the user and distort the use? The question therefore reaches far back; it begins when man first harnessed a power greater than his own, the power of animals. Every machine is a kind of draught animal – even the nuclear reactor. It increases the surplus that man has won from nature since the beginning of agriculture. And therefore every machine re-enacts the original dilemma: does it deliver energy in response to the demand of its specific use, or is it a maverick source of energy beyond the limits of constructive use? The conflict in the scale of power goes back all the way to that formative time in human history.

Speaking

1 The art of being wrong. Discuss with your partner the implications of each of the statements below. They were all made by scientists who were highly respected in their day even if they lacked a certain accuracy of foresight.

Rail travel at high speed is not possible, because passengers, unable to breathe, would die of asphyxia.
Dr Dionysys Lardner (1793-1859), Professor of natural philosophy, London University.

Flight by machines heavier than air is unpractical, insignificant, if not utterly impossible.
Simon Newcomb (1835-1909)

I can accept the theory of relativity as little as I can accept the existence of atoms and other such dogmas.
Ernst Mach (1838-1916), Professor of physics, University of Vienna.

2 Discuss predictions that scientists are making now which are likely to prove to be equally unreliable.

Writing

Scientific progress does not always contribute to improving the quality of life. Discuss. (Use about 350 words.)

There is always one discussion question in the exam, so it is important to know how to prepare for it. The question is usually in the form of a controversial statement which the candidate is asked either to discuss or comment on. Before starting to write, plan an outline for each paragraph and have a clear idea of how the composition is going to begin and end. Study the example at the top of the next column.

The style should be similar to that found in an article in a magazine or scientific journal. The passage from *The Ascent of Man* provides an excellent model. It is important to make a distinction between ideas, comments and opinions which are subjective and those which are more objective. The language on the right can be used to introduce objective and subjective statements.

Paragraph 1: Introduction. Explain what the statement means, with particular reference to key terms: here, *scientific progress* and *quality of life.* Give one or two examples, but do not go into great detail, as this will be done in later paragraphs.

Paragraph 2: Discuss the positive aspects of scientific progress. Refer to specific examples, but also mention briefly any drawbacks these may have. For example here, computers have improved the quality of life by speeding up many processes, but they have also caused unemployment and could threaten privacy.

Paragraph 3: Discuss the more negative effects of scientific progress. Refer to specific examples. Here, pollution is an obvious example. In Paragraphs 2 and 3, try to remain objective by discussing the examples from a general point of view.

Paragraph 4: Express your own feelings by using more emotive language, but try to maintain the balance by mentioning both positive and negative aspects.

Paragraph 5: Conclusion. Say categorically whether or not you agree with the statement by referring back to the points that have already been made. The opinion should be subjective but backed up by logical argument.

Phrases introducing objective statements.
It is generally agreed (that) ...
Most people would argue (that) ...
It is common knowledge (that) ...
According to influential opinion, ...
The consensus view seems to be / is that ...

Phrases introducing subjective statements.
In my opinion, ...
My point of view is that ...
As far as I am concerned, ...
I think/believe (that) ...
I am convinced (that) ...

![icon]

There is always room at the top.

Daniel Webster

Speaking

1 It is often said that experience is the best teacher and that you cannot really learn anything until you have tried to do it.

1 When you pass your driving test, do you really know how to drive or does this happen only after you have been driving for some months?
2 Is it true to say that the only way to learn to speak a foreign language is to speak a foreign language?

2 Look at the photographs on the right and discuss with a partner what they have in common.

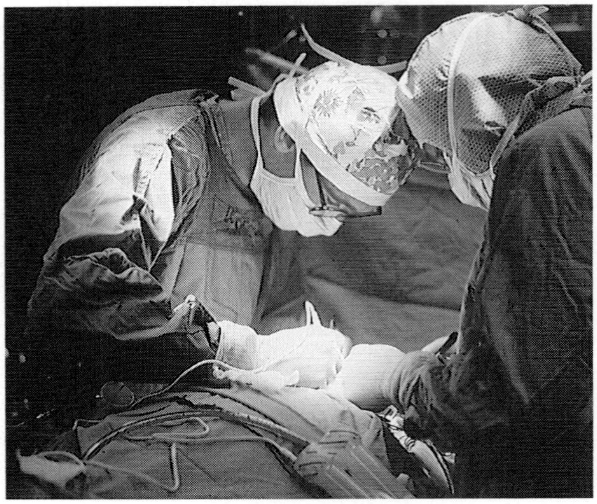

3 Read the passages below. Discuss how they develop the themes introduced in the photographs by:

1 deciding who is speaking.
2 discussing what points each of them is making about learning.
3 relating what each person says to experiences you have had.

Yea, of course we bunk off school to come down here – who needs it anyway? I learn a darn sight more doing this! It takes real skill to persuade people to part with their money, but if you've got the knack and really work at it you can clean up. I want to start my own business and get on – how can I do that stuck behind a desk?

Well, it had to happen sooner or later. Reading about it is one thing, but when you have to face the sight of blood and see people in pain it's a completely different matter. I must say I felt pretty squeamish, but at least I didn't faint. I just hope that after this initial experience I'll get used to it.

You've got to have a feel for it if you're working with animals. It's no use otherwise. We get people straight down from the Agricultural College. They're hopeless – wet behind the ears. They don't know what's hit them. I've been doing it all my life and I'm still learning. Animals are great teachers, you know.

Reading

The following passage is taken from *News from Nowhere* by William Morris. Writing in 1890, Morris describes a journey along the River Thames which enables him to give his views on an idealised society. In it, people can live in equality and harmony and conventional forms of education have no place.

1 Choose the most appropriate completion, a – d, for statements 1 – 5.

1 According to the passage, *the struggle for life* was a
a fight against slavery.
b fight against slaves.
c slave's fight for food.
d slave's fight for privileges.

2 The old man believed that
a children benefited from going to school.
b children were incapable of rebelling.
c schools could be damaging to children.
d schools developed children's minds and bodies.

3 *Twaddle* means
a useless facts and information.
b information that is well known but important to learn.
c a method of torturing people.
d a way of keeping people in poverty.

4 The narrator
a had never studied mathematics.
b believed that mathematics should never be taught.
c believed that only people over fifty should study mathematics.
d had been taught mathematics.

5 The old man, Hammond, laughed quietly because
a he felt he had made his point.
b he was amused by the narrator's ideas on education.
c the narrator had made a joke.
d he wanted to make fun of the narrator.

Said I: 'I want an extra word or two about your ideas of education; although I gathered from Dick that you let your children run wild – and in short, that you have so refined your education, that now you have none.'
'Then you gathered left-handed,' quoth he. 'But of course I understand your point of view about education, which is that of times past, when "the struggle for life", as men used to phrase it (i.e. the struggle for a slave's rations on one side, and for a bouncing share of the slave-holder's privilege on the other), pinched "education" for most people into a niggardly dole of not very accurate information; something to be swallowed by the beginner in the art of living whether he liked it or not, and was hungry for it or not: and which had been chewed and digested over and over again by people who didn't care about it in order to serve it out to other people who didn't care about it.'
I stopped the old man's rising wrath by a laugh, and said: 'Well, you were not taught that way, at any rate, so you may let your anger run off you a little.'
'True, true,' said he, smiling. 'I thank you for correcting my ill-temper: I always fancy myself as living in any period of which we may be speaking. But, however, or put it in a cooler way: you expected to see children thrust into schools when they had reached an age conventionally supposed to be the due age, whatever their varying faculties and dispositions might be, and when there, with like disregard to facts, to be subjected to a certain conventional course of "learning". My friend, can't you see that such a proceeding means ignoring the fact of growth, bodily and mental? No one could come out of such a mill uninjured; and those only would avoid being crushed by it who would have the spirit of rebellion strong in them. Fortunately most children have had that at all times, or I do not know that we should ever have reached our present position. Now you see what it all comes to. In the old times all this was the result of poverty. In the nineteenth century, society was so miserably poor, owing to the systemized robbery on which it was founded, that real education was impossible for anybody. The whole theory of their so-called education was that it was necessary to shove a little information into a child, even if it were by means of torture, and accompanied by twaddle which it was well known was of no use, or else he would lack information lifelong: the hurry of poverty forbade anything else.
All that is past; we are no longer hurried, and the information lies ready to each one's hand when his own inclinations impel him to seek it. In this as in other matters, we have become wealthy: we can ▶

◀ afford to give ourselves time to grow.'
'Yes,' said I, 'but suppose the child, youth, man never wants the information, never grows in the direction you might hope him to do: suppose, for instance, he objects to learning arithmetic or mathematics; you can't force him when he is grown; can't you force him while he is growing, and oughtn't you to do so?'
'Well,' said he, 'were you forced to learn arithmetic and mathematics?'
'A little,' said I.
'And how old are you now?'
'Say fifty-six,' said I.
'And how much arithmetic and mathematics do you know now?' quoth the old man, smiling rather mockingly.
Said I: 'None whatever, I am sorry to say.'
Hammond laughed quietly, but made no other comment on my admission, and I dropped the subject of education, perceiving him to be hopeless on that side.

Speaking

The passage raises questions about both what we learn and how we learn it. Discuss with your partner which of the subjects you have studied is the most useful in real life and which is the least useful.

Use of English

Something to be swallowed by the beginner whether he liked it or not, and was hungry for it or not: and which had been chewed and digested over and over again by people who didn't care about it in order to serve it out to other people who didn't care about.

This is an example from the passage of an extended metaphor. In it, all the language used metaphorically is connected with eating food: *swallowed, hungry, chewed, digested.*

This is a very effective linguistic device when used appropriately. It is, however, very easy to become confused and mix metaphors, so undermining the effect. The writer or speaker starts off in one subject area and then arbitrarily switches to another. For example:

Although she may have the courage of a lion, the chances are she will still be blown off course.

In this example, of course, the metaphor starts by referring to an animal, but then moves on to refer to a boat. It, therefore, sounds ridiculous, whereas a sustained metaphor can be very effective. For example:

Although Newman had been dealt a weak hand in the negotiations, he played his cards close to his chest, bluffed shrewdly and finally scooped the jackpot. The contract was his.

1 Read sentences 1 – 5 below. In each of them, an extended metaphor is used to enhance the message. Decide which are effective, which are less so and why.

1 When Margaret realised her job was on the line, she took the bull by the horns and jumped ship before the hovering vultures could throw her to the lions.
2 Dawn crept over the downs like a sinister white animal followed by the snarling cries of the wind eating its way between the black boughs of the thorns.
3 My head is a city in which pains have taken up residence in various parts of my face.
4 He has the sort of hawk-like expression that can open an oyster shell from forty paces.
5 Beneath the bludgeonings of Fate, his head is bloody but unbowed.

2 Complete each of sentences 1 – 7 by linking it with the most appropriate ending a – g.

1 Marlene snaked into the crowded ballroom …
2 Polly strutted around proudly …
3 Bernard entered regally …
4 Simon wrestled his way to the front …
5 John sailed through his exams but had difficulty getting a job …
6 Elizabeth took the lion's share of the responsibility …
7 Sweeney acted incisively …

a and performed with surgical precision.
b and coiled up in the most comfortable chair.
c and proceeded to dance majestically.
d in order to muscle in on what was happening.
e and sank without trace.
f and devoured anyone who stood in the way.
g managing to ruffle a number of feathers.

3 Read the advertisement for IWC watches which contains two extended metaphors: about time and Leonardo da Vinci.

1 Find the exact language which is used to extend each of these metaphors in the text.
2 Explain how the two metaphors are linked together.
3 Discuss the audience that the advertisement is aimed at.
4 Discuss how effective it is.

The automatic Da Vinci chronograph, with perpetual calendar and moon phase display, by IWC.

For gentlemen who have centuries at their disposal.

The little Da Vinci chronograph with perpetual moon phase display banishes forever a popular misconception: that IWC watches are crafted exclusively with gentlemen in mind.

The little Da Vinci is a tour de force, the Mona Lisa of our own 'old masters'. Within her firm yet gentle contours she contains a complex movement hitherto at home exclusively in the man's world.

Her alluring face betrays, nay documents, the ineluctable passage of time, exact to the second, minute, date and phase of the moon. Beyond that, her ability to withstand the ravages of time remains a well-kept feminine secret.

The little Da Vinci will continue to be a source of pleasure to the woman of the world for many moons to come. But of which she, alas, will ultimately have only too few.

Reading, writing and speaking

The article on the next page is about qualified success. It describes an interview with Bala Ambati, a prodigy from New York who, at the age of thirteen, expects to become the world's youngest doctor.

1 Read the passage. Find a word or phrase in the passage that means the same as each of the following words and phrases.

1 how to do something in a very careful way
2 to make something happen more quickly than usual
3 talented
4 to prevent someone developing fully
5 to continue with what is accepted as normal
6 a logical puzzle
7 a theory that developing too quickly has negative consequences
8 illnesses
9 desire
10 self-satisified

2 This article raises a number of questions about the education process. Respond to questions 1 – 4 with a partner.

1 Bala has not had a normal childhood, but has this done him any harm? Or has it only done him good?
2 Were the teachers right to worry that Bala was being pushed too hard?
3 Are academic excellence and successful social interaction mutually exclusive?
4 What is the attitude of the interviewer towards Bala? Which comments from the passage led you to this conclusion?

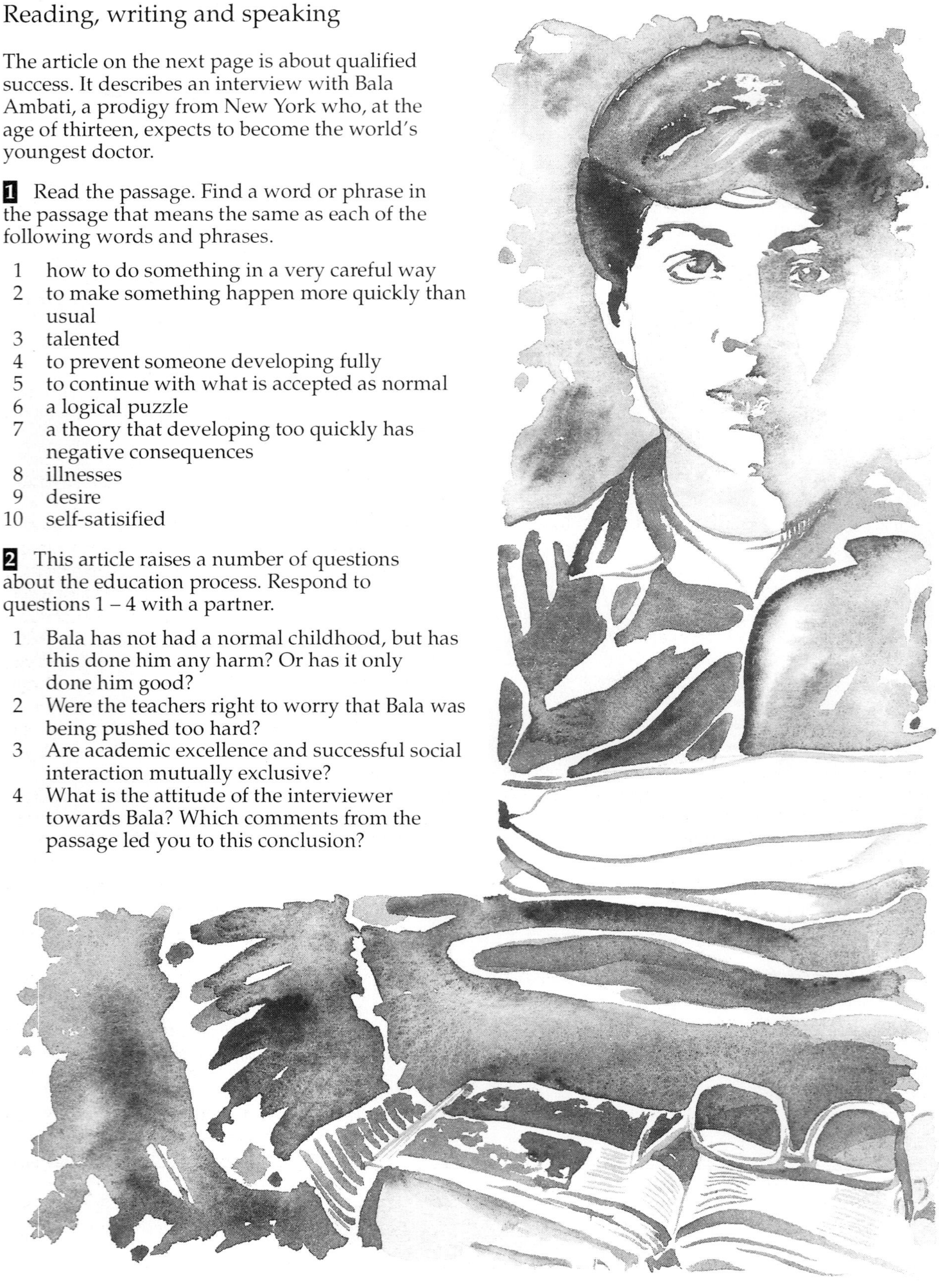

Bala carefully wrote out a note, giving the full names of every member of his family, to make sure they would be spelled and published correctly. The prodigy's printing is meticulously legible but slightly wobbly – no better than you would expect from a 13-year-old. From the first moment you find yourself gratified by signs of imperfection in him. 'We are from the same planet,' your subconscious whispers.

His diction, for example, is a joke. He speaks a sentence as if it's a formula in a learned speech to an academic gathering.

Their father, Ambati Rao, who holds a PhD in industrial engineering, used to give private lessons in mathematics in the family's front room. As a very young child, aged five or six, Bala would sit under the blackboard during these lessons. 'One day,' according to the father, 'he could answer the questions on calculus,' without having been given any specific teaching himself. 'He had had guidance and talk rather than instruction,' says Dr Rao.

The family left Madras in 1980 and emigrated to America because Dr Rao felt that he and his boys would get their best chance there. They have had four homes in four different states, the latest in New York where Dr Rao has been working in the Data Processing Agency of the city government's Human Resources Administration.

At every stage of his son's formal education, Dr Rao has been battling with school managers and educational administrators who felt he was trying to force the pace of Bala's development faster than would be good for him. At every step the father won.

By the time he was eight he was studying modern algebra, set theory, topology and logic through the Children Gifted at Mathematics Course organised by the State University of New York.

Halfway through third grade, when he was seven, Bala had already completed the academic curricula for grades four and five. His teachers wanted him to go through those years and classes in the orthodox way. His father was furious. 'I said to them: what are you going to do about this boy? Isn't it your responsibility to help him rather than to hold him back?'

Were the teachers right when they worried that Dr Rao was pushing Bala too hard? He says, 'I never pushed anybody. All children have these abilities. Everybody is a genius up to the age of 10. The parents' task is to discover the field in which the child's genius lies.'

Hearing this, Bala said: 'Many bureaucrats are the personification of inertia. They want to perpetuate the status quo. Their opposition came from ignorance rather than scepticism. It is my belief that academic excellence and social interaction are not mutually exclusive: I've shown that that is false. Many of these abilities are latent in most children but they are not developed. Unfortunately, parents tend to be divided into two categories and are seen either as pushy or passive.'

The Ambati family's idea of a good time after dinner is to 'sit and propose maths problems to each other.' Bala's outstanding contribution to family fun has been his solution to 'The Travelling Salesman Problem' (a well-known brain bender which asks how a man can visit a number of cities in the US without repeating or crossing his path). Bala's solution won the Navy Science Award. His prize was to be taken on a tour of a nuclear submarine in the Navy dockyards in San Diego – a treat he recalled with such enthusiasm and innocence that, for a moment, he sounded just like a 13-year-old kid.

It didn't last. He was soon speaking again in sentences which sound as if they've come out of a digital translating machine. You ask, 'Don't you ever feel like saying, "Give me a break, I'm only 13" to some of the adults who expect adult achievements from you?' And he replies: 'The need for that does not arise. I am able to adjust my front according to the peer group in which I find myself.'

If you ask him whether he ever worries that such rapid intellectual development at such an early age might lead to trouble in later life, he says: 'There is a strong research base to refute the early ripe / early rot hypothesis. The vast majority of happy geniuses are not given attention because they do not fit this hypothesis. The media have perpetuated the idea that an academic prodigy must have a bad social life.'

It is awful to imagine oneself receiving medical advice and treatment from a 17-year-old who speaks in textbook paragraphs; but perhaps he will have humanised his speech by the time he starts diagnosing the ailments of live humans. Bala says he wants to do a combination of research and hands-on practice because 'I have always been drawn to practice, having always enjoyed working with people', and he likes the idea of 'helping people out of devastating illness' because he was badly scalded when he was three years old and was in hospital for three months. 'My ambition is to be the best doctor I can be. I am keen to help some of the people who have helped me. I have a strong yearning to help humanity through medicine.'

'Wouldn't the world be a better place if everybody was as good as they could possibly be? If everybody was encouraged, throughout their lives, to find the highest level to which they could aspire?'

This is the question every prodigy poses. For the complacent adult, it is likely to be an infuriating question.

3 Over two hundred years ago similar questions were being asked about the boy genius Wolfgang Amadeus Mozart.

Read the passage and discuss with your partner:

1 what similarities and what differences there are between Bala Ambati and Mozart.
2 whether a person has to be born a genius or whether this level of ability can also be achieved through application and hard work.
3 what criteria should be used to identify a genius.
4 who else, either living or dead, you would call a genius.

Listening

Listen to a group of people discussing someone whose reputation as a genius is open to question. Complete the notes.

Name of subject:	....
Achievements:	....
Special qualities:	....
Speakers' reservations:	....
Consensus view:	....

A Composer At Five

At the age when most children are struggling with the basics of reading and writing, Mozart was already composing music and performing to great acclaim at the courts of Europe.

Child prodigies are rare in any age, and Mozart was surely one of the youngest and most prodigious of all time. Small wonder, then, that, especially in his early years, he should have been regarded with that mixture of awe and admiration that such a degree of talent inevitably attracts almost to a freakish extent. Leopold Mozart has often been criticised for exploiting his son's musical talents for his own material advantage, of taking the young boy around Europe as if he were a circus act, but the fact is that, even if there were an element of truth in this, Leopold's own character and the conditions that such travelling brought contributed enormously to the rapid development of those talents.

There is no doubt that the young Wolfgang had an extremely high degree of natural musical talent, manifest in a purely physical way in his having what we call today 'perfect pitch' and a highly-developed sense of coordination. This is suggested by Leopold's description of his son's first encounter with the organ at the start of the Mozart family's extended tour of Europe between 1763 and 1766, when the seven-year-old boy stood on the pedal-board and played 'as if he had been practising for several months. Everyone was amazed. Indeed this is a fresh act of God's grace, which many a one receives after much labour.'

Wolfgang's exceptional aural ability is confirmed by a Salzburg newspaper report from a few months earlier which claims that he could name any note that was sounded as well as being able to play like an adult, to improvise in different styles, to sight-read any accompaniment perfectly and to add a bass to any given melody. He is also said to have taken a second violin part and played it perfectly at sight, without error, although he had not had a single lesson on the instrument.

Indeed, the whole question of Mozart's education, musical or otherwise, is a curious one. It would appear that he never received any formal education other than lessons conducted father to son. He certainly seems to have enjoyed arithmetic and to have learnt Latin (which Leopold knew) and other languages during his childhood travels round Europe, yet to have had no other musical training than that afforded by his father's corrections of his early compositions, and hearing the music of others.

By the age of four he could play some of the keyboard pieces in his elder sister Nannerl's music book, and within the next year he had completed some little works of his own. The example of his almost equally talented sister, five years his senior (of whom he was inordinately fond), must surely have served as an additional spur to his own early development. What he missed in the schoolroom was more than compensated for by his extended travels through Europe: to Vienna in 1762; to Germany, Brussels, Paris, London, Holland and Switzerland in 1763-6; to Vienna again in 1767-8; and to Italy in 1769-71 and 1772-3.

Travels of this kind brought the young boy direct experience of many of the harsh realities in life – discomfort, homesickness, illness, hard work – as well as bringing him into constant contact with exciting new places, strange faces and most important of all for his development as a composer, music he would not have heard if he had stayed in Salzburg. When Leopold wrote from London in 1764 that 'my boy knows in this his eighth year what one would expect only from a man of forty,' he was exaggerating no more than when he lopped a year off his boy's age in the advertisements for his concerts; Mozart's skill and maturity at least musically were undeniably quite remarkable.

Use of English

The following passage comes from the novel *On the Road* by Jack Kerouac. Set in the United States in the early 1950s, it describes what happens when a writer, based on Kerouac himself, leaves the comparative security of city life and heads out West to experience life as a traveller. In this extract, because he and his girlfriend Terry are short of money, he decides to try his hand at picking cotton.

1 Read the passage. Then complete it with one word in each space.

Nothing was going to happen except starvation for Terry and me, so in the morning I walked around the countryside asking for cotton picking work. Everybody ... (1) me to go to the farm across the highway from the camp. I ... (2), and the farmer was in the kitchen with his woman. He came out, listened to my story and warned me he was paying only three dollars per hundred pounds (fifty kilos) of ... (3) cotton. I pictured ... (4) picking at least three hundred pounds a day and took the job. He fished out some long canvas ... (5) from the barn and told me to start the ... (6) day. I rushed ... (7) to Terry, all glee. On the way a grape truck went ... (8) a bump in the road and threw off great ... (9) of grapes on the hot tar. I ... (10) them up and took them home.

We ate the grapes with a loaf of ... (11). In a larger tent next to ours lived a whole family of cotton pickers. ... (12) dawn I went to work with them. They said the cotton was ... (13) in the early morning because of the dew and you could make more money than in the afternoon. ... (14) they worked ... (15) day from dawn to sundown.

We ... (16) down and began picking cotton. It was beautiful. Across the fields ... (17) the tents, and ... (18) them were the cottonfields that stretched out of ... (19) to the brown foothills and then the ... (20)-capped Sierras in the blue morning air. But I knew nothing about picking cotton. I spent too much time disengaging the white ball from the crackly bed; the others did it in one flick. Moreover, my fingertips began to bleed. I needed gloves or more experience.

2 The passage is written in a very straightforward style without complex structures. The sentences are short and to the point. This is a good example of how a narrative can be written without using elaborate language. Kerouac termed it *spontaneous prose*.

Read the last paragraph again and note how each of the sentences is started. He could have connected the sentences together as follows to make more continuous prose:

As I knew nothing about picking cotton I, unlike the others who did it in one flick, spent too much time disengaging the white ball from the crackly bed and because I had neither gloves nor experience, my fingertips began to bleed.

Why do you think Kerovac chose to write in his rather simple way rather than using the more complex sentence structure in the example? Which do you think is more effective?

Writing

Choice of style depends on the type of message the writer wants to convey to the people who are expected to read it. The style itself depends on the writer's choice of language and especially on the way that sentences are constructed and connected.

Connectors fall into three main groups which are characterised by the connectives *and*, *or* and *but*.

1 Complete sentences 1 – 10 using an appropriate connector from the list below.

besides otherwise alternatively moreover nevertheless notwithstanding likewise consequently despite conversely

1 ... writing numerous novels, Graham Greene fought tirelessly for causes he believed in.
2 Greene's enormous contribution to world literature is well-known; ..., he was not awarded the Nobel prize.
3 In his later years, Greene found life in England had become increasingly restrictive and ... chose to live in the South of France.
4 Greene's characters often lived in conflict with society and its conventions, but ... were depicted as having high moral standards.
5 After Greene's death, many lesser literary figures criticised his writing. ..., they condemned his novels on the grounds that they were too popular.
6 Many of Greene's novels are set outside England: *The Quiet American* is about Vietnam; ... *Our Man in Havana*, which is set mainly in pre-revolutionary Cuba.
7 Readers wishing to experience Greene's work for the first time should try his entertaining novel *Travels with my Aunt*. ... his short stories are very readable.
8 ... his personal wealth, Graham Greene was not interested in money and never gave up his comparatively simple lifestyle.
9 His antipathy towards England ..., he visited the country on occasions and was a regular contributor to the letters columns of English newspapers and magazines.
10 Greene felt it was his duty to make people aware of corruption in high places through his writing. ... nothing would be done to stop it.

2 Write a brief biography (about 150 words) of a person you know a lot about. It is to be published in a serious magazine or newspaper. Use the list of connectors in the previous exercise to help you.

Vocabulary development

Complete each of the following sentences with the most appropriate item a – d.

1 Following a tip-off, the police conducted a ... search of the property in the hope of finding even a trace of the missing goods.
a morbid b mendacious c meticulous
d meteoric

2 Rita seems to have the ... of always getting her own way.
a nick b knack c lack d crack

3 Freddie claims not to be ... but he didn't look at the screen once when the alien had his head knocked off at the end of the film.
a fiendish b heroic c frightful
d squeamish

4 Cleopatra managed to escape the ... of time and remained youthfully beautiful until the end of her life.
a passages b hours c ravages
d eternity

5 The vicious brute ... at every passer by and fully justified the sign 'Beware of the dog'.
a snarled b smirked c winked
d bowed

6 ... these accusations of indecisiveness, the selection committee is certain that Maurice Minor should be appointed as the next Managing Director.
a Regarding b Notwithstanding
c Siting d Banking

7 Mick, who was obsessively shy, used to ... around outside the café where Marianne worked in the hope of catching a glimpse of her.
a glower b soar c strut d hover

8 A whole ... of us, all working in the same office, go skiing together every year.
a lunch b crunch c bunch
d brunch

9 Once you have ... all the relevant material and memorised it, please return the document to Mr Smersh to ensure its confidentiality.
a digested b shredded c chewed
d swallowed

10 Harry Hassell is a lion of a man with a ... of blond hair and a ferocious temper.
a mane b wig c hank d dreadlock

Reading

The extract opposite comes from the novel *The Big Sleep* by Raymond Chandler. The plot is sometimes difficult to follow but it was written with such style that this hardly seems to matter.

1 Read the passage opposite. Decide whether each statement 1 – 8 is true or false.

1 The girl was probably not very strong.
2 It was fashionable, at that time, for girls to have very short hair.
3 Her teeth were discoloured.
4 She was obviously a very thoughtful person.
5 She moved her eyelashes in a way that was designed to be attractive.
6 The narrator was a professional boxer.
7 She fell into his arms because she had fainted.
8 She quickly disappeared the moment the butler came in.

2 Identify the language which is used metaphorically. Discuss with your partner how effective the imagery is in conveying the scene and the writer's ideas.

Writing

Write a story, in about 350 words, which begins:

The traveller surveyed the scene and thought, 'I have reached the end of my journey. This is where my new life begins.'

A narrative composition often requires you to continue a story from an introductory sentence. In this type of composition it is extremely important to read the sentence carefully, as it is phrased in such a way as to give several possible opportunities for extended writing. Words such as *traveller, scene* and *new life* can be interpreted in a number of different ways.

Before starting to write have a clear idea of:

1 who the traveller is and where this person has come from.
2 what the scene is and how it should be described.

Make sure you have the range of vocabulary to describe both the person and the place and that their detailed descriptions remain consistent throughout the composition.

As the traveller is about to start a new life, it is also necessary to give some idea of what the old life was.

Also think about how the story is going to end. Be careful about tenses. The opening sentence is set in the past (*surveyed*) and even though the traveller is thinking about the future, the story should be set in the past by use of appropriate tenses.

Look back over the language you have studied in the Unit and where appropriate incorporate it into your composition.

She was twenty or so, small and delicately put together, but she looked durable. She wore pale blue slacks and they looked well on her. She walked as if she were floating. Her hair was a fine tawny wave cut much shorter than the current fashion of pageboy tresses curled in at the bottom. Her eyes were slate-grey, and had almost no expression when she looked at me. She came over near me and smiled with her mouth and she had little sharp predatory teeth, as white as fresh orange pith and as shiny as porcelain. They glistened between her thin, too taut lips. Her face lacked colour and didn't look too healthy.

'Tall, aren't you?' she said.

'I didn't mean to be.'

Her eyes rounded. She was puzzled. She was thinking. I could see, even on that short acquaintance, that thinking was always going to be a bother to her.

'Handsome too,' she said. 'And I bet you know it.'

I grunted.

'What's your name?'

'Reilly,' I said. 'Doghouse Reilly.'

'That's a funny name.' She bit her lip and turned her head a little and looked at me along her eyes. Then she lowered her lashes until they almost cuddled her cheeks and slowly raised them again, like a theatre curtain. I was to get to know that trick. That was supposed to make me roll over on my back with all four paws in the air.

'Are you a prize fighter?' she asked, when I didn't.

'Not exactly. I'm a sleuth.'

'A a ...' She tossed her head angrily, and the rich colour of it glistened in the rather dim light of the big hall. 'You're making fun of me.'

'Uhuh.'

'What?'

'Get on with you,' I said. 'You heard me.'

'You didn't say anything. You're just a big tease.' She put a thumb up and bit it. It was a curiously shaped thumb, thin and narrow like an extra finger, with no curve in the fist joint. She bit it and sucked it slowly, turning it around in her mouth like a baby with a comforter.

'You're awfully tall,' she said. Then she giggled with secret merriment. Then she turned her body slowly and lithely, without lifting her feet. Her hands dropped limp at her sides. She tilted herself towards me on her toes. She fell straight back into my arms. I had to catch her or let her crack her head on the tessellated floor. I caught her under her arms and she went rubber-legged on me instantly. I had to hold her close to hold her up. When her head was against my chest she screwed it around and giggled at me.

'You're cute,' she giggled. 'I'm cute too.'

I didn't say anything. So the butler chose that convenient moment to come back through the French doors and see me holding her.

It didn't seem to bother him. He was a tall, thin, silver man. Sixty or close to it or a little past it. He had blue eyes as remote as eyes could be. His skin was smooth and bright and he moved like a man with very sound muscles. He walked slowly across the floor towards us and the girl jerked away from me. She flashed across the room to the front of the stairs and went up them like a deer. She was gone before I could draw a long breath and let it out.

The butler said tonelessly: 'The General will see you now, Mr. Marlowe.'

The Earth does not argue and shuts no-one out.

Walt Whitman

Reading and speaking

Read the following poem by Philip Larkin about how the environment is changing and answer questions 1 – 3.

1 Is this poem optimistic or pessimistic?
2 Why is the title suited to it?
3 How far do you agree with the sentiments expressed?

Vocabulary development

Choose the paraphrase which best explains these words and phrases from the poem.

1 *louts*
a animals kept as pets
b badly behaved young people

2 *bleak high-risers*
a angry builders who take stimulants.
b depressing modern tower blocks

3 *snuff it*
a finish a cigarette
b die

4 *a cast of crooks and tarts*
a people with no sense of morality
b people who want to preserve old buildings

5 *thick-strewn*
a densely covered
b intelligently positioned

GOING, GOING

I thought it would last my time –
The sense that, beyond the town,
There would always be fields and farms,
Where the village louts could climb
Such trees as were not cut down;
I knew there'd be false alarms

In the papers about old streets
And split-level shopping, but some
Have always been left so far;
And when the old part retreats
As the bleak high-risers come
We can always escape in the car.

Things are tougher than we are, just
As earth will always respond
However we mess it about;
Chuck filth in the sea, if you must:
The tides will clean beyond.
– But what do I feel now? Doubt?

That before I snuff it, the whole
Boiling will be bricked in
Except for the tourist parts –
First slum of Europe: a role
It won't be so hard to win,
With a cast of crooks and tarts.

And that will be England gone,
The shadows, the meadows, the lanes,
The guildhalls, the carved choirs.
There'll be books; it will linger on
In galleries; but all that remains
For us will be concrete and tyres.

Most things are never meant.
This won't be, most likely: but greeds
And garbage are too thick-strewn
To be swept up now, or invent
Excuses that make all needs.
I just think it will happen, soon.

Listening

1 What effects does the environment have on the people who live in it?

Listen to four people talking about where they now live and what adjustments they have had to make in order to adapt to a change in their environment. Number the people below in the order in which they speak.

- ☐ a recently released prisoner
- ☐ a castaway
- ☐ a lottery winner
- ☐ someone who has moved from town to country

2 Complete the notes below.

The first speaker has adjusted …
The second speaker implies …
The third speaker dislikes …
The fourth speaker has changed …

Reading

The following two extracts are taken from *King Fisher Lives* by Julian Rathbone. Lewis Fisher, a celebrated writer and a role model for the younger generation, decides to put his ideas about the development of civilisation to the test. His theories are challenged by a university lecturer called Mark Southam.

1 The first extract describes Lewis Fisher's theories. Read it and decide whether each of the following statements is true or false.

1 Lewis believes that his theories provide answers to the question of human evolution.
2 According to Lewis, survival depends on being able to change one's living conditions to suit a different environment.
3 The dramatic changes in climate which occurred proved that people could adapt to any conditions.
4 Complex social organisations enable people to come to terms with their own mortality.
5 Lewis could not be described as arrogant or self-opinionated.

'Right then,' Olivia shifted in a business-like fashion and the cushions squeaked. 'Lewis has been looking at the different theories of our beginnings, that is at homo sapiens when he first appeared, not at our forebears.' I realised that she was now talking not to us but to the recorder. 'Lewis is trying to interpret the scientist for the technologist in this, showing the practical applications of what the scientist has discovered. And right off, what does he discover but that most of these theories are contradictory. Was homo sapiens a hunter? Was he a tree-man, a bush-man, a plains-man? Was meat essential or an occasional luxury? Did the women stay at home? How essential were tools? Weapons? Lewis has found that each theory confidently asserts different answers to each and every one of these questions and that the questions therefore remain virtually unanswered.' She took breath. 'How'm I doing, Lewis?'
'Fine. But that bit about science and technology is your rationalisation. I don't aim to save the human race. What I want to know is how I should live.'
'Right,' she gulped. 'All the theories about our origin start with evolution and assume that established species are the survivors of mutations best adapted to their environment. But there is such a multiplicity of environments for humans, we seem so adaptable we'll fit in anywhere. So that clue to our nature led nowhere too. One thing seemed sure though. From Eskimos to Pygmies, natural man survived in small groups, without forming large, heavily organised societies, and this was true for many, many millennia. Probably only in response to cosmic catastrophe did that final evidence of our adaptability occur, long after our physical and mental evolution was complete. Ice ages, drought, maybe even planetary interference causing terrible convulsions ...'
'For Christ's sake,' I tried again, 'does he really have to justify his dislike of social systems by inventing a War of the Worlds?'
'So,' she went on, more hurriedly than ever, 'specific environment, so long as it was not too hostile, was not important; complex social organisation is not part of our nature ... there is a third factor. The higher mammals, the primates, the cats, and so on, have one basic instinct in common, and the higher the mammal the more developed it is: that is the instinct for their self-preservation. Every higher organism is a system refined and adapted to preserve itself; just as lower organisms are adapted to preserve their species. This perhaps is the importance of consciousness, self-awareness. Because we know we will die, we aim to try harder than any other animal to avoid death.'

2 In the second extract, Lewis and his friend Nadia, who is Mark Southam's sister, have cut themselves off from civilisation completely and gone to live up in the mountains, taking nothing with them except bows and arrows. After nine months, Mark becomes worried about his sister, so he goes to find them. He discovers that they are living entirely off the land in what he later terms *primitive conditions*. After realising that there is nothing to eat, Mark is persuaded to join Lewis and Nadia in their hunt for deer. He describes what happened.

Read the text and answer questions 1 – 8.

1 Why did Mark think that the deer were lovely when he first saw them?
2 Would Fisher and Nadia have reacted towards the deer in the same way?
3 Immediately after the buck was hit by the first arrow, how did the other deer, the does and their young, react?
4 What prevented the buck from escaping?
5 What is implied in the last sentence?
6 Is there any connection between the theories that Lewis was propounding and the experience that Mark had?
7 Do you believe that the need to survive changes the way that people behave? If so, to what extent and how? If not, why not?
8 How do you think you would react to deer being hunted and killed in this way if you were in the same situation as Mark?

3 Summarise in between 50 and 60 words what Mark actually did during the deer hunt. Begin the summary:

After the deer had been sighted, Mark …

And at last there they were. They had now moved a hundred yards to the left of the two pines Nadia had mentioned. At about two hundred and fifty yards two of them, the buck with his short antlers and one of the does, were clearly visible and in a moment I could make out the others in a patch of scrub oak which came just about up to the buck's head, between four and five feet. They were browsing off the leaves. They were lonely. Even at that distance their miniature daintiness in bright russet coats was lovely.

Nevertheless it was a long wait, but not now a boring one indeed, as the minutes piled on top of each other I began to feel drunk with apprehension and anticipation, a growing euphoria that began to well up from my stomach and sent tingles down the backs of my arms.

But I could not dare to allow these times of relaxation to extend beyond a minute, I had to be back, spread-eagled on the hot rock, with the sun burning into my neck and the flies crawling over my shoulders, for fear that after all I should miss the climactic moment.

I nearly did miss it, even though I was watching, the moment when the arrow struck, for it was so quick that a blink of the eye would have cost me an image which will endure till I die.

The buck suddenly lifted his head and froze. It will be said that at that distance I could not have seen his muzzle quiver-testing the air for taints, his ears moving independantly like radar detectors.

He barked twice, loud, deep, and sharp, and the scrub exploded as the does and young scampered away to my right along the edge of the forest, fast but stealthy they were, yet airborne in long leaps over rocks and bushes that must, one thought, shatter their legs on impact. The buck, though, stayed for a moment where he was, giving odd, quick, tortured jumps, twisting his neck, reaching with muzzle and tongue at the shaft, then as another arrow seered across his exposed neck his head swung forward and low and he came bounding up the slope towards me.

What should I do? What was I meant to do?

In spite of the slope, in spite of his wounds he had covered half the distance between us in the time it took me to slither off the rock, fumble for a spear, find one, and get back to where I was, and he was still running, speed undiminished. Behind him, a hundred yards behind and to the left, the brown figure of Fisher had broken cover and was coming after him at an angle, almost as fast but at the moment not quite so fast, the buck was widening the gap, would get away.

I leapt out brandishing my spear and hallooing; he saw me, stumbled and veered off in a course that would cut across Fisher's line, and in that moment I could hear the buck's snorted breath.

I hurled my spear, it fell short and wide, stooped for another and launched myself helter-skelter in pursuit, knees and palms skinned on rocks as I took fall after fall, breath dragged in and out of aching lungs, blood roaring in my ears. He stumbled too, stayed with haunches sunk to the ground, neck and head twisting in an agony of desire for the strength that was leaking out of him, searching for the will to go on, then he hauled his rump up again and the white, heart-shaped flash bounded away from me. As it did I heard the zip of the arrow that parted the air a yard from my head, heard never saw it, and I flung myself to the ground hugging myself into it as flat as I could go.

'Stand still.' It was a scream, a shout, not recognisably Nadia's but high and shrill.

I half turned my head though my feet and arms were rigid leaving me crouched over the boulder I was on like a white, shell-less crab and first I saw Fisher, quite close now, almost level with me and then behind him some way off but between us, Nadia with bow and arrow poised. All this I saw in the blink of an eye: I saw her legs splayed and one knee bent for the slope she was on, bow arm muscles swelling hard, arrow arm bending back to her ear, eyes, neck, vunerable breasts, flat firm stomach and thighs well-braced, her whole being centred on the diagram of energy between the hoop of the bow now almost a semi-circle and the equal lines of the string, lines pulled to perfect straightness by the pounds of pressure that held them.

The moment of release was too quick for the eye to catch, but the sound of it came and went with the arrow that passed between Fisher and me like a meteor between planets, and homed into the neck of the buck above us.

He hardly staggered, moved on, slowly relentless, one hoof, then the next, he went on moving, walking up the slope away from us, head down almost to his knees swaying and lifting, and I could hear the wheeze and bellow of his breath.

Fisher reached him first, but Nadia and I were close, close. Fisher seized the small, strong antlers and as the beast settled on its haunches he pulled the head up and back, and the eye whites rolled. He sank his bowie knife into its throat. The fresh, hot smell, metallic and sour, filled my nostrils, and my stomach turned, not with nausea, but with hunger.

Vocabulary development

1 The following verbs taken from the previous extract describe different types of movement.

slither fumble break cover leap brandish stumble veer haul scramble stagger

Read through the extract again to check how the verbs are used in context. Then complete each of the following sentences with a verb from the list. Make sure each verb is in the correct form.

1 Watson watched helplessly as Holmes ... over the smooth, wet rocks desperately searching for something to cling to, to prevent him from falling into the waterfall below.
2 ... a baseball bat for protection, Bertie Wooster confronted the masked intruder.
3 If Robin Hood had wished to see Marion, he ... sooner and emerged from the shadows of those enormous trees into the open.
4 As the yacht changed tack, a sudden gust of wind caused it ... suddenly, throwing the crew onto the deck.
5 After being hit by Wilcox, Leonard ... around the room holding his head before collapsing in a heap on the sofa.
6 Tess and Angel ... on their hands and knees into a ditch to avoid being seen by the mounted police.
7 Free from the pull of gravity, Neil Armstrong ... joyfully across the Moon's surface.
8 While Henry Wilt ... in his pocket in a vain attempt to find the key, the neighbours peered at him suspiciously from behind their curtains.
9 The little people of Lilliput tied ropes to Gulliver's arms and legs, ... him out of the sea and up onto the beach.
10 Christine ... over the protruding root, lost her footing and fell into the icy pond.

Reading and speaking

Read through the true story below and discuss with your partner:

1 what the farmers should have done to stop the indiscriminate hunting.
2 whether or not the hunting of wild animals is ever justified.
3 what alternative methods there are to control the wild animal population when it poses a threat to crops or farm animals.

Four-legged Works of Art

IN the 1920's, in New York State, USA, deer-hunting was very popular. So popular, in fact, that at weekends the countryside was crawling with hunters who hardly knew one end of a gun from the other. They shot at anything that moved. Sometimes they even shot each other, though they usually missed!

By 1927, farmers were so fed up with having their milk cows shot at in mistake for deer that they came up with an idea. They painted their cows in shades of khaki, green and brown so that they blended into the countryside and could graze undisturbed. This didn't work very well as the hunters still spotted movement – and shot at the cows. The next year the farmers painted their cows again, but this time they used bright, vivid colours, and painted their cows in stripes, spots and other bright patterns so the hunters just couldn't mistake them for deer. After all, who ever saw a pink deer with blue polka dots? The hunters certainly saw the cows now, but the painted cows idea failed in the end. The normally docile cows didn't like the bright colours and patterns, and became upset and hard to handle. When they stopped giving milk, the farmers had to wash the paint off and go back to the drawing board.

Use of English

1 The verb *need* in English can be used in various ways. Study the examples. Then match each of them with one of the explanatory notes a – f.

Nadia and Fisher need to kill deer to be able to eat.
(They have no other alternative.)

The deer needs cooking / to be cooked before it can be eaten.
(Something has to be done to it before eating it.)

Carrots don't need cooking / You don't need to cook carrots.
(They can be eaten raw.)

You needn't have cooked the carrots.
(But they are delicious, so I'm glad you did.)

He didn't need to wash the car.
(It had not been used since its last wash.)

a passive requirement
b active general need
c unnecessary action which was not carried out
d unnecessary action which was, however, carried out
e negative passive requirement
f negative active need

2 Rewrite each of the following sentences so that it means the same as the sentence above it, using the appropriate form of the verb *need* and beginning each sentence in the way shown.

1 The law requires all dangerous dogs to be licensed by their owners.
All owners ...
2 A dangerous dog cannot enter a public park unless it is kept on a lead.
A dangerous dog...
3 I know it's the height of fashion but why wear sunglasses in the dim light of a trendy restaurant?
You ...
4 Regular maintenance checks will be a thing of the past with these new electric cars.
These ...
5 Keep your voice down. I'm not deaf.
You ...
6 I spent all day in a queue in order to get a ticket to see the brilliant musical *Dogs* by Tozo Barker and then five minutes before the show started my friend walked in and bought a ticket straight away.
I ...
7 Gordon Globetrotter, the famous basketball player, was so tall that he could put the ball in the basket without jumping.
Gordon Globetrotter ...
8 All that worry was for nothing as the police have now decided not to take me to court for dangerous driving.
I ...

Reading

In the struggle to protect the environment, it is often thought that individuals have little influence. Significant improvements can only be brought about by governments or multinational organisations. However, it is surprising what can be achieved by members of the public.

The magazine articles on the next page describe individual successes in this continuing battle. Read the texts and the examples below. Then summarise each of the other individuals' actions in a similar way, using the connectors given on the right.

Reason: *To save the black rhino, one of the world's most endangered species.*

Action: *Michael trekked thousands of miles across Africa and Europe.*

Consequences: *He raised over $1 million. The black rhino population has been steadily increasing.*

Summary
In order to help save the black rhino, one of the world's most endangered species, Michael Werikhe trekked thousands of miles across Africa and Europe and as a result raised over $1 million which has partly contributed to a steady increase in the black rhino population.

Connectors
if
as a result (of)
because (of)
due to
as a consequence of
the result is (that)
therefore
so
consequently
thanks to
in order to
after seeing / experiencing / discovering
when he / she found out about / realised
instead of
in response to

Walks On The Wild Side

A long-distance walk for a worthy cause is hardly a new idea, but Kenyan MICHAEL WERIKHE has taken the concept to new lengths. Over the past eight years, Werikhe, 33, has trekked thousands of miles across Africa and Europe to raise money to save the black rhino, one of the world's most endangered species.

Elephant tusks, rhino horns and leopard skins confiscated from poachers were a common sight in the 'ivory room' of the Kenyan Game Department's Mombasa office, where Werikhe used to work. But a pair of 50-kg (110lb.) tusks brought in one day by a game warden induced him to start his one-man brigade. 'Being an African, I see wildlife as part of my heritage,' Werikhe says. 'If wildlife goes, then part of me is dead. I wanted to campaign for wildlife in my own private way.'

On his first wildlife walk in 1982, Werikhe travelled 2,400 km (1,500 miles), from Kampala, Uganda, through Kenya to Dar es Salaam, Tanzania, and back to Mombasa, with only a pet python named Survival for company. Lecturing to villagers and schoolchildren, he raised about $30,000 for conservation groups. In 1988 Werikhe went to Europe, covering 2,900 km (1,800 miles) in 135 days, and collected almost $1 million for rhino sanctuaries. Partly as a result of Werikhe's efforts, Kenya's black rhino population – once as low as 400 animals – has been slowly increasing since 1988. When Werikhe is not on one of his journeys, he works as superintendent of security at an auto plant. He plans to walk across the United States later this year and hopes to eventually visit the Far East.

LOVE CANAL'S FEISTY MUCKRAKER

She was a storybook Niagara Falls housewife, baking bread, keeping a spotless kitchen and raising her family in the neighborhood known locally as Love Canal. But in 1978 **LOIS GIBBS'** life took an abrupt turn. That was when she became convinced that the toxic goo seeping from an abandoned chemical-waste dump three blocks from her home was making her children and those of her neighbours sick. Stymied by stonewalling corporate and government bureaucrats, she summoned talents she did not know she had. Over a period of two years, Gibbs knocked on doors, passed out petitions, gave speeches, picketed, sat in, got arrested and, finally, took hostage a couple of Environmental Protection Agency officials until the FBI ordered her to release them. That got President Carter's attention and ultimately forced the Government to evacuate the neighbourhood.

The woman who transformed Love Canal into an international symbol of the dangers of toxic waste has become a role model for a generation of homemaking ecocrusaders.

A Children's Can-collecting Crusade

What can one boy or girl do to preserve the world's rain forests? Ask Jiro Nakayama. He's the twelve-year-old leader of a band of schoolchildren in Nagano, Japan, who have already saved 40 acres of forest land in Costa Rica. On their way to and from school, they collect old newspapers and aluminium cans for sale to a recycling plant at 63 cents per kg. The proceeds, augmented by donations from parents and neighbours, are sent to the International Children's Rainforest Program, which buys and preserves virgin parkland at the rate of $50 an acre. So far, Jiro and his friends have raised more than $5,000.

The program began in Sweden where some 100,000 schoolchildren, helped by matching government grants, have been able to buy 160,000 acres of Costa Rican forest. A similar venture affiliated with the Nature Conservancy has enlisted thousands of American students to preserve 110,000 acres of tropical parkland in Belize. Among the participants: a class of autistic children in the Bronx who cashed in enough cans to buy an acre of species-rich jungle.

Reading and Listening

You have just read about individual efforts to improve a potentially damaging situation. Sometimes, however, it is extremely difficult to bring about change because the consequences of any actions are cyclical and you end up at the point where you started. This is known as a vicious circle.

A famous example of this can be found in the novel *Catch 22* by Joseph Heller. People often say a situation is a *Catch 22* when it is a vicious circle.

Listen to a group of actors describing their *Catch 22*. Answer the questions below.

1 Why did they want to become actors?
2 How difficult was it to get the type of work they wanted?
3 What is *the fringe*?
4 Did they receive help from more established actors?
5 Why was it difficult for them to become established themselves?
6 How optimistic are they about the future?

Speaking

Paradise Island is an island of great natural beauty. It is easy to get to and would attract a large number of tourists if there were suitable accommodation. However, any new hotels could only be high-rise buildings as the island is very small. The island has no other industry or resources. Up until now the island has been self-sufficient but recently a drought has led to a water shortage.

Work with a partner and discuss:

1 what action the islanders should take.
2 what the possible consequences of those actions might be.

Reading

Read the article opposite about the effects of tourism. Complete each statement 1 – 5.

1 Tourists are attracted to faraway places because
a the resorts are in developing countries.
b the Mediterranean is too adventurous.
c they want to learn about different cultures.
d they want more exciting experiences.

2 Tourism in Goa has not had a negative effect on the
a water supply.
b fishing industry.
c service industry.
d local culture.

3 The tour operators claim that tourism brings
a a wide variety of cultural exchanges.
b opportunities to exploit the environment.
c the government into closer contact with local people.
d a substantial boost to local economies.

4 Tourism Concern believes that
a tourism can never have a beneficial effect.
b the present policies are environmentally friendly.
c this is not the right time to intervene.
d tourists themselves should take a more responsible attitude.

5 The writer of the article is
a highly critical of the tour operator.
b very unsympathetic towards tourists.
c laying the blame solely on governments for this exploitation.
d generally even-handed in his approach to the parties involved.

Travellers' Check

As mass tourism spreads, so does opposition to its highly detrimental economic and environmental effects.

As tourists tire of the Mediterranean and become more adventurous in their choice of holiday, the popularity of faraway countries is growing. But, in some developing countries, the locals have begun to fight back by drawing attention to the problems caused by tourism, and trying to embarrass the tour operators into changing their ways.

Holiday resorts in the Caribbean, Africa, South America and Asia are promoted as idyllic and unspoilt, offering the chance of an exotic dream holiday away from it all. The reality is often somewhat different. While tourist beaches and hotel compounds are luxurious, a short distance away the local population, often living in poverty, gains little from the arrival of the wealthy Western tourists.

Critics of the travel industry, who claim that mass tourism not only pollutes a delicate environment, but also exploits unorganised and powerless groups of people, point to the example of Goa. A large tourist hotel in India's most popular resort uses about 60,000 gallons of water each day, but the one million Indians who live there are lucky if their taps produce water for two hours a day. Most tourists who stay in Goa are unaware of this shocking fact, although only a few hundred yards from the most luxurious hotels, Goans can be seen queueing patiently to draw water from wells almost drained by the tourist industry's high-pressure pumps.

Although the issue of water highlights the impact of mass tourism on India's most popular resort, Goa offers many other examples. Hotels, which deny fishermen access to beaches, are built without the necessary roads and electricity to support them. Local traditional skills are lost as an economy dependent on servicing the growing numbers of tourists is developed. Alien cultures are also imposed which frequently involve contradictions and antagonisms.

The tour operators deny they are exploiting the countries where they send tourists and are also keen to draw attention to the advantages that it claims tourism brings, as vast quantities of badly needed foreign exchange pour into government coffers from visiting tourists and development creates a valuable infrastructure which also benefits locals.

Hard-up governments, believing that tourism offers an easy route to foreign exchange, encourage the tour operators, often by way of tax breaks and other incentives, to build ever-larger hotels and holiday facilities. Anthropologist, Dr Tom Selwyn, who runs the only academic course of its kind into the study of tourism, at London's Roehampton Institute, believes that few people living in holiday resorts in the Third World actually derive any financial benefit from tourism. He says indigenous industries and traditional skills are wiped out by the arrival of mass tourism, to be replaced by temporary unskilled jobs in the holiday business.

There is now growing concern about the economic and environmental effects of Third World tourism throughout the world. Campaign groups are establishing themselves and preparing to challenge the travel industry by drawing attention to the problems caused by what they see as badly managed tourism. Goa offers an example of the way a local protest movement can be born out of the fight to protect the local environment from mass tourism. An Indian government tourist plan proposes the construction of up to 52 luxury hotels on Goa's 65-mile coastline by the mid-1990s. Jagrut Goenkaranchi Fauz, or the JGF civil rights movement, has pledged to fight the plans, claiming they will destroy Goa's fragile environment and further distort its economy. It is also concerned about the rising number of charter flights that will bring even more tourists to Goa this year. Each new flight is greeted by JGF supporters handing out leaflets explaining to tourists, in their own language, what effect their stay in Goa is having.

A new organisation, Tourism Concern, intends to develop policies for an environmentally friendly and less exploitative form of tourism which doesn't destroy the very countries it seeks to promote. Tourism Concern's intervention is timely: as the world gets smaller, more and more people want holidays in ever more exotic and faraway places. But its success will depend on how far tourists can be persuaded to think about the effect their holiday may have on the country and people they want to visit.

Speaking

1 Refer back to your discussion about what should happen to Paradise Island. Discuss with your partner whether or not your opinions have changed in the light of this article.

2 Consider the statements below. Discuss their effects in the short term (over the next five years) and in the long term (twenty years from now).

Tourists visit faraway places in the belief that they will be idyllic and unspoilt.
In order to provide for these tourists more facilities have to be built.

3 Mass tourism is generally considered to have negative effects, but it can bring many benefits. Discuss with your partner what you think these might be.

Use of English

The text below comes from an advertisement for a travel company which claims that it has found a way of breaking the vicious circle of tourists destroying previously unspoilt areas. Read it and then complete it with one word in each of the spaces provided.

Writing

The advertisement in the previous exercise continues:

Cox and Kings' expert planning and impeccable service apply both for pre-arranged tours and individual itineraries. Wherever you want to go, your needs will be accommodated.

Write a letter to the company, telling them that you are interested in an individual itinerary. Give them details of where you would like to go, what you wish to do and the different types of environment you would like to experience. (Use about 200 words.)

Wild At Heart

As descriptions of 'secluded' and 'unspoilt' become increasingly rare in the enviromentally aware Nineties, ... (1) concerned are realising that vast ... (2) of sightseers cannot trample on areas of natural beauty and ... (3) them to remain beautiful.

No-one ... (4) this more than Cox and Kings which is celebrating its 233rd anniversary with the launch of a far-reaching and unique tour package.

The aim of Environmental Journeys is simple: to ... (5) the destruction which is occurring worldwide ... (6) allowing travellers to express appreciation through long-term support.

... (7) the exquisite and colourful islands of the Seychelles to the dramatic wilderness of Alaska, botany enthusiasts, wildlife lovers and photographers ... (8) are offered a huge ... (9) of landscapes, flora and fauna. There is something for every taste.

An Environmental Journey is guaranteed to prove... (10) memorable and rewarding and, ... (11) up by Cox and Kings faultless hospitality, both you and the areas you visit will ... (12) all the richer. ... (13) every traveller who books on ... (14) holidays, Cox and Kings will make a donation to special conservation projects ... (15) the relevant areas.

Language awareness

There need not always be a conflict between people and the environment. As the first extract on the right from the novel *The Rainbow* by D.H. Lawrence shows, they can work together in harmony.

1 Read the extract. Find a word or phrase that means the same as each of items 1 – 6.

1 moving as if carrying a heavy weight
2 a state of being less well-off than before
3 indicating that a place is full of life
4 a line cut in the soil before planting
5 the shine on a surface
6 looking intently in a certain direction

2 Read the passage again and answer questions 1 – 8.

1 What does *this* refer to? (line 8)
2 What became *smooth and supple after ploughing?*
3 Who are *they*? (line 15)
4 What exactly was *enough for the men*?
5 What is *the source of generation*?
6 Why do you think they were *unable to turn round?* (the last two lines)
7 What language does the writer use, both metaphorically and literally, to show the harmony that exists between the people and their environment?
8 There are many examples of words being repeated: *land, heaven and earth, cows, men.* What is the reason for this?

The Brangwens had lived for generations on the Marsh Farm, in the meadows where the Erewash twisted sluggishly through alder trees separating Derbyshire from Nottinghamshire. Living on rich land, on their own land, near to a growing town, they had forgotten what it was to be in straitened circumstances. But heaven and earth was teeming around them and how should this cease? They knew the intercourse between heaven and earth, sunshine drawn into the breast and bowels; feeling the pulse and body of the soil that opened to the furrow for the grain and became smooth and supple after ploughing. The young corn waved and was silken and the lustre slid along the limbs of the men who saw it. They took the udder of the cows, the cows yielded milk and the pulse against the hands of the men, the pulse of the blood of the teats of the cows beat into the pulse of the hands of the men. It was enough for the men, that the earth heaved and opened its furrows to them, that the wind blew to dry the wet wheat and set the young ears of corn wheeling freshly round about. So much warmth and generating and pain and death did they know in their blood, earth and sky and beast and green plants, that they lived full and surcharged, their senses full fed, their faces always turned to the heat of the blood, staring into the sun, dazed with looking towards the source of generation, unable to turn round.

Reading and writing

Some people feel in harmony with an urban environment. The second extract on the right is taken from *Money* by Martin Amis. In it, the hero, an English film producer, describes the effect that New York has on him.

Describe the surroundings which bring out either the best or the worst in you. Explain how they do this and why. (350 words)

Now you've seen me in New York before, and you know how I am out here. I wonder what it is: something to do with the energy, the electricity of the place, all the hustle and razz it fills me with that get up and go. I'm a different proposition in New York, pulled together, really on the ball. I was at it again first thing this morning, straight down to business despite my jet-lag and the kind of hangover that would have poleaxed any lesser man.

Lying in bed, with telephone, address book, ashtray and coffee cup efficiently arranged on the pouffe of my gut, I now buckled down to the first item of business.

Do you think at your age it is right?

Lewis Carroll

Listening

1 Is there ever a right or a wrong age to do things? Listen to various people talking about when they started to do activities which are generally restricted to certain age groups. Number them in the order in which they speak.

- ☐ a granny undergraduate
- ☐ a ten-year-old chess champion
- ☐ a veteran marathon runner
- ☐ a sixteen-year-old PhD student
- ☐ a glamorous actress

2 Answer the following questions.

1. What differences did age make to what each person was doing?
2. How did each of their contemporaries react?
3. How did people working with each of them react?
4. Why and how were each of them able to break down the age barrier?

Speaking

How important do you think age is when deciding who is best suited to carry out certain tasks?

Discuss with a partner what you think the ideal age is to perform each of the following jobs and sports as effectively as possible. Give your reasons. If, however, you think that age is immaterial to how well a person in any of these categories can perform, explain why.

1. a motor racing driver
2. a high court judge
3. a sprint runner
4. a foreign exchange dealer
5. a nursery school teacher
6. a university professor
7. a gymnast
8. a government leader
9. a novelist
10. a foreign language learner

Reading and speaking

The extract on the next page is taken from *The Prime Of Miss Jean Brodie* by Muriel Spark.

1 Read the extract and answer questions 1 – 10.

1. Why could the girls not take off their hats?
2. What was the headmistress's attitude towards *the Brodie set*?
3. Why did *the Brodie set* count on its fingers?
4. What does *that time* refer to?
5. What exactly is meant by *a new plot is afoot*?
6. What is the difference between *a crank school* and *an education factory*?
7. Why are *Roman profile* and *assassinated* particularly appropriate as used in this context?
8. Who might *the gang* be?
9. What does Miss Brodie mean by *the years of my prime*?
10. Why does she say *the age of chivalry* is past?

2 The following adjectives might be used to describe Miss Brodie. Some have a negative connotation and would be more likely to be used by the people who want her to resign. Others have a positive connotation and would be the sort of descriptions used by the Brodie set.

Work with a partner and discuss which adjectives are positive and which are negative. Then match each positive adjective with its negative equivalent. Number each pair 1 – 8 in the boxes provided.

☐ strong-willed	☐ idiosyncratic
☐ obsessive	☐ bizarre
☐ arrogant	☐ dynamic
☐ over-active	☐ thick-skinned
☐ insensitive	☐ self-assured
☐ single-minded	☐ resilient
☐ vulnerable	☐ assertive
☐ sensitive	☐ aggressive

3 *Give me a girl at an impressionable age and she is mine for life.*

1. What do you think Miss Brodie meant by this?
2. Discuss with your partner the advantages and disadvantages of being influenced by a strong personality like Jean Brodie.

The boys, as they talked to the girls from Marcia Blaine School, stood on the far side of their bicycles holding the handlebars, which established a protective fence of bicycle between the sexes, and the impression that at any moment the boys were likely to be away.

The girls could not take off their panama hats because this was not far from the school gates and hatlessness was an offence. Certain departures from the proper set of the hat on the head were overlooked in the case of fourth-form girls and upwards so long as nobody wore their hat at an angle. But there were other subtle variants from the ordinary rule of wearing the brim turned up at the back and down at the front. The five girls, standing very close to each other because of the boys, wore their hats each with a definite difference.

These girls formed the Brodie set. That was what they had been called even before the headmistress had given them the name, in scorn, when they had moved from the Junior to the Senior school at the age of twelve. At that time they had been immediately recognizable as Miss Brodie's pupils, being vastly informed on a lot of subjects irrelevant to the authorized curriculum, as the headmistress said, and useless to the school as a school. These girls were discovered to have heard of the Buchmanites and Mussolini, the Italian Renaissance painters, the advantages to the skin of cleansing cream and witch-hazel over honest soap and water, and the word 'menarche'; the interior decoration of the London house of the author of Winnie the Pooh had been described to them, as had the love lives of Charlotte Brontë and of Miss Brodie herself. They were aware of the existence of Einstein and the arguments of those who considered the Bible to be untrue. They knew the rudiments of astrology but not the date of the Battle of Flodden or the capital of Finland. All of the Brodie set, save one, counted on its fingers, as had Miss Brodie, with accurate results more or less.

By the time they were sixteen, and had reached the fourth form, and loitered beyond the gates after school, and had adapted themselves to the orthodox régime, they remained unmistakably Brodie, and were all famous in the school, which is to say they were held in suspicion and not much liking. They had no team spirit and very little in common with each other outside their continuing friendship with Jean Brodie. She still taught in the Junior department. She was held in great suspicion.

Marcia Blaine School for Girls was a day school which had been partially endowed in the middle of the nineteenth century by the wealthy widow of an Edinburgh bookbinder. She had been an admirer of Garibaldi before she died. Her manly portrait hung in the great hall, and was honoured every Founder's Day by a bunch of hard-wearing flowers such as chrysanthemums or dahlias. These were placed in a vase beneath the portrait, upon a lectern which also held an open Bible with the text underlined in red ink, 'O where shall I find a virtuous woman, for her price is above rubies.'

Two of the Andrews wheeled their bicycles out on to the road and departed. The other three boys remained defiantly, but looking the other way as if they might have stopped to admire the clouds on the Pentland Hills. The girls crowded round each other as if in discussion. 'Good afternoon,' said Miss Brodie when she approached the group. 'I haven't seen you for some days. I think we won't detain these young men and their bicycles. Good afternoon, boys.' The famous set moved off with her, and Joyce, the new delinquent, followed. 'I think I haven't met this new girl,' said Miss Brodie, looking closely at Joyce. And when they were introduced she said: 'Well, we must be on our way, my dear.'

Sandy looked back as Joyce Emily walked, and then skipped, leggy and uncontrolled for her age, in the opposite direction, and the Brodie set was left to their secret life as it had been six years ago in their childhood.

'I am putting old heads on your young shoulders,' Miss Brodie had told them at that time, 'and all my pupils are the crème de la crème.'

Sandy looked with her little screwed-up eyes at Monica's very red nose and remembered this saying as she followed the set in the wake of Miss Brodie.

'I should like you girls to come to supper tomorrow night,' Miss Brodie said. 'Make sure you are free.'

'The Dramatic Society ...' murmured Jenny.

'Send an excuse,' said Miss Brodie. 'I have to consult you about a new plot which is afoot to force me to resign. Needless to say, I shall not resign.' She spoke calmly as she always did in spite of her forceful words.

Miss Brodie never discussed her affairs with the other members of staff, but only with those former pupils whom she had trained up in her confidence. There had been previous plots to remove her from Blaine, which had been foiled.

'It has been suggested again that I should apply for a post at one of the progressive schools, where my methods would be more suited to the system than they are at Blaine. But I shall not apply for a post at a crank school. I shall remain at this education factory. There needs must be a leaven in the lump. Give me a girl at an impressionable age, and she is mine for life.'

The Brodie set smiled in understanding of various kinds.

Miss Brodie forced her brown eyes to flash as a meaningful accompaniment to her quiet voice. She looked a mighty woman with her dark Roman profile in the sun. The Brodie set did not for a moment doubt that she would prevail. As soon expect Julius Caesar to apply for a job at a crank school as Miss Brodie. She would never resign. If the authorities wanted to get rid of her she would have to be assassinated.

'Who are the gang, this time?' said Rose, who was famous for sex-appeal.

'We shall discuss tomorrow night the persons who oppose me,' said Miss Brodie. 'But rest assured they shall not succeed.'

'No,' said everyone. 'No, of course they won't.'

'Not while I am in my prime,' she said. 'These years are still the years of my prime. It is important to recognize the years of one's prime, always remember that. Here is my tram-car. I dare say I'll not get a seat. This is nineteen-thirty-six. The age of chivalry is past.'

Writing

Write a description of a person who has influenced you, in either a positive or negative way, and give some examples of how this has been achieved. Use about 200 words.

Reading and speaking

The newspaper advertisements opposite are for a European marketing director and a managing director. In the former, the requirement is for a person in his/her early thirties and in the latter for someone aged thirty-five to forty-five.

1 Read through the advertisements and discuss with your partner why you think it is necessary to specify the age range of potential applicants for the job. What would prevent someone of forty-four being a marketing director and someone of thirty being a managing director?

2 List the qualities required for each job.

3 Discuss the main differences that there are likely to be between the candidates applying for the two jobs.

Entertainment Computer Software

EUROPEAN MARKETING DIRECTOR

Cotswolds, c. £45,000, car

The company is one of the world's leading publishers of home computer entertainment and simulation software and its name is synonymous with many of the best-selling computer game titles.

Its rapid expansion in recent years has seen a significant increase in market share in both the UK and prime European countries, with distributor agreements now well established.

The requirement is for an ambitious marketeer to head a broad-based function and devise the marketing strategy to take the company through the 1990's. It calls for an individual who has the perception and vision to formulate challenging marketing objectives in what is a diverse and fast-changing market. You can also expect to play a highly influential role in both product development and PR activity and maintain a high profile with the retail sector.

Preferably a graduate in your early 30's, you should have gained comprehensive marketing experience in a consumer-orientated environment with sound knowledge of retail.

Possibly seeking your first board appointment, it is important to have taken a prominent stance in leading the marketing team of a company operating in European markets.

Adaptability, creativity and flair are regarded as essential personal skills, along with tenacity and proven business acumen. In return you can expect an opportunity of unrivalled scope for personal development.

Managing Director

NORTH MIDLANDS, £50,000 PACKAGE

This successful company has a well-earned reputation for manufacturing and supplying products of the highest quality to a wide range of clients.

A high calibre executive is required to lead the company on a path of substantial growth.

Aged 35-45 and well qualified, it is essential that you have a proven background at a senior level in a market-led manufacturing business and possess a strong knowledge of shopfitting and/or contracting. You will ideally have some experience of estimating, buying, contracts management and surveying but above all you must be a strong and innovative Managing Director, capable of taking the company forward by capitalising on product and business development opportunities, both in home and overseas markets.

Personal qualities will include the communication skills, personality and presence necessary to control and take the company forward. The renumeration package consists of a first class salary, highly attractive bonus scheme and a full range of executive benefits.

Reading

Some people seem to be ageless, as reflected in the famous quotation, *Age cannot wither her.* To illustrate this further, consider the passages opposite from a short story called *Jane* by W. Somerset Maugham. In it, he examines the effects of age and appearance on people's relationships.

1 In the first extract, the narrator, who has just returned from a period of time spent in China, meets an old friend, Mrs Tower. Read his description of her.

2 While he is there, Mrs Tower's sister-in-law, Jane Fowler, comes to visit. Her appearance is somewhat different to that of Mrs Tower, even though they are about the same age. Read the description of Jane.

3 Decide whether each of the following statements is true or false.

1. Mrs Tower was always honest about her real age.
2. Mrs Tower made no secret of the fact that she dyed her hair.
3. The narrator believed that Mrs Tower looked older than she really was.
4. The narrator suggests that make-up did not improve Mrs Tower's appearance.
5. Mrs Fowler looked a good deal younger than fifty-five.
6. Mrs Fowler had her hair done by Monsieur Marcel.
7. Mrs Tower approved of Mrs Fowler's dress sense.
8. Although unusual, Mrs Fowler's clothes were still fashionable.

4 Now read on. Complete this summary of Mrs Tower's reactions.

Before Gilbert arrived she felt …
She predicted what he would be like …
But when she was introduced to Gilbert, her attitude changed …

I had no notion what her age was. When I was quite a young man she was married and a good deal older than I, but now she treated me as her contemporary. She constantly said that she made no secret of her age, which was forty, and then added with a smile that all women took five years off. She never sought to conceal the fact that she dyed her hair (it was a very pretty brown with reddish tints), and she said she did this because hair was hideous while it was going grey; as soon as hers was white she would cease to dye it.

'Then they'll say what a young face I have.'

Meanwhile it was painted, though with discretion, and her eyes owed not a little of their vivacity to art. She was a handsome woman, exquisitely gowned, and in the sombre glow of the alabaster lamps did not look a day more than the forty she gave herself.

'It is only at my dressing-table that I can suffer the naked brightness of a thirty-two-candle electric bulb,' she added with smiling cynicism. 'There I need it to tell me the first hideous truth and then to enable me to take the necessary steps to correct it.'

'Mrs Fowler,' he announced.

'Jane,' cried Mrs Tower, springing to her feet. 'I wasn't expecting you today.'

I chuckled inwardly when I recollected that the two ladies were contemporaries. Mrs Fowler looked a good fifty-five. She was a rather big woman; she wore a black straw hat with a wide brim and from it a black lace veil hung over her shoulders, a cloak that oddly combined severity with fussiness, a long black dress, voluminous as though she wore several petticoats under it, and stout boots. She was evidently short-sighted, for she looked at you through large gold-rimmed spectacles.

'Won't you have a cup of tea?' asked Mrs Tower.

'If it wouldn't be too much trouble. I'll take off my mantle.'

She began by stripping her hands of the black gloves she wore, and then took off her cloak. Round her neck was a solid gold chain from which hung a large gold locket in which I felt certain was a photograph of her deceased husband. Then she took off her hat and placed it neatly with her gloves and cloak on the sofa corner. Mrs Tower pursed her lips. Certainly those garments did not go very well with the austere but sumptuous beauty of Mrs Tower's redecorated drawing-room. I wondered where on earth Mrs Fowler had found the extraordinary clothes she wore. They were not old and the materials were expensive. It was astounding to think that dressmakers still made things that had not been worn for a quarter of a century. Mrs Fowler's grey hair was very plainly done, showing all her forehead and her ears, with a parting in the middle. It had evidently never known the tongs of Monsieur Marcel.

Early next morning Mrs Tower rang me up and I heard at once from her voice that she was in high spirits.

'I've got the most wonderful news for you,' she said. 'Jane is going to be married. Her fiancé is coming to dine here tonight and I want you to come too.'

When I arrived Mrs Tower, very splendid in a tea-gown a little too young for her, was alone.

'Jane is putting the finishing touches to her appearance. I'm longing for you to see her. She's all in a flutter. She says he adores her. His name is Gilbert and when she speaks of him her voice gets all funny and tremulous. It makes me want to laugh.'

'I wonder what he's like.'

'Oh, I'm sure I know. Very big and massive, with a bald head and an immense gold chain across an immense tummy. A large, fat, clean-shaven, red face and a booming voice.'

'Has Marion told you my news?' she said, turning to me with that really charming smile of hers as if we were already old friends.

'I must congratulate you,' I said.

'Wait to do that till you've seen my young man.'

'I think it's too sweet to hear you talk of your young man,' smiled Mrs Tower.

Mrs Fowler's eyes certainly twinkled behind her preposterous spectacles.

'Don't expect anyone too old. You wouldn't like me to marry a decrepit old gentleman with one foot in the grave, would you?'

This was the only warning she gave us. Indeed there was no time for any further discussion, for the butler flung open the door and in a loud voice announced:

'Mr Gilbert Napier.'

There entered a youth in a very well-cut dinner jacket. He was slight, not very tall, with fair hair in which there was a hint of a natural wave, clean-shaven, and blue-eyed. He was not particularly good-looking, but he had a pleasant, amiable face. In ten years he would probably be wizened and sallow; but now, in extreme youth, he was fresh and clean and blooming. For he was certainly not more than twenty-four. My first thought was that this was the son of Jane Fowler's fiancé (I had not known he was a widower) come to say that his father was prevented from dining by a sudden attack of gout. But his eyes fell immediately on Mrs Fowler, his face lit up, and he went towards her with both hands outstretched. Mrs Fowler gave him hers, a demure smile on her lips, and turned to her sister-in-law.

'This is my young man, Marion,' she said.

He held out his hand.

'I hope you'll like me, Mrs Tower,' he said. 'Jane tells me you're the only relation she has in the world.'

Mrs Tower's hands trembled slightly.

'There is of course a certain disparity of age between you,' she smiled.

'Twenty-seven years,' said Jane. 'Do you think it's too much? Gilbert says I'm very young for my age. I told you I shouldn't like to marry a man with one foot in the grave.'

Vocabulary development

1 *Having one foot in the grave* is an expression describing someone who is old. Because of its associations with death, it is usually said in an ironic or humorous way. It would be considered extremely impolite to use this expression in front of an old person.

Growing older is something that is not always easily accepted, so people often use euphemisms, such as *he's getting on a bit* or *she's not as young as she was*, expressions where the true and more negative meaning is implied in a more positive expression. Another example of a euphemism is the description of a person who is overweight and fat as *well-built* or *not all skin and bones*.

Look at the statements below and decide how they could be expressed more directly.

1. Things have been better.
2. Their marriage was dissolved.
3. Your grandfather passed away peacefully during the night.
4. She is a woman of a certain age.
5. There was considerable collateral damage as a result of the bombing.
6. His services are no longer required.
7. We look forward to receiving a cheque for the outstanding amount.
8. We would be grateful for a reply to our recent letter at your earliest convenience.
9. The Company has called in the receiver.
10. The referee told him to take an early bath.
11. She does not suffer fools gladly.
12. His domestic arrangements are somewhat fluid.
13. He behaves rather strangely at times.
14. She is being economical with the truth.

2 Work with a partner and decide what euphemisms you would use to:

1. explain to your boss that you have made a mistake in your work.
2. tell your boss that she has made a mistake.
3. tell the waiter that your food tastes awful.
4. describe an outing that you found boring to the friend who recommended it to you.

3 Advertisements for unattractive jobs which might not receive many applications are often full of euphemisms that make them appear much more desirable than they actually are. Read the following job descriptions and decide what job is being advertised in each of them.

1. Sleeping at night could be costing you money. Turn those dark hours into earning opportunities and enjoy the freedom to spend your days how you wish.
2. If you care about environmental protection, enjoy the open air, relish a physical challenge and are not afraid of hard work come and join the Gleam Team.
3. Are you:
   keen on computation?
   familiar with a consumer environment?
   Do you enjoy contact with people?
   Then come and work for us. You'll have hands-on experience of the very latest in retailing technology and be responsible for ensuring that customers are provided with the most efficient service in itemising and pricing their purchased goods.

4 Write an advertisement for one of the following jobs. Make it sound as attractive as possible.

1. a prison officer
2. a typist
3. a hospital porter
4. an assistant in a fast food outlet
5. a door-to-door salesman

Reading

Read the article opposite about the relationship between age and bad driving and answer questions 1 – 10.

1. What are the main points made in the report by the Automobile Association?
2. What does *If only* refer to?
3. What is the writer's opinion of his own driving skills?
4. How does his driving differ from that of the reckless young executive?
5. What is likely to improve the writer's driving?
6. What is the writer's attitude towards women drivers?
7. How do people who suffer from direction-blindness differ from most bad drivers?
8. Why do you think the writer was driving in an open field when he was aged sixteen?
9. How might the writer have *clocked up more than £1,400 in motoring fines*?
10. What is the significance of the Zsa Zsa Gabor quote?

Cars and real men

As someone whose driving gets worse every year, I was surprised to see an AA report last week claiming that driving ability improves with age.

The two-year study of young driving behaviour by transport and psychology experts at Southampton University singled out men aged 17 – 25 as the most lethal on British roads, contributing to a quarter of crashes. While not all young men are bad drivers (and believe me, I am), the AA Foundation for Road Safety Research found that most became more skilled and safer as they got older.

If only! Bad drivers, I suspect, are born rather than made. Ever since passing my test on the fifth attempt seven years ago, I have been worrying motoring colleagues, cyclists and lollipop ladies. Worse, my chances of improving my driving skills are about as great as a bubble car winning next weekend's San Marino Grand Prix.

But my sort of motoring is, to be fair, rather different from the AA's reckless young executive who gets macho enjoyment out of his car, likes to jump lights, and thinks he is Nigel Mansell. The report says this young man is at his worst when driving with friends to a party to the sound of blaring pop music, and at his best when driving with his girlfriend or wife.

Some people are simply born rotten drivers – even, or especially, men.

For me the reverse is true. I warn passengers of my mechanical ineptitude before starting the engine. If an attractive girl is sitting in the passenger seat, my driving falls to pieces: I talk too much, get lost, cannot keep my eye on the road, battle to find the gears and have to make embarrassing emergency stops. And I find pop music helps my driving; I have some heavy metal pop tapes in my car which I put on full blast when I start to fall asleep at the wheel. Classical music, however, can be dangerous. I have sympathy with the Royal Marines major who, when arrested on the M5 for speeding, said he had been listening to Beethoven's Wellington victory march and had simply joined in the cavalry charge.

The AA's dangerous young drivers have flashy cars with powerful acceleration and go-faster looks. My bad driving has nothing to do with a car's performance. I once drove a throaty Lancia sports car, but swapped it for a nice old 1100cc hatchback.

Useless motoring has little to do with gender. Just as men wobble about the road as they shave and make phone calls in the morning, so women whizz along putting on their make-up and varnishing their nails. The police recently arrested this women in London for steering with her knees as she used both hands to tie her pony tail.

Bad driving cannot always be put down to a lack of co-ordination. Nor has it much to do with age. As a friend of mine has found with his 'direction blindness' – he cannot drive, and gets lost in his own flat – such afflictions are with you for life. When a friend gives him a lift, for example, and ushers him towards the car, he often makes for the driving side. He cannot remember, without actually peering inside it, which side the steering is on. Ever since the day when, aged 16, I took my mother's car for a spin in a 20-acre open grass field and drove it off a cliff, my driving career has been both costly and inglorious. A year later I drove a moped up onto the bonnet of a Mini belonging to the headmaster's secretary of my school. During my first driving test in Ludlow the examiner had to take control. Since 1983, I have clocked up more than £1,400 in motoring fines (excluding parking tickets).

Motoring, for me, is just a means of getting from A to B, and I rank it as a basic skill somewhere in difficulty between wallpapering, learning Dutch or aquiring 100wpm shorthand. I cannot see how it is possible to confuse driving a car with having sex, and suspect many people boast of their driving prowess, simply because they are not much good at anything else. 'Being macho,' to quote Zsa Zsa Gabor, 'does not prove mucho.'

WILLIAM CASH

Speaking

Bad drivers are born rather than made. Discuss with your partner:

1 the reasons the writer gives to support this statement.

2 whether or not you agree with it and the reasons for your opinions.

3 which of the following skills people are more likely to acquire naturally than through experience, practice and hard work.

understanding computers
learning a foreign language
learning to play a musical instrument
singing in tune
playing a ball game
reading a map
ice-skating
writing poetry

4 whether it is ever justifiable to say that a person is too old or lacks the natural ability to learn a new skill.

Use of English

Bad drivers are born rather than made.

1 *Rather than* is used to make a distinction between one fixed state and another. It could be replaced by *not*, but in doing so any element of doubt is removed. Study another example. Rephrase it using a negative construction. Discuss which style you prefer and why.

Some people eat to live rather than live to eat.

2 Rewrite each of the following sentences using *rather than*.

1 I hope I die before I get old.
2 The Government had to decide whether to control inflation and thereby create unemployment or to reduce unemployment allowing inflation to rise. They chose the former policy.
3 The rebels agreed that starving in the mountains was better than living under a dictator.
4 Mrs Harris, an octogenarian, prefers listening to heavy metal rock and does not really like the middle of the road music that people expect her to.
5 My younger sister is happier in the company of older men and does not usually go out with boys of her own age.
6 Actions speak louder than words.

3 *Bad driving cannot always be put down to a lack of co-ordination.*

The verb *put down to* is used to indicate why something has happened. Study another example.

On her hundredth birthday Maggie Smith said that her long life *was due to* a lack of exercise and a diet of red meat.
Maggie Smith said her long life *could be put down to* a lack of exercise and a diet of red meat.
Maggie Smith *put* her long life *down to* a lack of exercise and a diet of red meat.

Read the extract on the next page from the poem *Father William* by Lewis Carroll. Complete the sentences using *put down to* in the appropriate tense.

1 Father William's desire to stand on his head …
2 His prowess to turn a back-somersault …
3 He … his capacity to eat a goose …

4 Discuss with your partner what you would put each of the following down to.

1 success at exams
2 achieving an ambition
3 failing a driving test
4 enjoying a long life

5 *Put* can be used to form a very wide range of two- and three-word verbs.

Use a good dictionary to help you complete the following with an appropriate verb with *put*. Make sure the verb is in the correct form.

1 The horse was in agony after breaking its leg and had … .
2 At the end of the examination, all candidates must … their pens and stop writing.
3 The ideas on reversing the ageing process that Professor Wyman … to the medical research committee will cause controversy.
4 Lady Blott … the plan to build a six-lane motorway through the grounds of Blott Castle, her family's home for the last six hundred years.
5 There is a rumour … that the treasure amassed by the Knights Templar is about to be discovered.

6 Kimberley … a transfer to another department when she found out that her boyfriend would also be her boss.
7 After Reginald Spode's conviction for fraud, the people who had lost money through his failed business demanded that he … for a very long stretch.
8 Despite … a tremendous fight, the veteran player was finally defeated by her more youthful opponent.

Writing

It is never either too early or too late to start something that you really want to do.

Discuss this statement using about 350 words.

YOU ARE OLD, FATHER WILLIAM

'You are old, Father William,' the young man said,
'And your hair has become very white;
And yet you incessantly stand on your head
Do you think, at your age, it is right?

'In my youth,' Father William replied to his son,
'I feared it might injure the brain;
But now that I'm perfectly sure I have none,
Why, I do it again and again.'

'You are old,' said the youth, 'as I mentioned before,
And have grown most uncommonly fat;
Yet you turned a back-somersault in at the door
Pray, what is the reason for that?'

'In my youth,' said the sage, as he shook his grey locks,
'I kept all my limbs very supple
By the use of this ointment – one shilling the box
Allow me to sell you a couple.'

'You are old,' said the youth, 'and your jaws are too weak
For anything tougher than suet;
Yet you finished the goose, with the bones and the beak
Pray, how did you manage to do it?'

'In my youth,' said his father, 'I took to the law,
And argued each case with my wife;
And the muscular strength which it gave to my jaw
Has lasted the rest of my life.'

Work is more fun than fun.

Noël Coward

Speaking

1 Do you think work can ever be fun?

2 How do people generally view the idea of working for a living?

Listening

Listen to the following people talking about a typical working day of theirs. Match each speaker with one of the occupations below. Number the occupations in the order in which they occur on the recording.

- ☐ a barrister
- ☐ a bricklayer
- ☐ an aristocrat
- ☐ an architect
- ☐ a night cleaner
- ☐ a taxi-driver
- ☐ a doctor
- ☐ an engineer
- ☐ an advertising copywriter

Reading

The extract on the next page is from *Tess of the D'Urbervilles* by Thomas Hardy. Tess, a beautiful young woman, has been abandoned by her husband, Angel Clare, so she has to find work. She joins an old friend, Marian, who used to work with her at a dairy but now has a job as a farm labourer.

1 Read the extract. Choose the most appropriate definition for each of the following vocabulary items as it occurs in this context.

1 *starve-acre*
a prosperous
b unfertile

2 *swede-field*
a an area of land where root vegetables are grown
b an area of land farmed by foreigners

3 *livestock*
a farm workers
b farm animals

4 *lot*
a situation
b gamble

5 *stoicism*
a calm acceptance
b extreme anger

5 *magnanimity*
a generosity
b meanness

2 Read the extract again. Answer questions 1 – 6.

1 What enabled Tess to cope with the harsh conditions in which she had to work?
2 What, unlike Tess, did Marian do to come to terms with the situation?
3 What extended metaphor is used to create the impression of a bleak landscape?
4 What does *by that* in the last line of the left-hand coloumn refer to?
5 What, in this context, is meant by *the circumstantial will*?
6 Which of the following would be the most appropriate title for this extract? Why?
a Down on the farm
b Frozen to the roots
c All in a day's work
d The woman pays

There was no exaggeration in Marian's definition of Flintcomb-Ash farm as a starve-acre place. The single fat thing on the soil was Marian herself; and she was an importation. Of the three classes of village, the village cared for by its lord, the village cared for by itself, and the village uncared for either by itself or by its lord, this place, Flintcomb-Ash, was the third.

But Tess set to work. Patience, that blending of moral courage with physical timidity, was now no longer a minor feature in Mrs. Angel Clare; and it sustained her.

The swede-field in which she and her companion were set hacking was a stretch of a hundred odd acres, in one patch, on the highest ground of the farm, rising above stony lanchets or lynchets, the outcrop of siliceous veins in the chalk formation, composed of myriads of loose white flints in bulbous, cusped, and phallic shapes. The upper half of each turnip had been eaten off by the live-stock, and it was the business of the two women to grub up the lower or earthy half of the root with a hooked fork called a hacker, that it might be eaten also. Every leaf of the vegetable having already been consumed, the whole field was in colour a desolate drab; it was a complexion without features, as if a face, from chin to brow, should be only an expanse of skin. The sky wore, in another colour, the same likeness; a white vacuity of countenance with the lineaments gone. So these two upper and nether visages confronted each other all day long, the white face looking down on the brown face, and the brown face looking up at the white face, without anything standing between them but the two girls crawling over the surface of the former like flies.

They worked on hour after hour, unconscious of the forlorn aspect they bore in the landscape, not thinking of the justice or injustice of their lot. Even in such a position as theirs it was possible to exist in a dream. In the afternoon the rain came on again, and Marian said that they need not work any more. But if they did not work they would not be paid; so they worked on. It was so high a situation, this field, that the rain had no occasion to fall, but raced along horizontally upon the yelling wind, sticking into them like glass splinters till they were wet through. Tess had not known till now what was really meant by that. There are degrees of dampness, and a very little is called being wet in common talk. But to stand working slowly in a field, and feel a creep of rain-water, first in legs and shoulders, then on hips and head, then at back, front, and sides, and yet to work on till the leaden light diminishes and marks that the sun is down, demands a distinct modicum of stoicism, even of valour.

Yet they did not feel the wetness so much as might be supposed. They were both young, and they were talking of the time when they lived and loved together at Talbothays Dairy, that happy green tract of land where summer had been liberal in her gifts; in substance to all, emotionally to these. Tess would fain not have conversed with Marian of the man who was legally, if not actually, her husband; but the irresistible fascination of the subject betrayed her into reciprocating Marian's remarks. And thus, as has been said, though the damp curtains of their bonnets flapped smartly into their faces, and their wrappers clung about them to wearisomeness, they lived all this afternoon in memories of green, sunny, romantic Talbothays.

So the two forces were at work here as everywhere, the inherent will to enjoy, and the circumstantial will against enjoyment. Marian's will had a method of assisting itself by taking from her pocket as the afternoon wore on a pint bottle corked with white rag, from which she invited Tess to drink. Tess's unassisted power of dreaming, however, being enough for her sublimation at present, she declined, except the merest sip, and then Marian took a pull herself from the spirits.

'I've got used to it,' she said, 'and can't leave it off now. 'Tis my only comfort.'

Amid this scene Tess slaved in the morning frosts and in the afternoon rains. When it was not swede-grubbing it was swede-trimming, in which process they sliced off the earth and the fibres with a bill-hook before storing the roots for future use. At this occupation they could shelter themselves by a thatched hurdle if it rained; but if it was frosty even their thick leather gloves could not prevent the frozen masses they handled from biting their fingers. Still Tess hoped. She had a conviction that sooner or later the magnanimity which she persisted in reckoning as a chief ingredient of Clare's character would lead him to rejoin her.

Use of English

These days much of the drudgery involved in manual labour is no longer necessary, as the work can be done more easily and cheaply by machines. Or can it? Complete the passage with one word to fill in each of the spaces.

> Workers at the Campbell's soup factory in Ohio USA, complained ... (1) the management that ... (2) heavy cases of soup caused them back trouble. The managers ... (3) sympathetic and ... (4) the problem a lot of thought. ... (5), they came ... (6) with a new worker to ... (7) out – a robot that cost the company more than $200,000 to develop. The idea was that the robot ... (8) lift the heavy cases of soup, ... (9) than the workers.
> It ... (10) good on paper, but when the robot started work, it caused ... (11). Whenever the robot found a faulty ... (12) it dropped it, causing many thousands of dollars- ... (13) of damage. Campbell's ... (14) to admit that their robot was a failure; it ... (15) fired and sent back to the local university. ... (16) the workers, it was a ... (17) of back to ... (18).

Reading

Contrary to popular belief, there are some jobs that are generally best left to humans, even though they may not necessarily be any more successful at them than the robot was at lifting tins of soup.

The extract opposite comes from *Prudence* by Jilly Cooper. Pendle, a barrister, has gone to visit his girlfriend, the narrator. One of the other guests, called Rodney, works in advertising. They are in the middle of having dinner.

1 Read the extract. Find a word or phrase that is similar in meaning to each of the following.

1 a television set
2 became extremely angry
3 very old-fashioned
4 verbal attack
5 incomprehensible language
6 very old people
7 greed
8 an argument between husband and wife
9 cannot be challenged
10 holds back the development of

2 Read the extract again. Complete the notes on the arguments for and against the legal profession and the advertising profession.

1 Rodney claims that:
lawyers have very old-fashioned attitudes.
...
...
...
Pendle counters that:
...

2 Pendle believes that advertising:
gives people false expectations.
...
...
Rodney argues that:
advertisements tell the public what's on the market.
...
...
...
...

'D'you mind if we look at the box during the News at Ten break?' asked Rodney, who had several crumbs in his hairy chest. 'I want to see the Virago Tyre commercial. I keep missing it. Have you seen it?' he added to Pendle.
'I don't watch television,' said Pendle.
Rodney flipped his lid. 'That's what I've got against lawyers,' he howled. 'Your attitude is positively antediluvian. How can anyone not watch television in this day and age?'
Oh God, he was about to launch into his anti-legal profession tirade. I leapt to my feet.
'Could you pass your plate up, darling?'
But Rodney was not to be halted, and when I staggered in with the beef en croute five minutes later he was still at it.
'Lawyers are a lot of incompetent hacks,' said Rodney, 'blinding people with their own mumbo jumbo. All you care about is reputation. You don't give a damn about the issues of the case; you just want to beat other lawyers.'
'The people who control our courts,' went on Rodney, splashing wine into everyone's glasses, 'are a lot of geriatrics in fancy dress. The whole system, in fact, is designed to isolate them from the pressures of modern life. Who, pray, are the Rolling Stones? Christ, you're cushioned against reality.'
'We deal with murders, rape, divorce every day,' said Pendle mildly. 'I'd hardly call that ...'
'Exactly my point,' interrupted Rodney. 'You can only deal with the horror of life by turning it into a play with a stage and a cast in period costume.'
Rodney was warming up now. 'Why do legal costs increase as the price of a house increases, although exactly the same amount of paper work is involved? And it's all geared to the rich, isn't it? Pay a fine or go to prison, so the rich pay up, and the poor go to jug.'
'It's time for drastic reform,' said Rodney, tipping back his chair. 'The crime rate's going up and up, the divorce rate's rocketing and parasites like you are cleaning up.'
'The reason why crime is going up,' said Pendle softly, 'is because people have never before been so well informed about what they're missing. And we've got your profession to thank for that. Every time we turn on a television set, or walk down a street, or go in the tube, we're bombarded by advertisements, tempting us with the promise of a better life. As a result everyone thinks they've got a right to a modern kitchen, a new car, a beautiful girl in a cornfield, a happy family life, children in permanently white jeans, a bouncing bright-eyed dog. No wonder marriages break up when people are constantly bombarded by an idealized picture of marital bliss.'
'Oh don't give me all that stuff,' spluttered Rodney. 'Advertising provides a service; we tell the public what's on the market.'
'Rubbish,' said Pendle. 'You create discontent, envy and avarice. You encourage a constant desire for novelty. Change the packaging, sell the product as new.'
'Everything is backed up by market research and statistics,' said Rodney pompously.
'Advertising people use statistics like a drunk uses a lamp-post,' snapped Pendle. 'For support rather than illumination. What sort of world d'you think you've created when there's no child whose unhappiness can't be dispelled by a sunshine breakfast, no romantic setback that can't be cured by using a new kind of toothpaste, no marital dust-up that can't be ended with a box of chocolates?'
He was playing with words now.
'Bravo,' I said.
'Advertising's fun; no one takes it seriously,' protested Jane.
'Oh yes they do,' said Pendle. 'Thousands of people write in for an amazing offer of a £2 so-called steak knife that's worth 99p. Dress anyone up in a white coat and the public think he's an unimpeachable authority. I came across an advertisement the other day which claimed its product was used by 90 per cent of actors who play doctors on television.'
'At least advertising keeps people in work – actors, writers, designers,' stuttered Rodney.
'Advertising stultifies creativity,' said Pendle crushingly. 'That's why hardly any decent poetry or painting or music's being produced in this country at the moment. All the creative talent is being frittered away in advertising.'
There was a silence. Tiger Millfield let out a huge belch, but no one giggled. Somehow when Rodney had attacked Pendle it had just been bluster, but with Pendle one felt it was the real thing.
'I must go,' said Pendle. 'I've got to drive down to Winchester early tomorrow morning. The brief only arrived this evening. I haven't studied it yet.'
He nodded a curt goodbye to everyone else, and I followed him out into the hall.
'You certainly floored Rodney,' I said. 'I didn't know you felt so strongly about advertising.'
His eyes gleamed wickedly.
'I don't. If I'd wanted to I could have argued the case for advertising just as well.'
'B-but you were so convincing,' I said.
'That's my job.'

3 The writer uses a number of different verbs and adverbs to indicate the way Rodney and Pendle speak to each other. Each of them gives the reader a clearer idea of how the words are expressed and so helps to bring the argument to life. They are:

verbs	adverbs
asked	*mildly*
added to	*softly*
howled	*pompously*
went on	*crushingly*
spluttered	
snapped	
stuttered	
interrupted	
protested	

Complete the following sentences by choosing the most appropriate verb or adverb to complete each of the following sentences.

1 'George Davis is innocent of the crime,' … the angry mob as the convicted man was led away.
2 'I have to confess that the weekly fluctuations in the sales of popular music is not high on my list of interests,' the judge said … .
3 'After a performance like that, Miss Newley should never find work as an actress again,' the critic remarked … .
4 'P-p-p-please will you marry me?' … the nervous suitor.
5 'Madelaine, I utterly forbid you to marry that ridiculous little man,'… her father, as his face turned a dark shade of red.

4 Imagine that you were one of the other guests at the dinner party described in the extract. Using the notes you have made, report the argument about the rights and wrongs of advertising to a mutual friend of Pendle's and Rodney's. Start:

Over dinner the other night there was a tremendous row between Rodney and Pendle over the merits of advertising. It started off when Pendle claimed he never watched TV and so Rodney laid into him about how out of touch the legal profession was and how lawyers were only interested in money. Pendle countered this by … .

Speaking

1 There may be more to advertising than meets the eye. Look carefully at this advertisement. Discuss with your partner:

1 what point the advertisement is making.
2 who the advertisement is aimed at.
3 how effective the advertisement is in drawing the reader's attention to what is being advertised.

2 Discuss with your partner your own views on advertising. You may find some of the following questions useful in your discussion.

1 Should advertising be restricted in terms of the products advertised?
2 Should there be special regulations for advertising that is targeted at children?
3 Should there be any restrictions on the wording of advertisements?
4 Should celebrities be used to endorse products?
5 Should there be a limit to the time given to advertising on TV?
6 Is advertising the most effective way of selling a product?
7 Has the industry become too sophisticated?
8 That is to say, are advertisers more interested in the style of their advertisements than in the products they are promoting?

ASTOUNDING
Chameleon Lamp
WHATEVER colour your room, we guarantee the original CHAMELEON LAMP will change colour to match it!
ONLY £16.99
SEND NO MONEY! FREE 10 DAY TRIAL.
GET TO WORK QUICKER!
£6.99 + 25p p+p
SPRING SHOES
Halve your TRAVELLING TIME to the office! Works on all kinds of ROADS and PAVEMENTS. Crash helmet extra.
10 DAY MONEYBACK TRIAL OFFER
DON'T STOOP TO SWEEP YOUR HOUSE
FOOTHOLD DUST PAN
Now DUSTBUSTING doesn't have to be BACK-BREAKING . . . with the original FOOTHOLD Dustpan.
SEND NO MONEY! Free 10 day trial! Pay postman on delivery only £3.49 (+p & p) or send £3.99 with order and we pay postage
DEPT. 1765
HAMSTER HOTEL ★★★★★
When you go away, GIVE YOUR PETS A BREAK . . . at the HAMSTER HOTEL. Rottweilers NOT welcome . . . £8.50 per night (including breakfast). No children. Bar. Restaurant. Training wheel
THE PERFECT RODENT RETREAT
FED UP WITH FRENCH CUISINE?
Then try this MOUTHWATERING new recipe book.
TRIPE DISHES OF THE WORLD
ONLY £4.99
You've never seen such a load of tripe!!!
. . . AND OTHER MOUTHWATERING RECIPES.
£4.99 each + 25p. p & p (including tax).
VISIT THE Haunted Castle
MANIFESTATIONS daily at ye olde haunted castle. SPIRITS everywhere. Also, Dungeon Cocktail Bar.
A GREAT NIGHT OUT FOR THE FAMILY.
ONLY 2 MILES FROM THE A30, Nr. BODMIN.
DISPOSABLE SUITS!
At LAST, an end to dry cleaning bills. Soil our suits and you simply THROW THEM AWAY!!!!
Lightweight suits
Also available in tweed.
£25
state size and style when ordering.
FAIRLY LONG LASTING CONTAINS NO CFC'S
REINFORCED ODOURLESS SOXS
The original guaranteed odourless sox. Take your shoes off in public and see the relief on your friends' faces. £2.50 a pair.
Amazing new Scientific
GUARANTEED to keep at least some of the rain off while you're cycling!!!
CYCLE UMBRELLA
ONLY £2.98 ON THE ROAD!
REVERSIBLE TROUSERS
For Men and boys
Change your trousers
surprise your friends.
AVAILABLE IN ALL SIZES
TWO for £14.99
Satisfaction guaranteed or your money back.
INFLATE-A-LOO
The EASY to inflate INFLATE-A-LOO
Use it anytime, anywhere.
From the MAKERS of the original INFLATE-A-URINAL.
ONLY £16.99
SATISFACTION GUARANTEED
send to Dept P15 NO cheques
CUT YOUR DRINKING BY ½ WITH A ½ PINT GLASS
Seen from the front it looks like a full pint. Lose weight and feel better.
Send £2.99 + 26p P&P. DEPT 69
STAND TALL! IN YOUR OWN "BUILT UP" HAT.
FED UP with being short? Then get the REMARKABLE "Built-up" bowler Hat. Stand TALL and gain the RESPECT OF your FRIENDS and COLLEAGUES.
From £12.50
48 STYLES (State size and colour.) Easy terms
ADDS INCHES TO MEN OF STATURE
TRAVELLING SET OF ENCYCLOPEDIAS
£25.99
This easy to carry portable set of encyclopedias means you never have to get caught short on holiday again.
A BOON TO THE MODERN TRAVELLER. PRINT NAME AND ADDRESS CLEARLY ON ORDER.
Eezy-cleen. Saves £££'s on redecorating!
MACHINE WASHABLE WALLPAPER
ONLY £3.99 PER ROLL
Before, dirty wallpaper meant redecorating, but now you can put it in the washing machine.
SUITABLE FOR AUTOMATICS
JUST USE A WARM IRON AFTERWARDS.
CATALOGUE. £1.99 (+25p. p & p) DEPT. 1173
ROSE-TINTED
LOOK AT LIFE IN A NEW WAY
INSTANTLY CURES DEPRESSION
FED UP? Depressed by those dull, dull days? Then get a pair of ROSE-TINTED SPECTACLES and see life as politicians do.
£7.99 Inc. VAT
SPECS
Buy 2 pairs get one FREE. No one should be without them.
PORTABLE TAXI METER
Ever wondered if the taxi driver was RIPPING YOU OFF? Now you can be sure . . . with the Portable Taxi Meter.
CARRY IT IN YOUR BRIEFCASE
and have solid proof when you call him a liar.
£10.99
BATTERIES INCLUDED
SOLAR POWERED NITE LIGHT
£8.99 inc vat
SAVE a fortune on electricity with the original patented solar powered nite light, use at any time – as long as the sun is shining. WORKS FROM DIRECT SUNLIGHT.
£8.99 (inc vat) + 75p p+p 10 DAY TRIAL MUST SATISFY OR MONEY WILL BE REFUNDED. STATE COLOUR PREFERENCE.
WHATEVER YOUR NEW BUSINESS IDEA, YOU'RE BETTER OFF TALKING TO BARCLAYS BANK.

Reading

What conclusions can be drawn about the world of advertising from this poignant tale?

The Most Unsuccessful TV Commercial

The comedienne Pat Coombs is the proud holder of the record for the largest number of unsuccessful 'takes' for a television commercial. In 1973, while making a breakfast cereal advertisement, she forgot her lines twenty-eight times. On each occasion she forgot the same thing – the name of the product. When asked five years later what the product was, she replied: 'I still can't remember. It was some sort of muesli, but the name was practically unpronounceable. They were very kind to me, but that only made it worse. I had total stage-fright every time the camera came near me. With each take I got worse. It's put me off cereal for life.'
The commercial was never finished and the product was taken off the market soon afterwards.

Speaking

1 Pendle said that he could have put up just as convincing an argument for advertising as against it, because that was his job. In fact, lawyers often have to present cases in court using arguments that they do not necessarily agree with.

Choose one of the following statements. Discuss with your partner what arguments you would use. Put the case both for and against it.

1 Watching television is a complete waste of time.
2 Eating meat is wrong.
3 Everyone should be taught to drive a car when they reach the age of fourteen.
4 There is no such thing as equality of opportunity.
5 Full-time education should be compulsory up to the age of twenty-one.
6 The damage to the environment caused by modern society has been greatly exaggerated.

2 Discuss the advantages and disadvantages of working as a lawyer.

3 What aspects of a lawyer's professional life might Noël Coward have considered more fun than fun?

Reading

The Law like the Ritz Hotel is open to all.
(Judge Darling)

The extract on the next page comes from *Bleak House* by Charles Dickens. In it he satirises the court system that existed in England during the nineteenth century, particularly the length of time it took to hear cases, the complexities of the legal system, the attitudes of the lawyers and the expense of bringing cases to court. Although there have been improvements, it could be argued that many of these shortcomings still exist.

The Lord High Chancellor was the most senior judge in the Court of Chancery, which dealt mainly with cases involving debt and taxation. In common with the barristers, he wore a wig made, as it still is today, out of animal hair.

Read the passage and answer questions 1 – 10.

1 Why is fog used as a metaphor to describe the Court of Chancery?
2 Which sentence indicates that this case involved a considerable amount of paperwork?
3 In the warning *Suffer any wrong that can be done you, rather than come here,* who does *you* refer to and where is *here*?
4 Why do the short-hand writers and the various reporters leave court as soon as the case of Jarndyce and Jarndyce is called?
5 Why do the Chancery lawyers find it so difficult to agree on the grounds for this case?
6 What point was Mr Blowers making when he said that such a thing might happen *when the sky rained potatoes* and what is the connection between that remark and the phrase *or we get through Jarndyce and Jarndyce*?
7 Why do you think that the author deliberately does not tell the reader what the case of Jarndyce and Jarndyce was actually about?

Fog everywhere. Fog up the river, where it flows among green aits and meadows; fog down the river, where it rolls defiled among the tiers of shipping, and the waterside pollutions of a great (and dirty) city.

Most of the shops lighted two hours before their time as the gas seems to know, for it has a haggard and unwilling look.

The raw afternoon is rawest, and the dense fog is densest, and the muddy streets are muddiest in Lincoln's Hall where, at the very heart of the fog, sits the Lord High Chancellor in his High Court of Chancery.

On such an afternoon, the Lord High Chancellor ought to be sitting here – as here he is – with a foggy glory round his head, softly fenced in with crimson cloth and curtains, addressed by a large advocate with great whiskers, a little voice, and an interminable brief, and outwardly directing his contemplation to the lantern in the roof, where he can see nothing but fog.

On such an afternoon, some score of members of the High Court of Chancery bar ought to be as here they are mistily engaged in one of the ten thousand stages of an endless cause, tripping one another up on slippery precedents, groping knee-deep in technicalities, running their goat-hair and horsehair warded heads against walls of word and making a pretence of equity with serious faces, as players might. On such an afternoon, the various solicitors in the cause, some two or three of whom have inherited it from their fathers, who made a fortune by it, ought to be – as are they not? – ranged in a line, in a long matted well (but you might look in vain for Truth at the bottom of it), between the registrar's red table and the silk gowns, with bills, cross-bills, answers, rejoinders, injunctions, affidavits, issues, references to masters, masters' reports, mountains of costly nonsense, piled before them. Well may the court be dim, with wasting candles here and there; well may the fog hang heavy in it, as if it would never get out; well may the stained-glass windows lose their colour, and admit no light of day into the place; well may the uninitiated from the streets, who peep in through the glass panes in the door, be deterred from the entrance by its owlish aspects, and by the drawl languidly echoing to the roof from the padded dais where the Lord High Chancellor looks into the lantern that has no light in it, and where the attendant wigs are all stuck in a fog-bank! This is the Court of Chancery; which has its ruined suitor, with his slipshod heels and threadbare dress, borrowing and begging through the round of every man's acquaintance; which gives to monied might the means abundantly of wearying out the right; which so exhausts finances, patience, courage, hope; so overthrows the brain and breaks the heart; that there is not an honourable man among its practitioners – who would not give – who does not often give the warning, 'Suffer any wrong that can be done you, rather than come here!'

Who happen to be in the Lord Chancellor's court this murky afternoon besides the Lord Chancellor, the counsel in the cause, two or three counsel who are never in any cause, and the well of the solicitors before mentioned? There is the registrar below the judge, in wig and gown; these are all yawning; for no crumb of amusement ever falls from JARNDYCE AND JARNDYCE (the cause in hand), which was squeezed dry years upon years ago. The shorthand writers, the reporters of the court, and the reporters of the newspapers, invariably decamp with the rest of the regulars when Jarndyce and Jarndyce comes on. Their places are blank.

Jarndyce and Jarndyce drones on. This suit has, in course of time, become so complicated that no man alive knows what it means. The parties to it understand it least; but it has been observed that no two Chancery lawyers can talk about it for five minutes without coming to a total disagreement as to all the premises.

Jarndyce and Jarndyce has passed into a joke. That is the only good that has ever come of it. It has been death to many, but it is a joke in the profession.

The last Lord Chancellor handled it neatly, when, correcting Mr Blowers, the eminent who said that such a thing might happen when the sky rained potatoes, he observed, 'or when we get through Jarndyce and Jarndyce, Mr Blowers.'

Listening

Listen to these extracts from a court case. Complete the journalist's notes.

```
Name of accused: ...
Alleged crime: ...
Plea: ...
Key witness for the
prosecution: ...
Key evidence for the
prosecution: ...
Key witness for the defence: ...
Key evidence for the defence: ...
Verdict: ...
Sentence: ...
```

Speaking

1 Discuss with a partner how each of the photographs relates to the theme of job satisfaction and the enjoyment of work.

2 Read through each of the passages and discuss how it extends and develops the theme.

1 Fruit and vegetable pickers required – no experience necessary. Enjoy the fresh air life down on the farm. Take your pick from over a hundred locations countrywide. No shirkers or late risers need apply, but for those willing to work hard there is free accommodation and a high earnings potential. We back you up rather than break your back. Apply to Bendover Farms plc, Scratches Lane, Plumstead.

2 Management was, of course, most concerned about employee reaction to the installations but following the inevitable reduction in the workforce – brought about mainly through natural wastage, I hasten to add – there has been a gratifyingly positive response to the new working practices and a considerable reduction in absenteeism.

3 The smell of the greasepaint and the roar of the crowd gives me a terrific buzz but I've had to train incredibly hard to get there. The main problem for most of us dancers is that we are over the hill by the time we get to thirty. Then what? Who knows? But I wouldn't miss it for the world.

Reading

1 Read the passage on workaholism on the next page and answer questions 1 – 11.

1 How would you define workaholism?
2 At what point does work become counter-productive?
3 In what way does *a short-term gain* become *a long-term loss*?
4 What does *it* refer to in the phrase *before he or she knows it*?
5 Why do some companies not want to admit that workaholism exists?
6 Why are managers not often asked questions about the effects of their working methods?
7 What do you think is meant by *a corporate culture*?
8 What is *this vicious circle*?
9 How might a senior executive react when told by his wife that she wants a divorce?
10 In what ways might an employee *wilt under pressure*?
11 What recommendations are made about how to counter the effects of workaholism?

2 Summarise the main dangers of workaholism in 80 – 100 words.

Use of English

Rewrite the following sentences using the words in italics. The meaning must remain the same, but this word must not be altered in any way.

1 The increase in sales of Virago tyres was attributed to their excellent TV commercial.
down

2 After complaints from the public, the company removed Geturoats muesli from the shops.
off

3 As soon as Pendle arrived at the court, he began the task of preparing his case.
set

4 Jones was informed that he had been dismissed by the organisation.
services

5 Jilly has decided to apply for that job in publishing.
put

Writing

Write *one* of the following compositions. Use about 350 words.

1 Describe the type of job you enjoy or would enjoy doing. Give reasons for your choice.
2 *Work is much more fun than fun.* Discuss.

WORKAHOLISM
The Industrial Disease of our Times

The days of the infamous British tea-break are over. There has been a swing of the pendulum towards hard work which, one might think, can only be a good thing. This thinking has proved to be naïve, however, and has created one of the pitfalls of modern management. Just as work-shyness used to be the scourge of the British shop floor, so workaholism has become the industrial disease of modern management. British executives are understandably loathe to admit this. Their failure to do so and, therefore, to take measures to cater for it may be costing British companies dear. Someone working over 45 hours a week may be up to 25% less efficient.

When assessing and interviewing applicants for jobs, personnel managers look for a positive attitude towards the company and the post in question. They welcome the kind of robust enthusiasm that will carry prospective executives through times of heavy workload, responsibility and stress. Once someone has been appointed, however, their performance is usually assessed in different terms: against targets, as a member or leader of a team, in terms of perceived efficiency and effectiveness, commitment and so on. Rarely do personal methods of work come under the microscope to have their impact assessed. The effect of these working methods on a manager's domestic life and leisure pursuits, what is more, are considered to be none of the company's business. Even to ask questions about this would be construed by many as an invasion of privacy.

It therefore passes unnoticed if a manager's commitment and enthusiasm lead to potentially damaging methods of work. Long hours, the pressure of targets and responsibilities, and mental fatigue combined can begin to erode quality of contribution. Before he or she knows it, the drive to work becomes an obsession. Interests in the family, loved ones, hobbies and other leisure pursuits wane and the time allocated to them is taken over by work. Commitment has become addiction, the manager has to a degree lost control, he or she has become a workaholic.

Rather than enhancing performance and contribution, workaholism undermines it – and not only for the manager concerned. All job-related managers and junior employees are at risk. Workaholism can rapidly become part of the corporate culture, particularly where senior management naïvely encourage long hours, seeing them as symbols of commitment and as a means of achievement. What they do not realise is how easily this short-term gain can become a long-term loss. Excessive commitment to work causes stress in domestic life, which in turn causes stress and damages performance. The ensuing poor performance in itself causes further stress and so the manager spirals downwards towards almost inevitable failure and the risk of serious stress-related physical or psychological illness.

So what can be done about this vicious circle? The first step would seem to be to persuade companies to accept that the problem exists. This meets resistance, however – as long hours are often seen as proof of commitment and one of the functions of management has long been to foster commitment and hard work – but research in Europe and the USA is beginning to be taken seriously by most well-run companies.

How do you then identify and handle existing cases? Some may wilt under the pressure, others may be brought up short by some sort of shock to the system: by a brief but serious illness or the threat of divorce, for example. In the latter instances, it is likely that the manager will reevaluate his or her lifestyle and take the measures necessary to avoid a personal tragedy.

As far as the remaining cases are concerned – and, for that matter, those who may well succumb in future – the experts recommend a systematic screening and information service with back-up counselling and support. Flexible working hours can be helpful, as they facilitate productive use of time and, at the same time, encourage each individual to plan the day to suit his or her particular lifestyle. Regular holidays should be seen as a necessity not a luxury and regular excessive overtime should be frowned on. Above all, the corporate climate has to foster quality not quantity of work.

Art first, then philosophy, lastly science.

Muriel Spark

Speaking

1 Should this be the order of importance of the great subjects of life? Say what you think.

2 In some countries artists, writers and poets apparently have higher status than scientists and engineers. In Westminster Abbey in London, for example, Poets' Corner honours leading English poets of the past, but there is no such place for the scientists who, arguably, have contributed far more to the nation's prosperity.

Explain how your country views and ranks scientists and engineers.

Reading and speaking

1 Read the poem by Wendy Cope. Choose the word or phrase closest in meaning to items 1 – 8 as used in this poem.

1 *blueprints*
a pornographic literature
b plans or drawings

2 *scrape by in cheerless garrets*
a live in poverty in an attic
b live unhappily in an old house

3 *had got it made*
a had achieved success
b had fallen in love

4 *well-heeled*
a very healthy
b comfortably off

5 *a crust*
a just enough money
b a fortune

6 *bust*
a notoriety
b statue

7 *spurn*
a repair
b reject

8 *going down the drain*
a becoming more literate
b becoming worse off

2 Read the poem again and complete each statement 1 – 5 in the most appropriate way.

1 Wendy Cope believes that engineers
a do not get the financial rewards they deserve.
b are well-paid for what they do.

2 Poets, on the other hand,
a are unlikely to find financial security.
b have a higher standard of living than engineers.

3 *It must be hell* suggests that
a engineers have a very hard life in reality.
b poets cannot usually live by writing poetry.

4 The poem implies that most small boys
a long to write poetry.
b want to work with machines when they grow up.

5 The tone of the poem is
a ironic.
b comic.

ENGINEERS' CORNER

Why isn't there an Engineers' Corner in Westminster Abbey? In Britain we've always made more fuss of a ballad than a blueprint ... How many schoolchildren dream of becoming great engineers?

Advertisement placed in The Times *by the Engineering Council*

We make more fuss of ballads than of blueprints
That's why so many poets end up rich,
While engineers scrape by in cheerless garrets.
Who needs a bridge or a dam? Who needs a ditch?

Whereas the person who can write a sonnet
Has got it made. It's always been the way,
For everybody knows that we need poems
And everybody reads them every day.

Yes, life is hard if you choose engineering
You're sure to need another job as well;
You'll have to plan your projects in the evenings
Instead of going out. It must be hell.

While well-heeled poets ride around in Daimlers,
You'll burn the midnight oil to earn a crust,
With no hope of a statue in the Abbey,
With no hope, even, of a modest bust.

No wonder small boys dream of writing couplets
And spurn the bike, the lorry and the train.
There's far too much encouragement for poets
That's why this country's going down the drain.

3 Discuss with a partner where society would be without (a) scientists and engineers and (b) writers and poets. Come to some conclusions about their relative value to society.

Use of English

The expression *no wonder* is often used to show that a person has understood the reasons behind something that had previously been puzzling them. It may be used either in a straightforward way or with additional implications. For example:

A There's something wrong with the lock.
B *No wonder my key wouldn't work.*

A Bernard came to stay for the weekend.
B *No wonder there isn't any food in the fridge.*

In the first example, the response is straightforward: B realises the reason why the key did not work.

In the second example, B implies that Bernard eats a lot and that that is the reason for the empty fridge.

1 Listen to the dialogues and decide whether there is any implicit meaning in the speaker's use of *no wonder*. If so, explain it.

2 *No wonder* can also be replaced by *It's hardly surprising (that). It* refers forward to whatever is not surprising. The respective reason why is often introduced by *given/considering (that).*

It's hardly surprising Jane's going to Majorca, given that John's in Florida.
Given that John decided to have a holiday on his own in Florida, it's hardly surprising that Jane's in Majorca.
Given the money John is paid, it's hardly surprising he can afford expensive holidays.

The implication is, of course, that Jane and John are no longer friends. Note that *given* is only followed by *that* when it comes before a subject and a verb.

Combine each set of facts below into one sentence using *it's hardly surprising, given (that)* and any other connecting devices that may be needed.

1 Not many graduates become science teachers.
Teachers' pay is low compared to that of other scientific professions.

2 Torrey Canyon used to be a very popular holiday resort.
Last year the beaches were polluted by an oil slick.
Holiday bookings this year are down by 70%.

3 John Self is a very rich man.
He works in Hollywood as a film director.
Hollywood film directors are extremely well paid.

4 Ronald Macdonald is overweight.
He eats nothing but fast food.

3 Complete each of the following sentences in an appropriate way.

1 Given the exorbitant prices the Hotel Ritzy charges, …
2 It's hardly surprising that so few people take their cases to court, …
3 No wonder Glenda Gloss got the starring role in the film, …
4 …, given that more and more roads are being built.
5 It's hardly surprising all those people are smiling, …

Reading

I think, therefore I am. Descartes.

What makes human beings different from other life forms – or even from machines – is a question which has been posed by both scientists and philosophers. The extract on the next page is taken from a short story by the American writer, Ambrose Bierce. It was written in 1935.

1 Read the passage opposite and answer questions 1 – 5.

1 When, according to Moxon, does a machine think?
2 What is the narrator's opinion of Moxon's ideas?
3 How does Moxon justify his argument that plants can think?
4 What, according to Moxon, is the phenomena of crystallisation?
5 What is ironic about the narrator's comment, *Ah, plants belong to the philosopher class*?

2 Summarise Moxon's arguments on machines in 70 – 100 words. Start:

Moxon's argument for saying that machines can think is based on …

'ARE YOU SERIOUS? Do you really believe that a machine thinks?'

I got no immediate reply; Moxon was apparently intent upon the coals in the grate, touching them deftly here and there with the firepoker till they signified a sense of his attention by a brighter glow. For several weeks I had been observing in him a growing habit of delay in answering even the most trivial of commonplace questions.

Presently he said: 'What is a "machine"? The word has been variously defined. Here is one definition from a popular dictionary: "Any instrument or organization by which power is applied and made effective, or a desired effect produced." Well, then, is not a man a machine? And you will admit that he thinks – or thinks he thinks.'

'If you do not wish to answer my question,' I said, rather testily, 'why not say so? All that you say is mere evasion. You know well enough that when I say "machine" I do not mean a man, but something that man has made and controls.'

'When it does not control him,' he said, rising abruptly and looking out of a window. A moment later he turned about and with a smile said: 'I beg your pardon; I had no thought of evasion, I can give your question a direct answer easily enough: I do believe that a machine thinks about the work that it is doing.'

That was direct enough, certainly. It was not altogether pleasing, for it tended to confirm a sad suspicion that Moxon's devotion to study and work had not been good for him. I knew, for one thing, that he suffered from insomnia, and that is no light affliction. Had it affected his mind? His reply to my question seemed to me then evidence that it had; perhaps I should think differently about it now. I was younger then, and among the blessings that are not denied to youth is ignorance. Incited by that great stimulant to controversy, I said: 'And what, pray, does it think with – in the absence of a brain?' The reply, coming with less than his customary delay, took his favourite form of counter-interrogation: 'With what does a plant think in the absence of a brain?'

'Ah, plants also belong to the philosopher class! I should be pleased to know some of their conclusions; you may omit the premises.'

'Perhaps,' he replied, apparently unaffected by my foolish irony, 'you may be able to infer their convictions from their acts. Observe this. In an open spot in my garden I planted a climbing vine. When it was barely above the surface I set a stake into the soil a yard away. The vine at once made for it, but as it was about to reach it after several days I removed it a few feet. The vine at once altered its course, making an acute angle, and again made for the stake. This manoeuvre was repeated several times, but finally, as if discouraged, the vine abandoned the pursuit and ignoring further attempts to divert it, travelled to a small tree, further away, which it climbed.

'Roots of the eucalyptus will prolong themselves incredibly in search of moisture. A well-known horticulturist relates that one entered an old drain pipe and followed it until it came to a break, where a section of the pipe had been removed to make way for a stone wall that had been built across its course. The root left the drain and followed the wall until it found an opening where a stone had fallen out. It crept through and, following the other side of the wall back to the drain, entered the unexplored part and resumed its journey.'

'And all this?'

'Can you miss the significance of it? It shows the consciousness of plants. It proves that they think.'

'Even if it did, what then? We were speaking, not of plants, but of machines.' Moxon replied. 'Is thought an attribute also of the mineral kingdom?'

'How else do you explain the phenomena, for example, of crystallization?'

'I do not explain them.'

'Because you cannot without affirming what you wish to deny, namely, intelligent co-operation among the constituent elements of the crystals. When soldiers form lines, or hollow squares, you call it reason. When wild geese in flight take the form of a letter V, you say instinct. When the homogeneous atoms of a mineral, moving freely in solution, arrange themselves into shapes mathematically perfect, or particles of frozen moisture into the symmetrical and beautiful forms of snowflakes, you have nothing to say. You have not even invented a name to conceal your heroic unreason.'

Speaking

People have more control over machines than machines have over people.

Using the photographs and the language you have studied in this Unit, discuss with your partner how far you would agree with this statement.

Listening

Discuss how modern technology may affect scientists' value to society and their social status.

Listen to a talk given by a leading scientist in the field of artificial intelligence. Choose the most appropriate answer for each question 1 – 5.

1 What is the main obstacle to be faced when making a machine with abilities similar to those of human beings?
a The length of time it takes to build them.
b The fact that nobody believes it is possible.
c The complexity of the human brain itself.
d The lack of the right software.

2 In what way are fifth-generation computers different from their predecessors?
a They are likely to be much more expensive to produce.
b They cannot think for themselves.
c They lack the power to take decisions.
d They are capable of abstract thought.

3 What effect will the new computers have on health care?
a They will make visiting the doctor cheaper.
b They will make it easier to visit the doctor.
c They will make visiting the doctor unnecessary.
d They will make people frightened about their health.

4 What will be one of the disadvantages brought about by the new computers?
a They will lead to a decline in educational standards.
b They will lead to a decline in health care.
c They will lead to a decline in the appreciation of art.
d They will lead to a decline in employment opportunities.

5 What is the speaker's general attitude towards the effects of artificial intelligence systems on our lives?
a Optimistic.
b Pessimistic.
c Frightened.
d Indifferent.

Speaking

Discuss with a partner what other qualities should be poured into this head in order to enable this person to cope with the demands of an increasingly technological society.

Reading and speaking

1 One of the disciplines that bring together art, philosophy and science most closely is architecture. This can cause tensions between them. The extract on the right is from *Hawksmoor* by Peter Ackroyd. It describes the time when Sir Christopher Wren was designing the new St Paul's Cathedral after it had been burnt down in the Great Fire of London in 1666. Read the passage and answer questions.

1. Why do you think the other subjects mentioned are important when designing a building?
2. What do you think is meant by *You cannot build out of books unless they be castles in the air*?

2 The magazine article on the next page is about a monument appropriate to the twentieth century, an airport terminal. Before reading it, discuss what you think are the most important factors to take into consideration when designing:

1. a house.
2. an airport terminal.
3. an office complex.

In the course of your discussion, consider the following:

a the appearance of the building.
b the building materials.
c the building's use of energy.
d the functions of the building.
e the surrounding environment.

3 Read the article. Find a word or phrase in it that is similar in meaning to each item 1 – 10.

1. general agreement
2. going forward very quickly
3. displaying in an extrovert way
4. empty of unnecessary items
5. an act done in the face of criticism
6. becoming less and less
7. leg-like building supports
8. rules restricting the design and siting of buildings
9. with many different applications
10. very difficult to find

◊

Thus did I learn of Architecture and, appriz'd that workmen could advance to the degree of Architect in these times, I coveted that office for myself: to become the Structorum Princeps, as Mr Evelyn has it, the ingenious Artificer who must be learned in Astrologie and Arithmetick, Musick no less than Geometry, Philosophy as well as Opticks, History no less than Law, was my set Purpose. But you cannot build out of Books, unless it be Castles in the Air, and I decided to step into the World for further Information: I listen'd to the Discourse of the workmen in my Master's yard (next St Paul's on which he was then employed) and held them in Conversation concerning matters of Practice; I also sought occasions to visit the brick-burnings in Whitechappel and here I learned of the earth which lies beneath London: these and like Matters I laid up in my Head, for there was no knowing to what Use they might come.

4 Read the passage again. Identify what conflicts exist between architects and each of the following:

1. the general public.
2. the government department responsible for future planning.
3. the environmentalists.

Discuss with your partner how each of these conflicts could be resolved.

5 *However much care an architect takes to design a building the way it is run depends on the people.*

Read the passage again. Discuss with your partner whether or not you have had similar experiences at airports.

Writing

Write one of the following compositions. Use about 350 words.

1. *There can be no real human progress without scientific development*. Discuss.
2. Describe the way in which you think scientists could most affect the quality of future human life.

ARCHITECTURE

There has probably never been a greater consensus in this country about the kind of architecture we don't want to see.

The emergence of giant office developments like Broadgate and Canary Wharf in London and giant shopping developments like the Metro Centre in Gateshead, the largest in Europe, remind us that this consensus hasn't prevented developers from forging ahead with more of the same. All it has done is to persuade the developers of Broadgate to apply a fin de siècle *gloss of bronze and mahogany, to conceal the evidence of fast-track technology that has made the building and the acres of information technology it contains.*

The Eighties alternative to hiding your technology was flaunting it, with Richard Rogers' Lloyds Building the best-known example. Now we also have Sir Norman Foster's Stansted Airport. The terminal got built only after a long and bitter planning battle, and the design reflects this history. On the face of it, Stansted is a single-storey building. Only when it is approached by train is it clear that the ground level roundabout has been raised to conceal a basement storey housing the railway station and all baggage-handling and other services. This allows the immense, single passenger floor to remain uncluttered, and the roof height to be fixed at a level that the architects claim is no higher than that of surrounding trees.

But Foster wouldn't be the architect he is unless there were a few technical innovations to drive the design. To hold up the roof and to bring up the ducts, cables and other services from below, he has designed structural 'trees' that are the single most memorable visual ordering device of the whole building. This is a typical piece of Foster bravado: the functional made beautiful. To claim then, as he does, that their form is direct reference to the real trees visible through the glass walls, is simply to introduce an unnecessarily apologetic note of post-rationalization.

If the majority of the designers of the pavilions for Expo 92 in Seville are to be believed, the future will consist of buildings whose form is defined by the services they provide and the hi-tech materials they are made of.

But for how much longer can the spirit of excess be sustained in the face of dwindling supplies of fuel and raw materials? Architects are taught that aluminium is six times more energy-intensive to produce than steel, which is three times more energy-intensive than concrete, which is four times more energy-intensive than timber ... Yet they continue to specify materials like aluminium.

Future Systems, a two-person architectural practice based in London, are regarded by many as a world leader in building research and development. This doesn't necessarily mean their buildings are hi-tech. The green building they recently designed as a research project for engineers Ove Arup, uses the wind, rather than air-conditioning, for ventilation, and natural daylight rather than artificial lighting. Visually, these requirements have resulted in something that looks like a giant glass egg on stilts. But Future Systems claim to be totally indifferent to stylistic questions: what the building looks like, they imply, is the inevitable corollary of what it does.

Actually, Future Systems are at their most persuasive in a context in which the look of a building is unimportant anyway. They have designed a collapsible structure of heat-reflecting PVC over aluminium ribs, which could provide shelter for 200 people in cases of natural disaster, one which could be used as a clinic or food distribution centre. They are understandably disappointed that none of the aid agencies has yet responded to this imaginative design.

Many innovative designers seem to feel that, if it is hard to imagine finding a place for futuristic design in the historic urban context of, say, London, then that is the past's problem, not the future's. But London is a city more restricted than most by often conflicting building and planning regulations.

The way forward for architects seems to be to design versatile buildings that can be made acceptable to planners whatever the context, while addressing the environmental problems that otherwise threaten to put architects and everyone else out of a job permanently.

As for the long-term-future, we have the technology now to make buildings look like anything we want, whatever their function. But what if the energy and raw materials become too scarce to go on building the buildings? The alternative may be to live our lives in a visual illusion instead, a world supplied by a virtual reality computer software package. That way we could buy our Future Systems-designed environment in the form of a diskette, slip it into our computers in the privacy of our decaying urban slums, and live a futuristic virtual life. And Future Systems would have sold a design without once having to consult the planners.

A good time was had by all.

Stevie Smith

Speaking and listening

1 Discuss with a partner:

1 whether or not each of the groups is having a good time.
2 what enjoyment people get from being spectators at these events.
3 which of the events you would choose to attend and why.

2 Describe events that you particularly enjoy and any that you find particularly boring.

3 Listen to the following people talking and decide:

1 what each speaker does for a living.
2 the situation each speaker is in.

Reading

The extract on the next page is from the novel *Howard's End* by E. M. Forster. Before reading it, discuss with a partner what comes into your minds when you hear the term *classical music*.

Read the passage and answer questions 1 – 13.

1 Rewrite *It will be generally admitted*, keeping the meaning the same without using 'it'.
2 What does *it* refer to?
3 Why does Mrs Munt tap?
4 Why does she feel she has to do this surreptitiously?
5 What does the full score contain?
6 How does Fräulein Mosebach's young man feel about the music?
7 What is meant by *the passion of your life*?
8 Why is *even if* appropriate in this context?
9 Why did Helen's attention wander?
10 What is implied by *listening to classical music*?
11 How did Herr Liesecke react to the music?
12 What did Aunt Juley do during the performance?
13 What is the main difference in attitude between Helen and Tibby when they are listening to the music?

It will be generally admitted that Beethoven's Fifth Symphony is the most sublime noise that has ever penetrated into the ear of man. All sorts and conditions are satisfied by it. Whether you are like Mrs Munt, and tap surreptitiously when the tunes come – of course, not so as to disturb the others – or like Helen, who can see heroes and shipwrecks in the music's flood; or like Margaret, who can only see the music; or like Tibby, who is profoundly versed in counterpoint, and holds the full score open on his knee; or like their cousin, Fräulein Mosebach, who remembers all the time that Beethoven is 'echt Deutsch'; or like Fräulein Mosebach's young man, who can remember nothing but Fräulein Mosebach: in any case, the passion of your life becomes more vivid, even if you hear it in the Queen's Hall, dreariest music-room in London, though not as dreary as the Free Trade Hall, Manchester.

For the Andante had begun very beautiful, but bearing a family likeness to all the other beautiful Andantes that Beethoven had written, and, to Helen's mind, rather disconnecting the heroes and shipwrecks of the first movement from the heroes and goblins of the third. She heard the tune through once, and then her attention wandered, and she gazed at the audience, or the organ, or the architecture. Much did she censure the attenuated cupids who encircle the ceiling of the Queen's Hall, inclining each to each with vapid gesture, and clad in sallow pantaloons, on which the October sunlight struck. 'How awful to marry a man like those cupids!' thought Helen. Here Beethoven started decorating his tune, so she heard him through once more, and then smiled at her cousin Frieda. But Frieda, listening to classical music, could not respond. Herr Liesecke, too, looked as if wild horses could not make him inattentive; there were lines across his forehead, his lips were parted, his pince-nez at right angles to his nose, and he had laid a thick, white hand on either knee. And next to her was Aunt Juley, so British, and wanting to tap. How interesting that row of people was! What diverse influences had gone to the making! Here Beethoven, after humming and hawing with great sweetness, said 'Heigho', and the Andante came to an end.

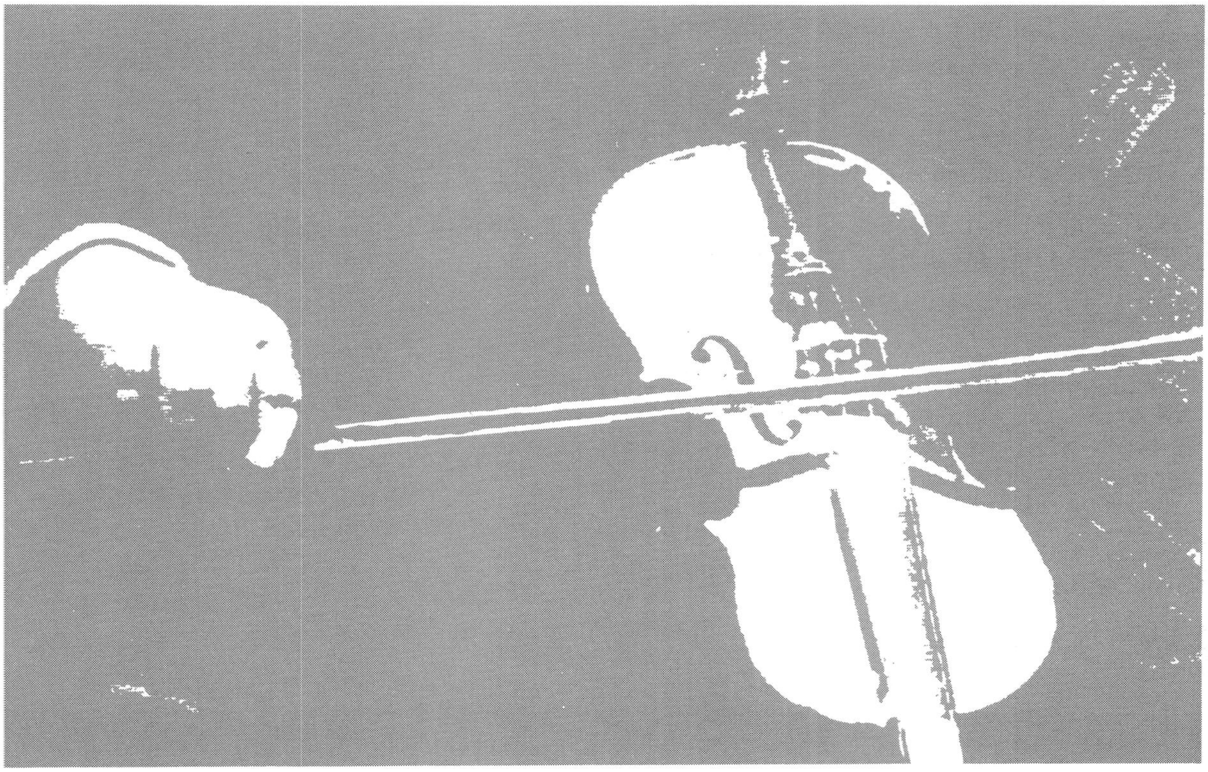

Listening

Listen to an extract from the radio programme Tape Measure. Choose the most appropriate completion for statements 1 – 5.

1 The type of music discussed
a often sounds ridiculous.
b is always controversial.
c is only understood by experts.
d is usually varied.

2 According to Reggie Jeeves, Light Years Ahead
a recorded their latest album in a concert hall.
b compose their own music.
c have three people in the band.
d are very talented.

3 Percy Pilbeam believes that
a Light Years Ahead produce highly original music.
b Beethoven composed soulless music.
c listening to electronic music improves his concentration.
d modern arrangements do not improve original compositions.

4 Joos Belgium
a has a high opinion of Light Years Ahead.
b enjoys sentimental music.
c agrees with Percy Pilbeams's opinion.
d enjoys sentimental music.

5 The three participants agree that
a the music is unsophisticated.
b the musicians are highly skilled.
c this type of music is very unusual.
d they want to buy the record.

Vocabulary development

1 Look at the list of adjectives which can be used to describe different types of music. Listen to the short musical extracts. Select the adjective(s) which you feel describe each extract appropriately. Number the adjectives appropriately, in the order in which the extracts occur. You may not select all the adjectives listed.

catchy	irritating
turgid	slow
melodic	strident
tuneless	flat
repetitive	beautiful
dramatic	magical
brilliant	brain-numbing
pedestrian	

2 Listen to each extract again. Compare your response to it with a partner.

3 Discuss other pieces of music that you would describe, using each of the adjectives listed.

Writing

You have seen this competition in *My Music*, a magazine which caters for a wide range of musical tastes. Submit your entry to the Editor. Use no more than 250 words. Write the review in the register you think is most appropriate to the atmosphere at the concert, not the type of music played. In other words, if you choose to describe a concert of classical music, it does not necessarily mean that you would use a more formal register than you would in a description of a rock concert. For a relatively informal or spontaneous occasion such as a school concert or, maybe, an outdoor concert, you could only reflect the atmosphere by using less formal language than you would when reviewing a formal concert by a symphony orchestra.

COMPETITION

YOUR concert choice
Top prizes to be won

Write a review of a concert you have recently been to.

Classical, rock, heavy metal, jazz, pop, easy listening – it's your choice. Describe – your reaction – the audience's reaction – the performance – why you went

Use ***no more*** than 250 words.
Submit your entry to
The Editor.

Use of English

... he had laid a thick white hand on either knee ...

Laid is the past participle of the verb *to lay, laid, laid* which is often confused with the verb *to lie, lay, lain.*

To lay is transitive and must be followed by an object (here, *a thick white hand*), whereas *to lie* is intransitive and cannot be followed by an object.

Remember also that the regular verb *to lie* and *lied, lied* means not to tell the truth.

Complete each of the following sentences using an appropriate form of the verbs *lay* and *lie* (irregular) or *lie(d)* (regular).

1 'You ... to me yesterday, didn't you. He was at the station, wasn't he?' Inspector Maurice Code shouted accusingly at the ticket collector.
2 According to the police, nobody ... eyes on Stephanie since she said goodbye to her boyfriend, Desmond, at the railway station. She seems to have disappeared into thin air.
3 'I'll ... any odds you like that the man with the broken nose is involved,' said Sergeant Arun categorically.
4 The newspapers were hounding our principal suspect so he ... pretty low all last week to try and stay clear of all the reporters.
5 'After she was murdered, Stephanie's body must have ... in the ditch for at least three days,' the doctor remarked sardonically.
6 'If you had ... a finger on my client you would never have heard the end of it,' said the lawyer menacingly. 'Just because he is the boyfriend doesn't make him guilty.'
7 'Perhaps we should ... off dubious Desmond for a while,' said Sergeant Arun hesitantly, 'I'm almost convinced he's telling the truth.'
8 '... your weapon down, put your hands in the air and walk this way,' the officer ordered the man with the broken nose.
9 'If you ask me,' Sergeant Arun remarked, 'the truth about the girl's murder ... hidden in these computer files.'
10 Inspector Code ... the blood-stained knife on the table and demanded an explanation from Desmond.
11 'Do you really expect me to believe that the knife ... around your kitchen for three days?' interrupted the Inspector.
12 'Money always seems ... at the bottom of cases like this and that's why I suspected our man with the rearranged features right from the start,' said Lewis effusively.
13 'It's hardly surprising the ticket inspector ..., given that he was being blackmailed,' mused Inspector Code.
14 As they left the police station, Code ... a hand on Arun's shoulder and congratulated him on finding the real culprit.
15 Maurice Code switched on his CD player, selected a track from his 'World of Opera' album, ... down on his comfortable sofa and allowed the music to transport him into another world.

Reading and speaking

Music is one way of stimulating the imagination. Another way of doing this is to use the technology which creates a computer-enhanced world so real that it is called virtual reality.

Read the magazine article on the next page and answer questions 1 – 6.

1 How do you think the following create their alternative realities?
a *writers*
b *big-budget film directors*
c *the illegally stimulated*
2 How are virtual reality games different from more conventional computer and video games?
3 What is meant by *imagination is the only limit*?
4 According to the passage, how are interactive systems most likely to be used at present?
5 What are the attractions of *paintball*?
6 What do you think are the main advantages and disadvantages of using virtual reality systems?

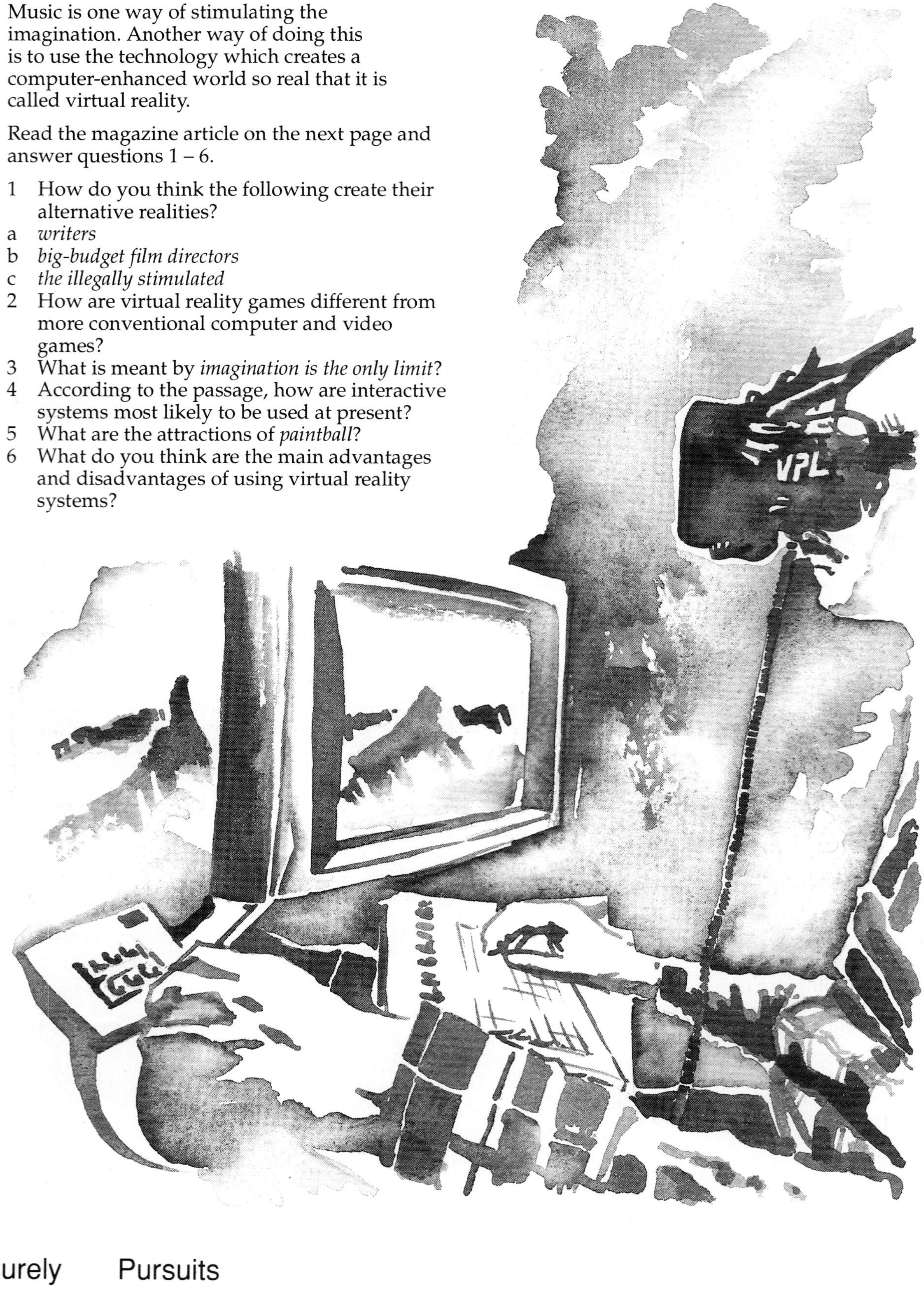

LEISURE

Escaping into an alternative reality has always been a favoured activity, but actually creating those realities is still largely the province of writers, the big-budget filmmakers and the illegally stimulated. Developments in the fields of virtual reality, interactive technology and imaginative role-playing games, however, mean that soon each of us will be able to spend our leisure hours relaxing in worlds of our own design.

With virtual reality, the details of your chosen world – a previous era, another country or a universe completely of your own design – are programmed into a computer. One enters the world by donning 'computer clothing': an electronic helmet which monitors head movement and relays appropriate video images on miniature screens inside the visor, and a glove filled with fibre-optic sensors with which one can manipulate objects and control one's slightest movements within the computer-graphic world.

Although its phenomenal price today limits virtual reality to certain practical and training uses, the possibilities for the future are almost endless. In a computer-induced world, you make your own rules: no need to be bound by conventional morality, or even gravity. Imagination is the only limit.

Interactive systems currently work on a more public level, as user-friendly information units in museums or as part of large displays. Laser discs or videos storing data are hooked into a computer, which is in turn linked to any number of other systems: lights, soundtrack tapes, even vibrating floors. By answering questions or activating touch sensors in a video wall or screen, individuals or teams can control the environment and the programme, choosing to move from a Venus scenario to Mars, or experiencing fully the consequences of their choices in role-playing games.

The potential is there for interactive leisure centres where the public can experience games and explore scenarios in large groups. The latest developers of both systems emphasize the participatory and exploratory nature of the technology: what will be on offer won't be glorified 3-D movies. Users will dictate the shape and setting of the programme, employing their own creativity and initiative rather than just 'playing' the computers.

For those who prefer more physical reality, favouring hardware over software, paintball offers real adventure. Initially an underground war game played with modified paint-firing airguns, then a hobby for bored executives, paintball has become a thrilling, well organized and rapidly expanding sport. Hardened players insist that there's no adrenaline rush quite like stalking and being stalked by an opponent armed with a powerful, paint-spitting gun.

It's likely that, as equipment becomes cheaper and more compact, the three systems will become increasingly entwined: paintballers will be able to play in virtual reality or interactive landscapes. The new computer-game or role-playing hobbyist of the future will no longer be a participating couch potato: mastery of your own world will be available at the press of a button, or the trigger of a paint gun.

Speaking

1 Look at the photographs and discuss with your partner what pleasure the participants derive from each of the leisure activities.

2 Read the passages below and discuss with a partner how each relates to one of the photographs and what further insights it gives into the motives of the people shown.

1 *Look who's stalking!*
Executive stress? Cut it out with a weekend away in the wooded terrain of the New Forest. Develop your skills of attack, defence, evasion, camouflage and leadership when you join a team of paintballers. Object? To capture your opponents' flag without being touched by a paintball gun. Don't just talk to your colleagues, come and stalk them as well.

2 As we climbed higher and higher, the valley looked small below us. When I looked down, I felt a frighteningly giddy sensation and thought I was going to fall. I turned to my colleague and murmured, 'Why do we do it?' He replied, 'Because it's there.'

3 I've got satellite, cable and a really good adjustable aerial, so I can tune in to stations almost anywhere in the world. What do I watch? Anything and everything. You name it, I've seen it. From ladies mud-wrestling through game shows to high opera and sophisticated drama, it's all there at the touch of a button. Go out? I've got no time. Besides, who needs it when you can get everything from a TV screen? Now, if you'll just excuse me, it's time for *The Weird World of the Wombat*, live from Australian TV. Unmissable!

Vocabulary development

Complete each of the following sentences with the most appropriate language item a, b, c or d.

1 Edward is a real … , he does nothing all day except watch television.
a couch potato
b salt of the earth
c lounge lizard
d brick

2 'It is outside the … of the script writer to tell me what to do,' bellowed the film director.
a walls
b jurisdiction
c scope
d province

3 … her protective headgear in order to reduce the risk of head injury, Alice rushed into the collapsing building.
a Conning
b Spurning
c Applying
d Donning

4 Some people feel that they are being … by unscrupulous operators so that they are no longer in control of their lives.
a manifested
b manipulated
c linked
d freed

5 My lawyer told me that I was not … by the terms of the contract as I had no knowledge of what was in the document.
a appreciated
b hounded
c bound
d dictated

6 Even after the earthquake was over, the whole house continued to … .
a shake up
b activate
c rebate
d vibrate

7 Interactive systems are innovative because they require the user to … at a high level rather than adopt a passive role.
a participate
b act
c involve
d combine

8 The equipment has been … so that it is suitable for use in role-playing.
a mollified
b modulated
c mooted
d modified

9 In order to catch the deer, Fisher had to … them through the woods for hours.
a stork
b stalk
c stake
d staunch

10 As the vine grew, it … itself around the wire.
a twinned
b climbed
c entwined
d hardened

11 The … of scientific opinion is that virtual reality systems will soon be commonplace.
a census
b common sense
c conference
d consensus

12 You're rich now, so you may as well … it and drape yourself in diamonds.
a flout
b flounder
c flip
d flaunt

13 Four days after Sid Perks' disappearance, all hopes of ever finding him alive began to … .
a kindle
b flounder
c riddle
d dwindle

14 During the exam, Marcie glanced … at the answers she had hidden up her sleeve.
a suspiciously
b superciliously
c subliminally
d surreptitiously

15 As Tess gazed glumly up at the leaden sky, her thoughts turned away from the … English weather to the beaches of Brazil.
a dowdy
b frumpy
c fiery
d dreary

Reading

1 The passage on the next page is taken from *The Great Gatsby* by F. Scott Fitzgerald. Gatsby is extremely rich, but few people have any idea how he acquired his wealth. He gives parties which are attended by the leisured classes of New York, in the hope of a chance reunion with the one love of his life, Daisy. They were separated when Gatsby had to go off and fight the war and when he returned he discovered that she had married someone else. The extract sums up the hedonistic light-heartedness of the 1920s Jazz Age. Read the passage and answer questions 1 – 6.

1. Why were the guests diving from the tower at high tide?
2. What were *the ravages of the night before*?
3. What is meant by *the bar is in full swing*?
4. Why were the introductions forgotten on the spot?
5. Why do the lights grow brighter?
6. What impression is the writer giving of the atmosphere at the party?

2 The writer uses colours to enhance the description. Write down what you think the writer was trying to convey with each of these images.

blue gardens
bewitched to a dark gold
gaudy with primary colours
yellow cocktail music

Vocabulary development

1 The expressions *like moths* and *like a yellow bug* have an immediate impact. Both these insects have particular characteristics that convey meaning in the context of the passage you have just read. Moths are attracted to light and a bug carries things backwards and forwards between two fixed points.

Discuss with your partner what characteristics each of the following creatures has.

a butterfly	a bee
a spider	a snail
a fly	a locust

2 Write sentences, using each of these insects metaphorically.

Writing

Write one of the following compositions. Use about 350 words.

1. Describe an event which you thoroughly enjoyed going to but which some of the people with you did not enjoy.
2. *The rat race of life is in pursuit of leisure.* Discuss.

There was music from my neighbour's house through the summer nights. In his blue gardens men and girls came and went like moths among the whisperings and the champagne and the stars. At high tide in the afternoon I watch his guests diving from the tower of his raft, or taking the sun on the hot sand of his beach while his two motor-boats slit the waters of the Sound, drawing aquaplanes over cataracts of foam. On weekends his Rolls-Royce became an omnibus, bearing parties to and from the city between nine in the morning and long past midnight, while his station wagon scampered like a brisk yellow bug to meet all trains. And on Mondays eight servants, including an extra gardener, toiled all day with mops and scrubbing-brushes and hammers and garden-shears, repairing the ravages of the night before.

Every Friday five crates of oranges and lemons arrived from a fruiterer in New York – every Monday these same oranges and lemons left his back door in a pyramid of pulpless halves. There was a machine in the kitchen which could extract the juice of two hundred oranges in half an hour if a little button was pressed two hundred times by a butler's thumb. At least once a fortnight a corps of caterers came down with several hundred feet of canvas and enough coloured lights to make a Christmas tree of Gatsby's enormous garden. On buffet tables, garnished with glistening hors-d'oeuvre, spiced baked hams crowded against salads of harlequin designs and pastry pigs and turkeys bewitched to a dark gold. In the main hall a bar with a real brass rail was set up, and stocked with gins and liquors and with cordials so long forgotten that most of his female guests were too young to know one from another.

By seven o'clock the orchestra has arrived, no thin five-piece affair, but a whole pitful of oboes and trombones and saxophones and viols and cornets and picolos, and low and high drums. The last swimmers have come in from the beach now and are dressing upstairs; the cars from New York are parked five deep in the drive, and already the halls and salons and verandas are gaudy with primary colours, and hair bobbed in strange ways, and shawls beyond the dreams of Castille. The bar is in full swing, and floating rounds of cocktails permeate the garden outside, until the air is alive with chatter and laughter, and casual innuendo and introductions forgotten on the spot, and enthusiastic meetings between women who never knew each other's names.

The lights grow brighter as the earth lurches away from the sun, and now the orchestra is playing yellow cocktail music, and the opera of voices pitches a key higher. Laughter is easier minute by minute, spilled with prodigality, tipped out at a cheerful word. The groups change more swiftly, swell with new arrivals, dissolve and form in the same breath; already there are wanderers, confident girls who weave here and there among the stouter and more stable, become for a sharp, joyous moment the centre of a group, and then, excited with triumph, glide on through the sea-change of faces and voices and colour under the constantly changing light.

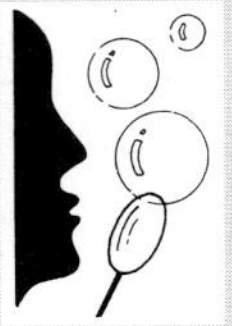

It was a dream of perfect bliss too beautiful to last.

Thomas Bayly

Speaking

It is said that there are two kinds of people: sunrise people and sunset people. Sunrise people have vision and look forward to what the future has to offer. Sunset people have dreams and look back nostalgically to a previous golden age which they hope will occur again. Which do you think you are?

Listening

1 Listen to five people answering questions about themselves. Complete the notes below.

2 Discuss with a partner which of the speakers you each have most in common with and why.

Reading

Read the extract on the next page from the novel *Of Mice and Men by John Steinbeck.*

It is set in the farming States of America during the Great Depression of the 1930s. The two main characters are Lennie, a rather simple-minded person, and George, who helps Lennie through the complexities of life.

1 Choose the word or phrase that is closest in meaning to each of items 1 – 5 as used in the extract.

1 *work up a stake*
a earn some money
b look forward to something to eat

2 *blow*
a lose
b spend

3 *poundin' their tail*
a talking emphatically
b working hard

4 *the jack*
a the money
b the equipment

5 *live off the fatta the lan'*
a have a lot of parties
b have plenty to eat

Questions	Speaker 1	Speaker 2	Speaker 3	Speaker 4	Speaker 5
Which do you prefer, sunrise or sunset?					
Why is that?					
Are you optimistic or pessimistic about the future?					
Do you see yourself more as a visionary or as a nostalgic dreamer?					

George said: 'I want you to stay with me, Lennie. Jesus Christ, somebody'd shoot you for a coyote if you was by yourself. No, you stay with me. Your Aunt Clara wouldn't like you running off by yourself, even if she is dead.'
Lennie spoke craftily: 'Tell me like you done before.'
'Tell you what?'
'About the rabbits.'
George snapped: 'You ain't gonna put nothing over on me.'
Lennie pleaded: 'Come on, George. Tell me. Please, George. Like you done before.'
'You get a kick outta that, don't you. A'right, I'll tell you, and then we'll eat our supper ...'
George's voice became deeper. He repeated his words rhythmically as though he had said them many times before.
'Guys like us, that work on ranches, are the loneliest guys in the world. They got no family. They don't belong no place. They come to a ranch an' work up a stake and then they go inta town and blow their stake, and the first thing you know they're poundin' their tail on some other ranch. They ain't nothing to look ahead to.'
Lennie was delighted. 'That's it – that's it. Now tell how it is with us.'
George went on. 'With us it ain't like that. We got a future. We got somebody to talk to that gives a damn about us. We don't have to sit in no bar-room blowin' in our jack jus' because we got no place else to go. If them other guys gets in jail they can rot for all anybody gives a damn. But not us.'
Lennie broke in. 'But not us! An' why? Because ... because I got you to look after me, and you got me to look after you, and that's why.' He laughed delightedly. 'Go on now, George.'
'You got it by heart. You can do it yourself.'
'No, you. I forgot some a' the things. Tell about how it's gonna be.'
'O.K. Some day we're gonna get the jack together and we're gonna have a little house and a couple of acres an' a cow and some pigs and ...'
'An' live off the fatta the lan',' Lennie shouted. 'An' have rabbits. Go on, George! Tell about what we're gonna have in the garden and about the rabbits in the cages and about the rain in the winter and the stove, and how thick the cream is on the milk like you can hardly cut it. Tell about that, George.'
'Why'm't you do it yourself. You know all of it.'
'No ... you tell it. It ain't the same if I tell it. Go on ... George. How I tend the rabbits.'

2 Answer questions 1 – 5.

1 According to George, what are the main differences between him and Lennie and the other people who work on the ranches?
2 Why was Lennie delighted?
3 What is meant by *you got it by heart*?
4 Why does Lennie say *It ain't the same if I tell it*?
5 What insights does the passage give into the dreams Lennie and George have?

Use of English

We're gonna have a little house.

Gonna is how *going to* sounds in some forms of spoken American English. In this context, this structure is used to express Lennie and George's definite plans for their future. As far as they are concerned, it is just a question of time before these plans are fulfilled.

The simple future tense is usually less assertive. It is more likely to be used when there is less concrete certainty in the speaker's mind, or that there are obstacles to overcome before something happens. It could be argued, therefore, that sunrisers use *going to* whereas sunsetters feel more comfortable with *will* when talking about future plans. For a complete review of future tenses and their use, see the back of this book.

The Wizard of Oz by L. Frank Baum is often regarded as an allegory of the American Dream, where anyone can achieve what they desire provided they put their minds to it. Dorothy, a determined young lady, and her new friends, a cowardly lion, a scarecrow who has no brain and a tin man with no heart, travel to the Emerald City to find the Wizard and to ask him to fulfil their wishes. By working as a team and compensating for each other's weaknesses, they make their way down the yellow brick road to success.

1 Complete items 1 – 10 with a verb in the appropriate future form.

1 'I ... see the Wizard of Oz and demand that he finds a way to get me home,' said Dorothy forcefully.
2 I ... ask him to give me back my courage, so I can pluck up enough of it to look him in the eye,' muttered the cowardly lion.
3 'Don't take that attitude,' said Dorothy. 'I ... stand right behind you and make sure you don't back out.'
4 'I ... plead with the Great and Powerful Wizard to give me a brain,' said the scarecrow. 'Please Dorothy ... you help me to decide what to say?'
5 'Of course I ... . Just remember that you ... get only what you deserve.'
6 'What about me,' groaned the tin man, '... you let me come with you to the Emerald City and ask the Great Oz to give me a heart?'
7 'I know your heart is in the right place already. We ... ask the Wizard to put a real one inside your chest just to make sure that everyone knows,' Dorothy replied gently.
8 'Let's go,' said Dorothy. 'We ... find him regardless of how hard the Witch of the North tries to stop us.'
9 'Do you think she ... cast a spell and turn me into a cat?' I do hope she ... ,' stuttered the cowardly lion in a quavering voice.
10 'Pull yourself together,' said Dorothy firmly. 'That wicked old witch ... stop us in our quest for courage, a brain, a heart and a ticket for my journey home.'

Speaking

Compare what you have written with your partner. If you have reached different conclusions about which form of the future to use, discuss the reasons for your choice.

Reading and Speaking

Read *The Lake Isle of Innisfree* by the Irish poet W. B. Yeats. Innisfree is a small island in Lough Gill in Eire. Yeats dreamed of living there alone in search of wisdom.

1 Answer questions 1 – 5.

1. What are *wattles*?
2. Why do you think the poet might want to keep *a hive for the honey-bee*?
3. What do you imagine *the veils of morning* are?
4. What different sounds does the poet imagine he will hear there?
5. Where do you think he is *now*?

2 Discuss the effect of the poem as a whole. The following adjectives may help you.

romantic
sentimental
contrived
mournful
sickening
soulful
rhythmic
evocative
beautiful
dreamy
sincere
fantastic
old-fashioned

3 Discuss the ways in which the poet uses future tenses.

4 Discuss the positive and negative effects of being alone on the way people think.

THE LAKE ISLE OF INNISFREE

I will arise and go now, and go to Innisfree,
And a small cabin build there, of clay and wattles made:
Nine bean-rows will I have there, a hive for the honey-bee,
And live alone in the bee-loud glade.

And I shall have some peace there, for peace comes dropping slow,
Dropping from the veils of the morning to where the cricket sings;
There midnight's all a glimmer, and noon a purple glow,
And evening full of the linnet's wings.

I will arise and go now, for always night and day
I hear lake water lapping with low sounds by the shore;
While I stand on the roadway, or on the pavements grey,
I hear it in the deep heart's core.

Use of English

1 *I will arise and go now.*
The sun rose over the western horizon.
As he lay there silently, he raised his eyes and looked at me pleadingly.

The verbs *arise, rise* and *raise* are easily confused. The following points may help to keep them separate in your mind.

1 *Rise, raise, risen* and *arise, arose, arisen* are intransitive, that is to say they can never have an object. *Raise, raised, raised* is transitive. For example:

The tiger raised its noble head and sniffed the air.
We must raise this question at the next meeting.
If the problem isn't raised, we'll never solve it.

2 For concrete statements of fact needing an intransitive verb, use *rise.*

The sun rises in the east.
Bread should rise before you put it in the oven.
The temperature rose steadily.
Our spirits rose in those glorious surroundings.
I tried not to rise to their rudeness, but I could feel my temper rising.

3 Both *rise* and *arise* can mean to get up, but are old-fashioned and, therefore, only found in literature or the most formal modern situations, when *rise* is used.

The conference rose and the delegates went home.
'Will the court please rise?' an official said as the judge walked in.

4 More abstract or complex issues *arise* in formal or informal contexts.

You have all read the minutes of the last meeting. Are there any matters arising?
If you'd used your common sense, the problem wouldn't have a risen.

2 Complete the following dialogue between Edward Eton, a business tycoon, and Bart Simpson, his personal assistant, with appropriate forms of *rise, arise* or *raise.*

1 Bart: There is something I would like … with you if I may.
2 Edward: Go ahead. What problem has … that you can't handle?
3 Bart: No problem from my point of view. I just thought you should know that the tide of protest … and unless you … your profile and act firmly there will be trouble.

4 Edward: Thank you for … this matter and bringing it to my attention, but I should inform you that until a specific incident … which requires me to take an active role, I … to these veiled threats but will continue to maintain a dignified silence.

3 *The sun sets in the evening.*
The glue has set hard.
The caravan set out into the desert in the cool of the evening.
At the onset of 'flu, take two tablets.

Set is an intransitive verb. It is also used in a very wide variety of two- and three-word verbs and of compound nouns.

Rewrite the following sentences so that the meaning is the same as the sentence above. Use the word in italics. Do not alter it in any way.

1 Your progress may have been blocked, but that is no reason to abandon the project.
setback

2 As soon as the monsoon season begins, a number of protective measures must be taken to avoid the danger of flooding.
onset

3 During the latter part of the football season, several teams lost matches they were expected to win.
upsets

4 In order to complete the experiment, the items must be grouped according to their colour.
sets

5 I wish to bring these points to everyone's attention the moment we open negotiations, so that we all know where we stand.
outset

6 The house is some distance from the main road and surrounded by beautiful gardens.
set back

7 As the beautiful Miss de Meena emerged from her limousine, the waiting journalists surged forward, firing questions, cameras clicking.
set on

8 It looks as though it is going to rain for a considerable period of time.
set in

Reading and speaking

For many people, Northern Ireland is a country ravaged by violence and bigotry. However, this image is far from reality for many of the people who live there.

1 Read the article opposite about the new generation of Belfast poets and decide whether each of the following statements is true or false.

1 Dublin is considered to be a romantic city.
2 Belfast is more glamorous than Derry.
3 Belfast prides itself on being a very artistic city.
4 Most of the young Belfast poets are very political.
5 They believe that the situation in Belfast is really no different from other cities.

2 Read the poem printed with the article and answer the questions below.

1 According to the poem, what is *a useful dream*?
2 Where can you find *the good life*?
3 What is *the secret*?

3 Discuss with a partner whether or not you agree with the sentiments expressed in the poem.

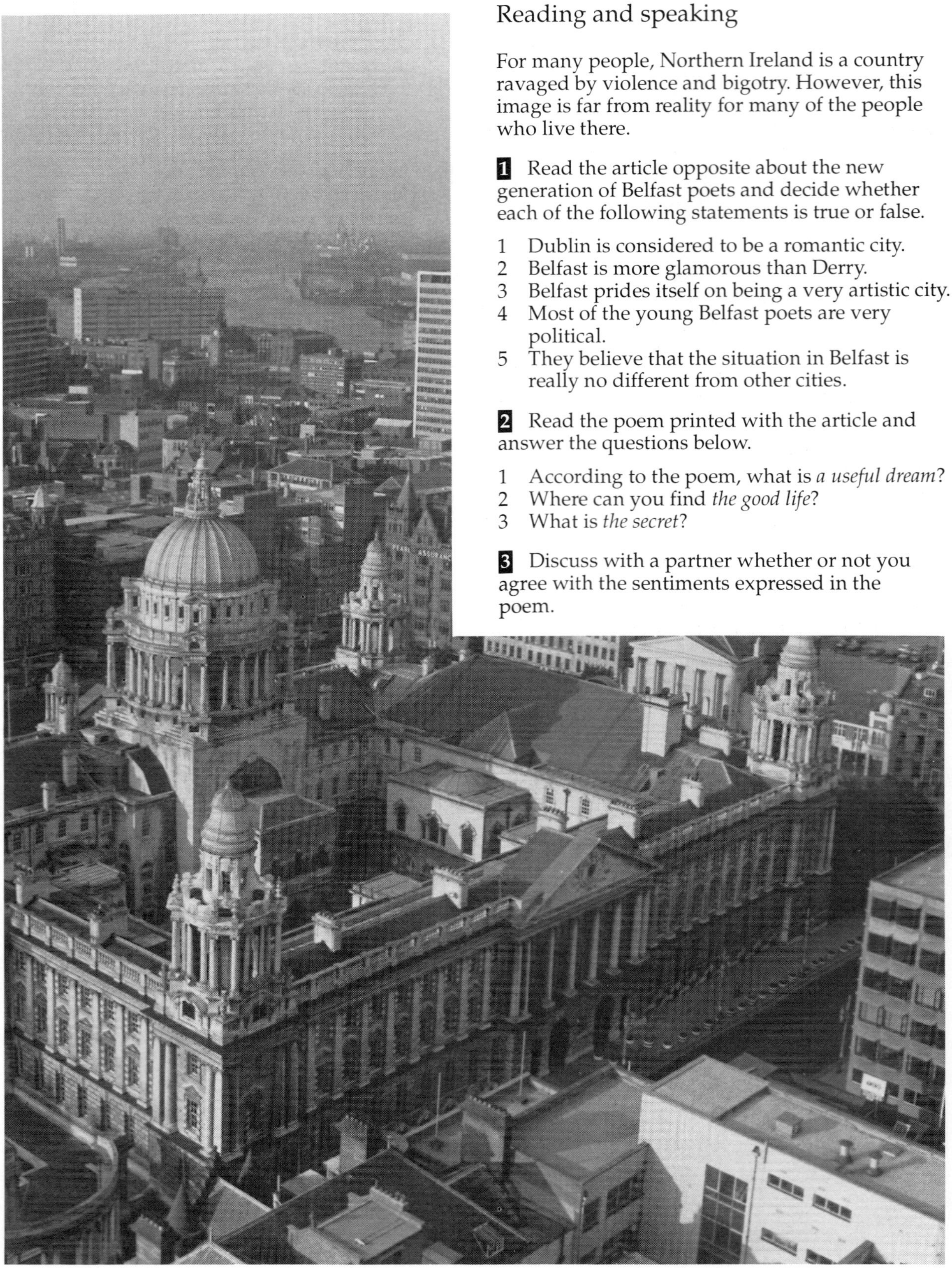

Bards Of Belfast

Belfast has an image problem. Trapped politically and culturally between Dublin and London, it has neither the romance of the former nor the big city buzz of the latter. Even within the six counties, this most provincial of capitals is overshadowed in the glamour stakes by the smaller, artier city of Derry.

The cityscape is almost wilfully unromantic. A succession of well-meaning face-lifts to the town centre can, at a pinch, lull you into thinking that you have been magically transported to Milton Keynes. But away from the 'Golden Mile' of shops, pubs and clubs stretching from the neoclassical City Hall to the neogothic university, long, low streets fall into sullen formation, outfacing each other with violently coloured end-of-terrace murals and even more violent slogans that scream at passers-by about Ireland's problems.

Despite and because of this, Belfast has a salty flavour all its own, with flashes of lyricism where you least expect them – the pony that grazes contentedly on a traffic island in the city centre, the 80-year-old in the pub who will suddenly stand up and sing a pure, clear treble while all around him hard men stare into their Guinness and try not to sob.

Belfast is not and never will be a hotbed of bohemian chic. It wears neither its heart, nor its art, on the sleeve. But the heart is there, despite the daily atrocities of extremists, in the solid decency of the place, and the art is in the talk of its people.

Ulster has bred poets for generations from the rhyming weavers of Antrim to the trade unionists of the 30s and 40s and the 'voices of conscience', who focused world literary attention on the civil rights struggles of the 60s.

Now there is a new generation of Belfast poets, young people who no longer feel the need to pin their colours to a political mast. Having grown up with the Troubles as a circumstance of daily life, they're not interested in picking over the dry bones of sectarianism. The issues they confront are shared by city dwellers everywhere and a new, confident, urban voice is rising above the ancient, muttered arguments. Above all, their poetry is a resounding affirmation that Ulster can be a place for living in not just an idea to die for, as seen in the poem below by Patrick Ramsey.

POEM OVERLOOKING BELFAST LOUGH *for David Trouton*

Looking out, you dream of distant shores,
Of loves in foreign cities, to be free,
Shrug off the dull responsibility
Of house, job, wife and kids – domestic chores

And start again with the ideals of youth,
Live energy and raw nerve. Find you're
Alone once more, slightly soiled, insecure,
Yet on amicable terms with the truth

Whatever that is. It's a useful dream
But that's all it is. The good life's here
Both prospective and real. Your proper sphere
Lies in the rituals of hearth and home.

The secret's remaining flexible, skilled.
Like anywhere, here is a place to build.

Listening

1 In *Of Mice and Men*, Lennie and George dreamed of having a farm with cows and rabbits. W.B. Yeats dreamed of finding solitude and peace on an island. For thousands of years, it has been believed that the interpretation of dreams can give an insight into our unconscious thoughts and inner selves.

Listen to this extract from a talk given by Cosmo Gurley, an authority on dream interpretation. Complete the notes below.

1 Fortune-tellers can predict the future because ….
2 To be a good interpreter of other people's dreams you need to be able to …
3 It is easier to understand …
4 Nineteenth-century scientists always …
5 Most modern scientists now believe that Freud …
6 Using dream interpretation as a method of foretelling the future …

2 Describe a dream you have had to a partner. Discuss it.

Reading

The extract on the next page is taken from the comic novel *Even Cowgirls get the Blues* by Tom Robbins, in which Sissy is determined to escape from her mundane existence in Richmond, Virginia. She consults a clairvoyant to try to find out what the future holds for her. Sissy is a very attractive girl whose physical beauty is somewhat marred by the fact that she has been born with abnormally large thumbs.

1 Find words or phrases in the extract which are similar in meaning to items 1 – 6.

1 an ornament
2 mysterious
3 burning slowly
4 a boring voice
5 false magic
6 strong feelings

2 Compare Sissy's attitude to fortune-telling with your own.

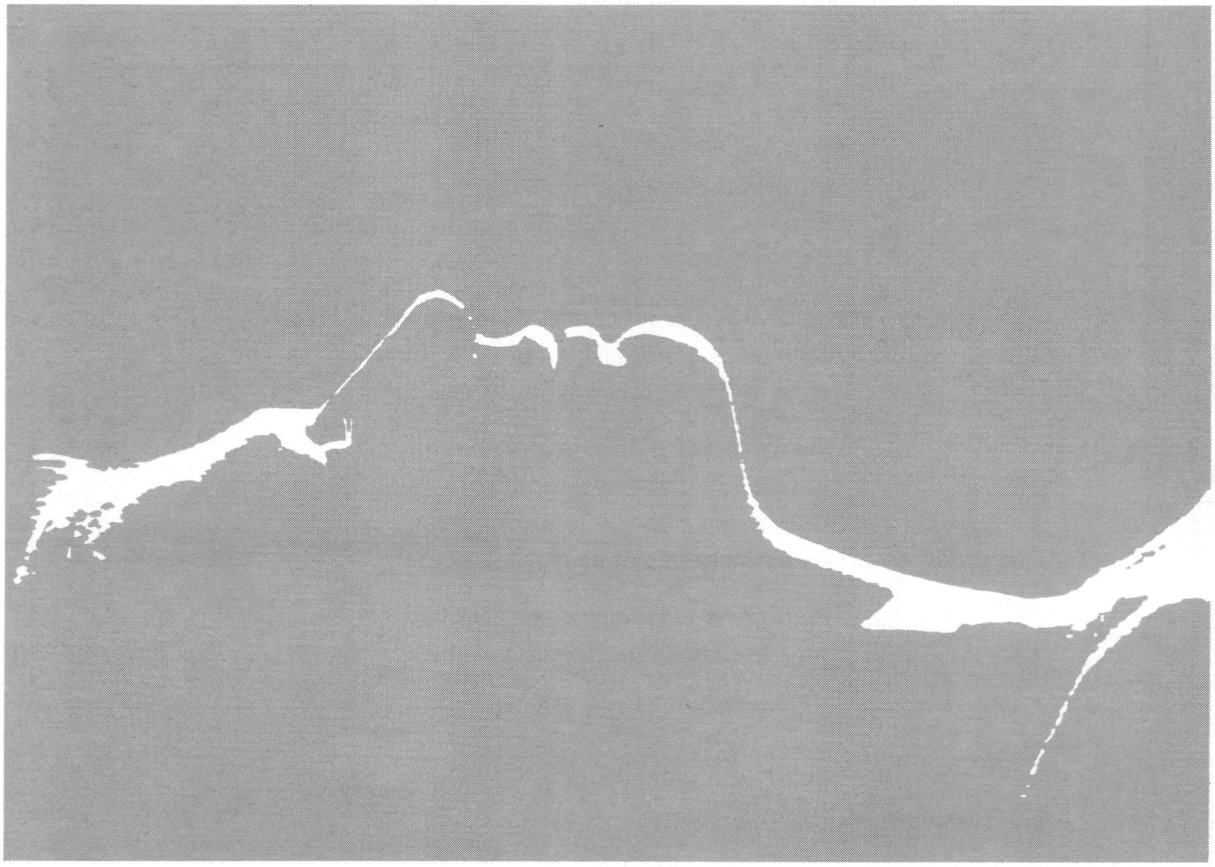

From the vortex of competing smells (this was outside the tobacco zone), Madame Zoe, in kimono and wig, asked them in. 'I am the enlightened Madame Zoe,' she began, stubbing a cigarette in one of those enlightened little ceramic ashtrays that are shaped like bedpans and inscribed BUTTS. The trailer was cluttered, but not one knick-knack, chintz curtain or chenille-covered armchair seemed to have come from the Beyond. The floor lamp was powered by electricity, not prana; the telephone directory was for Richmond, not Atlantis. Even more disappointing to the girl was the absence of any physical reference to Persia, Tibet or Egypt, those centres of arcane knowledge that Sissy was certain she would hitch to some day, although it should be made clear, here and now, that Sissy never really dreamed of hitching to anywhere; it was the act of hitching that formed the substance of her vision. It turned out that there was nothing the least bit exotic in that house trailer except for the smouldering incense, and although in the dead air of the Eisenhower Years in Richmond, Virginia, incense seemed exotic enough, that particular stick of jasmine was in the process of being kicked deaf, blind and dumb by a pot of cauliflower.

'I am the enlightened Madame Zoe,' she began, her voice an uninterested monotonous drone. 'There is nothing about your past, present or future that your hands do not know, and there is nothing about your hands that Madame Zoe does not know. There is no hocus-pocus involved. I am a scientist, not a magician. The hand is the most wonderful instrument ever created, but it cannot act of its own accord; it is the servant of the brain. It reflects the kind of brain behind it by the manner and intelligence with which it performs its duties. The hand is the external reservoir of our most acute sensations. Sensations, when repeated frequently, have the capacity to mould and mark. I, Madame Zoe, chiromancer, lifelong student of the mouldings and markings of the human hand; I, Madame Zoe, to whom no facet of your character or destiny is not readily revealed, I am prepared to ...'

Then she noticed the thumbs.

Reading

At the end of *The Great Gatsby*, Gatsby's dream of getting back together with Daisy results in failure and tragedy, which ultimately is the cause of Gatsby's own death. Read the extract on the next page , which forms the end of the novel. Answer questions 1 – 8.

1 Why did the narrator spend his Saturday nights in New York?
2 What is implied by *some final guest who had been away at the ends of the earth*?
3 Why are the houses described as *inessential*?
4 Who do you think the *Dutch sailors* were?
5 What does *Its* refer to?
6 What in this context is *the last and greatest of all human dreams*?
6 What is *the green light* a metaphor for?
7 *And one fine morning* – the end of the sentence is understood. How do you think it should be completed?
8 What message do you think is being given by the last sentence of the book?

Writing

Write one of the compositions below. Use about 350 words.

1 Describe your dreams for the future and how likely they are to become reality.
2 *Dreams are glimpses of reality and reality is but a dream.* Discuss.

Gatsby's house was still empty when I left – the grass on his lawn had grown as long as mine. One of the taxi-drivers in the village never took a fare past the entrance gate without stopping for a minute and pointing inside; perhaps it was he who drove Daisy and Gatsby over to East Egg the night of the accident, and perhaps he had made a story about it all his own. I didn't want to hear it and I avoided him when I got off the train.

I spent my Saturday nights in New York because those gleaming, dazzling parties of his were with me so vividly that I could still hear the music and the laughter, faint and incessant, from his garden, and the cars going up and down his drive. One night I did hear a material car there, and saw its lights stop at his front steps. But I didn't investigate. Probably it was some final guest who had been away at the ends of the earth and didn't know that the party was over.

On the last night, with my trunk packed and my car sold to the grocer, I went over and looked at that huge incoherent failure of a house once more. On the white steps an obscure word, scrawled by some boy with a piece of brick, stood out clearly in the moonlight, and I erased it, drawing my shoe raspingly along the stone. Then I wandered down to the beach and sprawled out on the sand.

Most of the big shore places were closed now and there were hardly any lights except the shadowy, moving glow of a ferryboat across the sound. And as the moon rose higher the inessential houses began to melt away until gradually I became aware of the old island here that flowered once for Dutch sailors' eyes – a fresh, green breast of the new world. Its vanished trees, the trees that had made way for Gatsby's house, had once pandered in whispers to the last and greatest of all human dreams; for a transitory enchanted moment man must have held his breath in the presence of this continent, compelled into an aesthetic contemplation he neither understood nor desired, face to face for the last time in history with something commensurate to his capacity for wonder.

And as I sat there brooding on the old, unknown world, I thought of Gatsby's wonder when he first picked out the green light at the end of Daisy's dock. He had come a long way to this blue lawn, and his dream must have seemed so close that he could hardly fail to grasp it. He did not know that it was already behind him, somewhere back in that vast obscurity beyond the city, where the dark fields of the republic rolled on under the night.

Gatsby believed in the green light, the orgiastic future that year by year recedes before us. It eluded us then, but that's no matter – tomorrow we will run faster, stretch out our arms further ... And one fine morning –

So we beat on, boats against the current, borne back ceaselessly into the past.

Language Summary

Guidelines

1 Whenever we use *would have done* and *could have done*, the action expressed by the verb is not actually performed. To make the correct choice as to when to use *would* and when to use *could*, think about the reason why the action was not performed.

Would is used when it was not possible to perform the task.

Could is used when it was possible to perform the task but another reason prevented it from being carried out.

I would have given you a lift, but my car had broken down.
I could have given you a lift if you had asked me.

2 In the negative, *would not (wouldn't) have done* and *could not (couldn't) have done*, the action is also not performed.

Would not is used when there may have been an opportunity to perform the action, but there was no wish or reason to do it.

Could not is used when it was not possible to perform the task, although there may or may not have been a wish to do so.

Although I had the key, I wouldn't have opened your suitcase.
I couldn't have opened your suitcase, because I didn't have the key.

3 Remember that the reasons why the actions were not performed may also be implied by the context.

I could have hit him.
(But I never hit anyone and he's bigger than me.)

Edna would never have said that.
(Edna is too polite to have made that sort of remark.)

Further practice

1 Complete each the following sentences in an appropriate way.

1 Melissa would have come to the cinema … .
2 Kent wouldn't have sold those secret documents to the enemy … .
3 Shylock could have lent them the money … .
4 Daniel couldn't have unlocked the door … .
5 Driving ace, Ricky Louder, … if he hadn't run out of petrol on the last lap.
6 Rosemary Leaf … in that dish, because she is a vegetarian.
7 The muscular Charles Atlas … with one hand tied behind his back.
8 Isabella … as she is absolutely terrified of heights.

2 Read between the lines. Note down the implication of each of these sentences.

1 Jane would have phoned me to say she wasn't coming.
2 Jane could have phoned me to say she wasn't coming.
3 Brian and Sue wouldn't have gone to a tennis match.
4 Diane couldn't have bought a ticket for the concert at the door.
5 Edgar would have walked on hot coals to see Cordelia.
6 Beverley's inheritance would only have paid her dressmaker's bill in any case.
7 I wouldn't have taken that route to get to London.
8 I couldn't have taken that route to get to London.

3 Answer questions 1 – 8 appropriately.

1 Why didn't you work harder for your exam?
2 Why do you think it was somebody local who burgled your house while you were away?
3 Why didn't you help yourself to the food in our fridge?
4 How did you feel when your solicitor told you that you'd inherited a fortune?
5 How did you know that it wasn't Miss Moneypenny who'd betrayed you, James?
6 How do I know it wasn't you who told the press all my secrets, Pamela?
7 Why didn't you tell us you weren't feeling well?
8 How did you react when the pilot told you all to prepare for a crash landing?

Guidelines

To make the choice between when to use the *-ing* form (*doing / being done / having done / having been done*) and when to use the infinitive (*to*) *do / be done / have done / have been done*) remember the following points.

1 Transitive and intransitive verbs which are followed by a preposition or adverbial particle are in turn usually followed by the *-ing* form.

Miriam put off going to the doctor.
Rupert took over running the company.
Martin started out thinking this was the best solution.
We look forward to hearing from you.
I am not accustomed to being spoken to in that way.
Martha was not used to eating English food.
The organisation is committed to maintaining the highest standards.

However, there are exceptions. These can often be explained by the sense of purpose behind the word *to*.

Brian sat down to write a letter.
Simon set out to swim the channel.

2 The verbs below are usually followed by the *-ing* form.

enjoy, deny, consider, avoid, evade, finish, suggest.

Paul enjoyed watching football.
Sonia denied stealing (having stolen) the gold watch.
Ada finished working and switched off the computer.
Colin suggested going to the cinema.

3 The verbs below are usually followed by *to* and the present or past infinitive. Remember that the two verbs may be separated by the object of the first verb.

refuse, tend, arrange, threaten, hope, intend, devise, be supposed, seem, used, expect, decide, want.

The police refused to open the gates.
Oliver devised the plan to steal the jewels.
Jeremy tends to forget his responsibilities.
Bruce threatened to resign.
Denny arranged to have the children looked after.
The representative was supposed to have met Miss Smith at the airport.
Am I supposed to bow when the Queen enters the room?
The immigrants seem to have adjusted well to their new environment.

4 The verbs below are followed by the *-ing* form or the infinitive, with little or no change in meaning.

write, start, begin, continue.

Tom started to work / working at 6 o'clock this morning.
Michaela intends to go / going to Florida.
The football match continued to excite / exciting the huge crowd.
I will write a letter to say / saying I am not satisfied.

5 The verbs below can be followed by the *-ing* form or the infinitive. The meaning changes depending on the form you use. To make the correct choice, it sometimes helps to decide whether the actions described by the verbs are separate or linked.

stop, try, regret, remember, forget.

He stopped to tie his shoe lace.
(First he stopped and then he tied his shoe lace.)
He stopped tying his shoe lace.
(The two actions are simultaneous.)

Try to keep your temper.
(Make an effort and don't lose it.)
Try adding some water.
(Experiment by doing this.)

I regret to say that your work is not up to standard.
(Saying this is making me feel bad.)
I regret saying / having said that.
(Now I regret what I said then.)

I remembered to post the letter.
(I reminded myself to do it.)
I remember coming here as a child.
(I'm recalling the past.)

I forgot to post the letter.
I'll never forget coming here as a child.

Further practice

1 Complete each of the following sentences by using a verb in the appropriate form with or without *to*.

1 The concert was expected … at 7.30 local time.
2 Although you have decided …, would you be interested in a different job with the same organisation?
3 The experts are suggesting … personal taxation so that we all have less to spend.
4 Unaccustomed as Marianne was to … in front of such a large audience, she still managed to cost her magic spell over everyone in the vast arena.
5 Farm workers in the Middle Ages used … their teeth with twigs from hazel trees and judging by their lack of dental decay they proved surprisingly effective.
6 Are you supposed … at this time of night It is after ten o'clock and all the other offices are closed.
7 At five o'clock in the morning Bill set out … fishing.
8 Mary always wakes up … the music which she has programmed on her automatic clock radio.
9 The fastest growing political party, at present, is the Turquoise Party, which is committed to … all forms of nuclear power within the next ten years or they believe the risks of a melt-down are considerable.
10 The menacing storm clouds threatened … the spectators' enjoyment of the open air parade.

2 Rewrite each of the following sentences so that it means the same. Use the word in italics. Do not change this word in any way.

1 The team gave the appearance that they had started the match well, but their disastrous performance in the second half proved otherwise.
seemed

2 Raffles decided not to steal Mr Pickwick's distinctive watch as it would be difficult to sell.
worth

3 Did it really slip your mind that you had to go for a job interview this morning?
remember

4 Two years ago, I had an argument with my uncle and since then we haven't spoken to each other.
stopped

5 That book about cosmology by Stephen Hawking is so complex that I gave it up before I had even finished the introduction.
tried

6 The manager has been very patient but she would appreciate payment of the bill as soon as possible.
forward

7 Must you wear those pink socks with your best suit?
insist

8 The Government has no plans at all to stop the provision of free treatment for all hospital patients.
committed

3 Respond appropriately to each situation 1 – 8, using a verb from the Guidelines for this Unit.

1 Someone has arranged a holiday abroad for you. It sounds wonderful. You ring them to tell them how you feel about their plans.

2 Diana's friends are asking her whether or not she is going to marry Charles. She isn't sure, but after a lot of thought, she takes the plunge.

3 You are writing the first line of a letter confirming that you will be at a meeting next Monday and that you are prepared to speak if required.

4 Looking back through a friend's photo album, you come across a photo of you on an outing you'd completely forgotten.

5 Luciano, a friend of yours, has a very sore throat. You think a drink of hot lemon juice sweetened with honey might help.

Guidelines

1 Both adverbs and adverbial phrases are used to indicate the way in which something is said.

'Do you mind if I open the window?' asked John politely.
'My daughter's graduating today,' Tom said with considerable pride.
People often act in a strange way if they are feeling embarrassed.

Usually adverbs can be formed from the adjective in a phrase and the meaning remains the same.

polite: *politely*
in a thoughtful manner: *thoughtfully*
in an adoring voice: *adoringly*

2 Where a noun is used, an adjective and, therefore, an adverb can also usually be formed from it.

with passion: *passionately*
out of respect: *respectfully*
with pride: *proudly*

3 However, in some cases, no adverb can be formed from the adjective, so an adverbial phrase is necessary. Adverbs formed from adjectives ending in *-ed* are rarely used.

'There is nothing to do except watch TV,' Joan said sounding bored.
'My client would like to hear the details of your offer,' replied the lawyer with considerable interest.
'Please don't touch me,' pleaded Hopkins in a frightened whisper.

4 In the same way, no adverb can be formed from some nouns.

'Help me!' gasped the pilot as he breathed with difficulty.
'I don't think Jane has arrived home yet,' said her aunt with concern.
'There's someone in our flat,' whispered Ann with alarm.
'Do you really want me to do it?' asked Gordon in surprise.

Further practice

Complete each of the following sentences with either an appropriate adverb or an adverbial phrase.

1. 'We are trapped. There appears to be no way out,' Smith yelled … .
2. 'I am always more than happy to oblige,' murmured the receptionist … .
3. 'Open all your suitcases,' demanded the customs officer … .
4. 'I do hope we shall meet again,' sighed Matilda … .
5. 'Don't tell me the plane's been delayed,' groaned Brian … .
6. 'Belinda has just won a round-the-world cruise in a competition, the lucky thing,' Colin remarked … .
7. 'The goalkeeper got a touch, but it's hit the crossbar and bounced over the net into the crowd,' yelled the commentator … .
8. 'Roxanne has no-one else to turn to. Please help her,' begged Andy … .
9. 'You are simply not good enough to enter for this exam,' said the Director … .
10. 'For goodness sake, I didn't mean to! Stop going on about it,' said Diana … .

Guidelines 1

1 Adjectives can be modified or intensified by adverbs to give a more precise description of a noun. The choice of adverb depends on the context and on whether or not it can be used appropriately (collocated) with a particular adjective. For example:

An awfully cold day collocates appropriately whereas *an awfully sunny day* does not, because *awfully* is negative in meaning but *sunny* is positive. You can, however, say *an awfully hot day* to indicate that the heat is uncomfortable.

The TV documentary was unbelievably / awfully / extremely / very / rather boring collocates appropriately, but *The TV programme was highly boring* sounds strange because *highly* is usually used to make an adjective more positive. *A highly enjoyable evening* or *a highly interesting programme* collocate appropriately.

2 Where an adjective has an absolute or fixed meaning, it cannot usually be modified or intensified with the adverb *very*.

Adjectives such as *unique, right, fine, appalling* fall into this category. They can, however, be intensified by *absolutely* or *quite*.

3 Remember that *too* is negative in meaning. If the weather is *too hot*, you feel uncomfortable. If the weather is *very hot*, you may be enjoying it. The only exception is the phrase *too good to be true*, meaning *unbelievably good*.

Further practice 1

Use the adverbs below to complete each of the sentences in the most appropriate way.

seriously	*refreshingly*
exquisitely	*indescribably*
immaculately	*highly*
surprisingly	*rather*
icily	*uncharacteristically*
absolutely	

1 That miniature painting is the most … beautiful example of this type of art that I have ever seen.
2 The documentary about the history of shoe making was … interesting and I watched every minute of it.
3 The hotel food was so … appalling that I always had my meals somewhere else.
4 Don't ever go to see the film version of 'Harry and her Brothers' starring Alan Trees because it is … boring.
5 Tim is now a … successful artist and has become extremely rich, but he still lives at home with his parents.
6 Olga, who is usually so reliable, was … late when she arrived at the meeting ten minutes after it had started.
7 The resort is always … quiet towards the end of the holiday season, but i prefer it when it is crowded with tourists.
8 The play was … different compared to the run of the mill musicals that all the other theatres were showing.
9 During the kidnap ordeal, Sandra Locke remained … calm and only when she was finally rescued did she show her feelings.
10 The … well-dressed P. J. Prober flung open the door of her new office and greeted all her employees with a wave.
11 All the … injured victims of the explosion have been taken to Holby Hospital.

Guidelines 2

Not only did Hilary play the classical violin, (but) she also played the drums in a rock band.

1 In certain structures, the subject and the verb are inverted. This usually occurs when a sentence begins with a word or phrase of the following types.

Adverbs of frequency

Rarely
Seldom
Once in a lifetime / blue moon
Many a time.

Time expressions

Only then
No sooner … than
Hardly
Scarcely
Never (again).

Negative expressions

Not only …, but also
Not only …, as well.
In / Under no circumstances
Nowhere

2 In order to use this structure correctly, follow the general guidelines below.

1 The inversion occurs immediately after the expressions listed above.

Note the exception, *Only when ...* . In this case, the inversion occurs in the second part of the sentence.

No sooner had the sun come out than it was time to pack up and go home.
Only when I saw her did I realise that we had met before.
Only then did I remember how we had first met.

2 The sentence must start with one of the expressions listed. If the expression is in another part of the sentence, the subject and verb are not inverted.

Rarely does the managing director come to the factory.
The managing director rarely comes to the factory.

3 Where there is inversion, the subject usually comes after the auxiliary part of the verb.

Never had the reporter seen such chaos.
Once in a lifetime do we have the chance to experience this phenomenon.

4 Inversion can be used with any tense, although it is rarely found with continuous tenses.

5 The inverted verb can be in either the active or the passive voice.

Seldom had the museum been visited by so many people.
Seldom had so many people visited the museum.

3 *No sooner ... than*, *Hardly ... when* and *Scarcely ... when* are usually used to describe actions which occurred in the past, where one action is very closely followed by another. The first action is in the past perfect tense because it occurred before the second action.

No sooner had I sat down than the telephone rang.
Hardly had I sat down when the telephone rang.

4 If a sentence starts with *Not only*, it may be completed with either *but also ...* or *... as well*. It is incorrect to use *but also* and *as well* in the same sentence. When *as well* is used, it must always be at the end of the sentence. Look at the examples in the next column.

Not only does sugar make you put on weight, but it's bad for your teeth as well.
Not only does sugar make you put on weight, but also it's / but it's also bad for your teeth.

5 It is possible to use *Not only* with a negative verb. In this case, however, *but also* and *but ... as well* must be replaced by *but ... either.*

Not only does John not eat fish, but he does not eat eggs either.

6 It is important not to over-use this structure. If you do, it loses its emphasis. Only use it for the purposes listed below.

1 To express strong feelings.

Never in my life have I been so angry.

2 To emphasise that something unusual has occurred.

Rarely do we see such large flocks of birds in winter.

3 To make a point in a definitive way, so as to preclude any argument.

Under no circumstances should books be removed from the library.

4 To emphasise how quickly one action comes after another.

Hardly had I entered the building than the security guard asked me to leave.

Further practice 2

1 Match each item 1 – 10 with one of the completions a – j. Then complete each sentence appropriately.

1 Seldom ...
2 Once every twenty years ...
3 Not only ...
4 Many a time ...
5 Hardly ...
6 In no circumstances ...
7 Nowhere ...
8 Never ...
9 Not only ...
10 No sooner ...

a such a beautiful view.
b to change the way people think.
c she runs ten kilometres every day as well.
d but today it was closed.
e than the music started.
f after midnight.
g be seen.
h in such an unfriendly way.
i either.
j the door was locked behind me.

2 Rewrite each statement 1 – 10 so that its meaning is similar but is expressed more emphatically.

1 The day after the show opened, the leading lady had a phone-call from a Hollywood director.
2 Our new lodger doesn't eat meat and doesn't like cheese or eggs.
3 You don't often see a documentary as good as that.
4 Those few weeks in March were the happiest days of Jake's life.
5 Claire had locked her keys in the car and had left her handbag on the back seat.
6 I'm so happy.
7 As soon as the programme was over, the phone began to ring.
8 Don't miss a unique opportunity to see an art collection of this quality.
9 Unauthorised personnel are not allowed beyond this point.
10 I don't think I'll ever be persuaded to go up in a hot-air balloon again.

Guidelines

1 The past continuous is used to describe a thought process which is interrupted by an event or by new information, or which continues uninterrupted for an unusually long time.

I was thinking of going to the beach, but I've just seen the weather forecast.
I was expecting a call from New York, but the phone hasn't rung all day.
I was wondering what time you'd arrive.
Jane was hoping to catch the six o'clock flight, but there are no seats left.
I'm sorry I couldn't be with you yesterday. I was thinking of you.
Brian's arrived early. Peter wasn't expecting him until nine o'clock.
I wasn't thinking of going away for the weekend, but maybe it's a good idea, now you come to mention it.

2 If the thought process stopped some time before another past event, the past perfect is the correct tense to use. Although it is possible to use the past perfect continuous, it is unnecessary and is usually more natural to use the simple form.

Simon had hoped to meet Louisa when he was in Spain, but when he saw his schedule, he knew he wouldn't have time.
The players hadn't expected their team to win, so they were delighted.

3 The continuous form of the infinitive is used with modal verbs in two ways.

1 to draw a conclusion based on circumstances which are still continuing at the time of speaking or writing.

   Despite their problems, Charles and Sally seem to be having a good time.
   They must be earning a lot of money now that their shop is so popular.
   Miss Brewster is not in the office at the moment, so she may be having lunch with a client.
   The plane landed twenty minutes ago, so they should be coming out of customs at any minute.
   He can't be having lunch in the canteen, because it is closed.

2 To contrast an activity that has been scheduled or it is one's duty to perform in theory with what is actually happening in practice. This structure can, therefore, be used to express criticism, concern or reluctance. Look at the examples in the next column.

   Harvey should be finishing his report, not sitting on the beach sunbathing.
   I should be going to Manchester, but I got the London train by mistake.
   You shouldn't be watching TV, you should be studying.
   Pauline shouldn't be living alone at her age.
   Those children shouldn't be wandering the streets at this time of night.
   They should be going out tonight, but they're tired.
   I should be going soon, I suppose.

Further practice

Complete each of the following sentences in an appropriate way, using one of the verb forms on the left.

1 Your examination is tomorrow morning, so don't you think you … revising?
2 In spite of the present bad weather, the holidaymakers … enjoying themselves.
3 I … to have a word with Dr Jones, but it is obviously not a good time at the moment.
4 Gillian … Mike back until tomorrow morning, but he turned up on the doorstep just after lunch.
5 I … if you'd like to have dinner with me on Saturday?
6 The Government … to reduce taxes before the end of last year but the economic situation prevented it.
7 My brother is a keen basketball fan so he … to the match but it depends on whether or not he has got a ticket.
8 The show … at any moment now as I can see the actors getting into position, through the gap in the curtain.
9 Look at the time. It's after half past nine and they said they would be here at eight. They obviously … coming.
10 You … playing tennis so soon after breaking your wrist. You know the doctor told you to rest it for another ten days.
11 Is James very busy? I … to have a word with him.
12 How did the interview go? I … of you.
13 I think that person over there … to meet the author, but he's gone now.
14 The cast … whether they could all go out for dinner after the show, but then they were too tired to enjoy it, so they didn't go.
15 We're so late! Everyone … where we are.

2 Use a continuous form to respond appropriately in each situation.

1 Your best friend took their driving test earlier today. You couldn't stop thinking about them and ring up to tell them so and find out how it went.
2 You are concerned because some young children are playing in a busy street.
3 You get a surprise present from a neighbour for whom you did some shopping.
4 You wanted to accept an invitation to stay with some friends for the weekend, but you're too busy to go.
5 You've gone to see some friends. Apparently they've just gone out, but their front door's open and a meal's cooking on the stove.

Guidelines

Sentence connectors can be divided into three categories under the general headings of *and*, *or* and *but*. They either replace these words or can be used in conjunction with them.

1 *And*. The connectors in this category are used:

1 to list or sequence a chain of events or comments.

first, secondly, thirdly, finally.
at first, then, next, eventually.
to begin with, thereafter, afterwards, lastly, to end with, finally.
in the beginning, in the end, at last.

First it's against the rules, secondly it's bad for you and lastly I won't allow it.
At first things are quite difficult for young artists, then they get a reputation and eventually they may become famous.

2 to add information, qualification or comment to the main part of a sentence.

besides, also, furthermore (formal), *anyway, in any case.*

There is no need for Brenda to go to Spain at the moment and anyway she has not got enough money for the flight.
The jury should bear in mind that the forensic evidence has been proved inadmissable and furthermore that there were no witnesses at the scene of the crime.

Note the difference in meaning between *lastly* and *at last / in the end.*

The British Government should do something for several reasons. Firstly, this is a serious problem, secondly it is their responsibility and lastly – and most importantly – only they have the power to legislate.
It took ten long years to persuade the British government to act, but then (in the end) they decided to legislate (at last).

3 to express similarity.

likewise, similarly, too, also, and so.

Hazel Dente feels that too much television is bad for children, and her husband Al does too.
Hazel Dente enjoys watching spaghetti westerns on TV and her husband Al likewise.
The general public like David Lynch's films and so do the critics.

4 to express similarity in the negative.

neither ... nor (more common in written English)
negative statement ... *either* (more common in spoken English)
(and) nor / neither + auxiliary or modal verb.

Neither my father nor my mother went to university.
My father didn't go to university and my mother didn't either.
The orchestra were not playing at their best and neither was the soloist.

5 to express positive or negative result or effect.

so, therefore, consequently, as a result, because

Eric Idle did not study and so he failed all his exams.
As a result of failing his exams, Eric Idle couldn't get a job.
Doctor Hide was convicted of murder and was therefore sentenced to life imprisonment.
Because he was found guilty of murder, Doctor Hide was sentenced to life imprisonment.
Doctor Hide was sentenced to life imprisonment because of the seriousness of his crime.

2 *Or*. The connectors in this category are used to express an alternative, especially more than one possible course of action.

otherwise, alternatively, on the other hand, instead of, either ... or.

Miss Prism can travel to Brighton by train or alternatively (go there) by bus.
Miss Prism can travel to Brighton either by train or by bus.
Instead of travelling to Brighton by train, Miss Prism can go there by bus.

3 *But*. The connectors in this category are used to express a contrast between two statements, especially when the connection between them seems unlikely or surprising.

nevertheless, nonetheless, notwithstanding (formal), *in spite of, despite, although, yet, even though.*

1 In the examples below, the connectors cannot come at the beginning of one sentence containing all the information. They may, however, be found at the beginning of a second sentence when the information is given in two sentences. Look at the examples on the next page.

Norman Sargent did not pass any exams when he was at school but (nevertheless) he became Prime Minister (nevertheless).
Norman Sargent did not pass any exams when he was at school and yet became Prime Minister.

2 In the example below, the connector usually comes at the beginning of the sentence.

Notwithstanding his first class degree, Robert Jackson works as a carpenter.

3 In the examples below, the connectors can come at the beginning or in the middle of a sentence.

Although / Even though Judy Wales is a qualified lawyer, she now teaches in a primary school.
Judy Wales teaches in a primary school although / even though she is a qualified lawyer.
In spite of / Despite being a pensioner, Gerry Attrick has completed an Open University course.
Gerry Attrick has completed an Open University course, in spite of / despite being a pensioner.

Further practice

Rewrite each of the sentences below using the word in italics. Make any changes that you think are necessary but do not change the word or the meaning of the sentence in any way.

1 Fred Gill and his brother John both enjoy fishing.
likewise

2 As the weather had become unsettled, the officials postponed the final match until the following day.
because

3 Samantha is unlikely to miss the train, but if she does, there are plenty of buses she can catch.
besides

4 John Ross is the drama critic of the Southmoor Gazette and has also written ten detective novels.
besides

5 Despite knowing that Jane Sativa'a suitcase contained smuggled goods, the customs officer did not search it to avoid arousing her suspicions.
nevertheless

6 Ferdinand apologised profusely to Miranda and offered to pay for the damage to her car, but she still would not open the front door to him.
notwithstanding

7 Even though Beethoven was deaf, he produced some of the world's most beautiful music.
yet

8 'If your car is not out of my parking space within one minute, I'll call the police,' warned Mr Sugden.
otherwise

9 'Your threats don't bother me. Anyway this parking space is not yours, it is shared by all the employees,' replied Miss Reason calmly.
furthermore

10 Miss Reason was absolutely furious with Mr Sugden, but she didn't say another word.
in spite of

Guidelines

1 The reasons for our actions or for events can lie in the past or in the future. Those that have their roots in the past are the causes of these actions and events. Those that are forward-looking are the purposes of them. Once they have taken place, they may bring about another event, a result. They may also change or modify the course of all further actions and events, thus having an effect. For example:

Cause	*Because Chris wasn't earning enough money in this country, he went abroad to work.*
Purpose	*In order to earn more money, Chris went abroad to work.*
Result	*Chris went abroad to work, so he earned more money.*
Cause and effect	*If you go abroad to work, you can earn some more money.*

2 The connectors most often used to express cause are *because (of)*, *as* and *due to*. Time words such as *after* and *when* can also carry some causative meaning. For example:

The motorway has been closed to traffic as / because there has been an accident.
Because of / Due to the storm, the port has been closed.
After seeing the film, Julie really wanted to read the book.
When Lucy read the letter, she understood why her parents had been so upset by it.

3 Purpose is usually expressed by *(in order) to* or *so as to* + an infinitive or by *so that* + a clause. Other expressions that can be used are *with a view to*, *with the aim of* or *with ... in mind*, all of which are followed by the *-ing* form of the verb or a noun. For example:

A lot of students take a holiday job (in order / so as) to earn some money.
Writers need peace and quiet so that they can concentrate on their work.
Some retired English people buy a house in southern Europe with emigration in mind.
Dickens wrote stories with a view to having them published as serials in magazines.

4 Result can be expressed by *so*, *thus*, *so ... that*, *as a result (of)*, *in response to*, *therefore*, *as a consequence (of)* and *consequently*. All can be followed by a clause, a noun or the *-ing* form of the verb. Look at the examples in the next column.

Beethoven went deaf as he got older, so he never heard his later works.
Racing drivers wear protective clothing, thus minimising the risk they take.
It is so hot that most people will stay indoors.
As a result of the success of Umberto Eco's novels, a number of other historical mysteries have been published.
Margaret Thatcher lost the support of her government and, therefore, she resigned.
As a consequence of the strike, the factory had to close.
The show has had wonderful reviews. Consequently, all performances are fully booked.

Note that *as a result* can be used at the beginning or the end of the second of two sentences.

The actors were nervous on the opening night. The performance was less good than the dress rehearsal as a result.
It is a simple play but beautifully acted. As a result it is worth seeing.

5 Cause and effect are usually expressed by *if* and various tense sequences. You can also express effect with expressions such as *The effect of this is that ...* followed by a clause or *have the (immediate/long term) effect of / that* followed by the *-ing* form of the verb or a clause, respectively. For example:

If there isn't enough oil in an engine, it breaks down.
If you don't put some oil in your car, the engine will seize.
Many drivers forget to put oil in their cars. The effect of this is that far more cars than necessary break down on the road.
The introduction of the breathalyser test had the long-term effect of reducing the number of accidents caused by drinking and driving.

Further practice

1 Rewrite sentences 1 – 8 below starting with the word in italics.

1 To provide for the increase in tourism on Alcomar Island, a bridge was built connecting it to the mainland.
Because ...

2 When people started using the bridge, the car ferries, which previously had provided the only link between the island and the mainland, carried fewer passengers.
As a result of ...

3 Fewer passengers meant that the company running the car ferries began to lose money.
As a consequence of ...

4 The Ferry Company cut the ticket prices by 60% so they would encourage more people to use the ferries.
In order to ...

5 However, this made little difference as using the bridge was still quicker and cheaper.
The bridge ...

6 The manager of the ferry company decided to take more drastic action after the Bank had threatened to close the company down.
In response to ...

7 Newspaper stories saying that the bridge was badly built and could be dangerous resulted in a dramatic fall in the number of cars using the bridge.
After ...

8 The company raised the price of tickets following a big increase in demand for places on the ferries.
Due to ...

9 Over-acting is something that today's audiences react very badly to.
If ...

10 The storm of protest about the content of my latest novel may mean it's being taken off the market.
Because ...

2 Join each pair of sentences below and rewrite them appropriately. Use a different connector in each case.

1 Water is heated. Steam is produced.
2 Shakespeare wanted a job in the theatre. He went to London.
3 Everyone wanted to see the film. It was on at the local cinema for three months.
4 The volcano threw dust, rocks and lava miles up into the sky. The islanders had to face living in perpetual darkness.
5 In an economic recession, people have less money to spend. They stop buying luxury goods.
6 The journalists went backstage after the performance. They wanted to interview the cast.
7 The marathon runners trained right through the winter. They were determined to be fit enough to complete the big race.
8 Tim didn't do any work before the exam. He failed.
9 Television and video brought films into people's homes. Fewer and fewer people went to the cinema.

Guidelines

1 The phrase *rather than* can be used:

1 to distinguish between two statements, where there is a strong belief in one of the statements over the other.

A person is sent to prison as punishment rather than for punishment.
Students want to go to university to get a degree rather than just to have a good time.

2 to express a preference for one option over another, where there is more than one alternative to choose from.

I (like to) eat fish rather than meat.
I would prefer to be poor and happy rather than rich and miserable.

2 To use the phrase correctly, bear in mind the points below.

1 *rather than* is a connective, joining two statements together. It cannot be separated. Do not confuse it with the expression *I'd rather* described in the next point.

2 When expressing a preference, you can use the expression *I'd (would) rather* and the infinitive of the verb. The alternative activity or object is often implicit. If it is mentioned, it is preceded by *than*.

Oh no! Not the cinema again! I'd rather go to the theatre.
I'd rather go to the theatre than to the cinema.
I'd rather not have a holiday than go camping in this weather!

3 The expressions below are exceptions to the rule, as *rather* and *than* are separated.

Rather you than me!
Rather the devil you know than the devil you don't know.

Language Practice

Rewrite each of the sentences below using *rather than*, *would rather* or *rather ... than*. Start each sentence with the word or phrase given.

1 John said that starving was preferable to eating the horrible hotel food.
'I ...

2 'Let's take the train as it's much quicker than the coach,' Trevor said to Max.
Trevor suggested ...

3 The opinion polls indicate that the Party of National Union is likely to defeat the Independent Alliance at the next general election.
According to ...

4 'I'm not interested in fashion. My choice of clothes depends on what I feel comfortable in,' claimed the ex-model Celia Shrimpton.
'I choose ...

5 The entertainer Noël Coward once said he was only interested in appearing on TV and not watching it.
'I ...

6 In a recent survey, 69% of the people interviewed said that watching a film on video was less entertaining than seeing the same film in the cinema.
Most people said, 'I'd ...

7 Barry wanted to be a dentist not a teacher, but he didn't pass the exams.
If Barry had passed ...

8 'If my father tries to make me marry the Duke of Malaria, I shall drown myself in goat's milk,' protested Princess Petulant.
'I'd ...

9 My friend Nathan West always tells people to save money and not to spend it.
It is ...

10 Veronica said that she didn't envy Sally.
'Rather ...

Guidelines

Before you know it, these people are not around any more.

The pronoun *it* usually applies to things and not to people. However, it can be used in other ways.

1 *It* can be used as the subject or object of the verb *to be* when the real subject follows after the verb.

It is difficult to understand the reason why he left.
Brian took it for granted that nobody would complain.

The sentences above could be written without using *it*. In doing so, however, the register changes and the sentences sound more formal.

The reason why he left is difficult to understand.
Brian took the fact that nobody would complain for granted.

2 *It* is used to refer to a source of information without having to say specifically what that source of information is.

It says here that nobody over the age of thirty-five can enter the disco.
It states categorically that no refunds can be given.
It is generally accepted that Japan is becoming one of the most important markets in the world.

3 *It* is used when describing what the weather is like.

It is raining.
It has been very windy recently.
It started to clear up later in the day.

4 *It* is used with expressions of time.

It's eight o'clock.
It is nearly my bedtime.
It's time we had lunch.
It's high time I was paid the money I am owed.

Note that in the last two examples, the verb which follows must be in the past tense even though the action takes place in the future.

5 *It* is used with expressions of distance.

It's only a short distance to the post office.
It's at least half an hour by car even on the motorway.
It's over 92 metres! What a throw!

6 *It* is used in colloquial expressions where its meaning is general and vague, often referring to a whole situation rather than to specific events.

Stuff it! I've had enough and I'm going home.
It's been pretty rough lately but I can take it.
Right, that's it! This time you've gone too far.
It'll be alright (on the night).
Don't worry. We'll make it.
If you don't like it, you can lump it!

Further practice

Keeping the same meaning, rewrite each of the sentences below so that it begins with *It*.

1 The general consensus was that the violin concert given by Nigel Nixon had been awful.
It ...

2 According to this, there are no non-stop trains after midnight.
It ...

3 We have stayed longer than we intended, but thank you for a lovely party.
It ...

4 The journey to the airport is not long, but I advise you to take a taxi.
It ...

5 There's one minute to go before the film starts, so hurry up.
It ...

6 Don't worry, everything's going to be fine.
It ...

7 The wind is getting stronger so we had better head for the shore.
It ...

8 Eating with your mouth open is bad manners.
It ...

9 Only the seriously rich can afford to play a game like polo.
It ...

10 According to all the newspapers, the veteran rock band, The High Rollers, are finally splitting up.
It ...

Guidelines 1

1 The expression *no wonder* is used, usually in spoken English, to show that the speaker has understood something that had previously been surprising or mysterious. For example:

A *There's an International Air Show on today at the local airfield.*
B *No wonder the traffic is so busy.*

A *I've just told the boss I can't complete that important assignment on time, so we may lose the contract.*
B *No wonder she looked so angry.*

2 In the examples above, the meaning is straightforward. The speakers mean what they say. The expression can, however, be used to carry sarcasm, irony or other implicit meaning. For example:

A *Susan spent the whole day lounging around on the sofa watching TV.*
B *No wonder she looks so tired.*

A *Frank hardly speaks to anyone and if he does, he's usually extremely rude.*
B *No wonder he's got so many friends.*

In these examples, the speakers are being ironic, as they mean the opposite of what they say.

3 In the expression *no wonder, wonder* is used as a noun. It is also used as a noun in the expression *It is a wonder (that)*, which is used to express surprise when something has happened in an unexpected way. For example:

A *Jane was sitting in the front carriage when the train hit the bridge, but she managed to escape with only cuts and bruises.*
B *It's a wonder that she wasn't more seriously injured.*

A *Billy didn't do any work before his exams.*
B *It's a wonder that he managed to pass a single one of them, let alone all six.*

4 *Wonder* is also a regular verb that is used:

1 to make a polite request.

I wonder if you could give me a lift to the station.
I was wondering if you would like to have dinner with me on Saturday.

2 to think aloud, voicing questions that are going through your mind, to which you cannot know the answer.

I wonder whether Jude will get married.
I wonder what the weather is like in Alaska at the moment.
I'm glad you've arrived safely, as I was wondering when you would turn up.

3 to express thoughts and questions about things that you find interesting, unusual or surprising.

I have often wondered how manufacturers manage to put the stripes into toothpaste.
I wonder whether there will be any significant change in the climate in the next twenty years as a result of global warming.
I wonder why that car is parked in the middle of the road.

Further practice 1

1 Complete the dialogues in an appropriate way using either *it is a wonder (that)* or *no wonder*.

1 A There hasn't been any rain for six weeks.
B ... the stream hasn't dried up completely.

2 A I found one of your earrings when I was cleaning out my car.
B I've been looking for that for ages. ... I could't find it.

3 A After the plane crashed, the pilot lived on nothing but wild berries for two weeks until she was rescued.
B ... she managed to survive.

4 A Barnes committed his third serious foul of the match with another late tackle on Venables.
B ... the referee didn't send him off.

5 A This is the third time I have seen this film.
B ... you can't keep your eyes open.

2 Read each of the following dialogues and decide whether B's reply is straightforward, is ironic or carries other implicit meaning and if so what.

1 A Gordon Roper achieved the success he deserved.
  B No wonder his business went bankrupt.

2 A Apparently, today is the birthday of the Great Dictator, that country's founder. To celebrate, everyone is allowed to touch his statue.
  B No wonder the people look so excited.

3 A I should get my final exam results today.
  B No wonder you are looking anxious.

3 Express your thoughts to another person about each of the following situations, using an appropriate form of the verb *wonder*.

1 You hear the doorbell ring but you are not expecting any visitors.
2 You want Bob Beckman to beat Pat Money in the final of the tennis tournament, but are not sure he will.
3 On many occasions you have tried to imagine what life a hundred years ago was like.
4 When you are looking up at the stars, you think about life forms that may or may not exist on other planets.
5 You would like to invite someone to lunch, but are not sure that he or she will accept unless you ask very politely.

Guidelines 2

1 The expression *it is hardly surprising (that)* can be used instead of *no wonder*. In this expression, *it* refers to what follows in the sentence. *Hardly* is an adverb modifying the adjective *surprising*, with a meaning similar to but not as absolute as *not*. The reason for the lack of surprise is introduced by *given / considering (that)*. For example:

It is hardly surprising that the beach is crowded, given that today is a public holiday.
It's hardly surprising that Maureen looks so relaxed, given that she has just come back from three weeks' holiday in the Bahamas.

2 Note that in this structure the order of the clauses can be reversed.

Given that today is a public holiday, it is hardly surprising that the beach is crowded.
Given that Maureen has just come back from three weeks' holiday in the Bahamas, it is hardly surprising that she looks so relaxed.

3 If *given* is followed by a noun or a noun phrase without a verb, *that* must be omitted. For example:

Given all the hard work Jane has done, it is hardly surprising she feels exhausted.
Given all her hard work, it is hardly surprising Jane feels exhausted.

4 When *hardly* is used to modify a verb, it must come immediately before the main verb. For example:

Since Brian injured his back, he has hardly worked.
Matilda speaks so fast that I hardly understand a word she says.

5 Note that the adverb formed from the adjective *hard* is *hard* and not *hardly*. When *hard* is used as an adverb, it always follows the verb. For example:

In order to win a place in the team, Mary trained hard.

6 *Hardly* is also used as an adverb of time to indicate a very short time between two events. For example:

She had hardly opened the door when the telephone rang.

Further practice 2

1 Read each of the following sentences and decide whether *given that* has been used appropriately. Put a tick next to the correct sentences and delete *that* from the sentences where it must be omitted.

1 Given that the people's disapproval of the Government's policies, it will be hardly surprising if they lose the next election.
2 Given that there has been a huge increase in taxes, the people's attitude towards the Government is hardly surprising.
3 It is hardly surprising that the Government has raised taxes, given that the increase in the rate of inflation.

4 Considering that all the money Cynthia spends on clothes, it is hardly surprising she looks so well dressed.
5 It is hardly surprising that the car won't start, given that it was left out in the snow last night with its lights on.

2 Complete each of the following sentences in an appropriate way.

1 Given the firefighters' devotion to duty, it is hardly surprising ...
2 It is hardly surprising that Mark did not get the job, given ... .
3 Considering the insulting way you have behaved, it is hardly surprising ... .
4 It is hardly surprising that the sea is no longer blue, given ... .
5 Given that Michael's favourite pastime is watching TV, it is hardly surprising ...

3 Complete each of the sentences with either *hard* or *hardly* in the appropriate space, either before or after the verb. Leave the other space blank.

1 The lecture was so boring I ... listened ... to a word that was said.
2 The lecture was very difficult to understand, so I had to ... listen ... to follow it.
3 Winning the competition was such a great surprise, I ... dreamt ... it would happen to me.
4 This ... is ... either the time or the place to be discussing these matters.
5 Although it ... was ... to understand Barry's motives, I am very grateful for what he has done.

Guidelines

The verbs below are often confused.

lay	*lie*	*lie*
laying	*lying*	*lying*
laid	*lay*	*lied*
laid	*lain*	*lied*

1 The verb *to lay* is transitive, which means that it must be followed by an object. It means *to put down* or *place*. It can also be used figuratively. For example:

Hens lay eggs.
Mary laid the cards on the table.
The builders are laying the foundations of the house.
Don't lay the blame on me!

2 The verb *to lie* is intransitive, so it cannot be followed by an object. It means *to be in a horizontal position*. It is usually followed by a preposition which indicates where the person or thing is. For example:

Ophelia lies in the bath for hours.
After the race, Sebastian lay on the ground to recover.
The Titanic has lain on the sea bed ever since it sank.

3 The verb *to lie*, meaning not to tell the truth, is regular and intransitive. An alternative expression is *to tell a lie / lies*. It is often followed by a preposition or adverbial particle. For example:

Jane always lies about her age.
I am sure Conrad lied to me about the money.
The judge accused the witness of lying about who caused the accident.

4 The verb *to lay* is used in a number of expressions and two-word verbs. For example:

The waiters lay the tables before the customers arrive.
The last time I laid eyes on Sandra was three years ago.
As a result of the recession, the company has laid off half the work force.
After the rebels had surrendered, they laid down their weapons.
The market traders have been laying out their stalls since five o'clock this morning.

Further practice

Complete each of the sentences below with the most appropriate form of one of the verbs, expressions or two-word verbs on the left. You may need to use more than one word.

1 The doctor told me to remove my shoes and … on the bed.
2 A priceless painting by Van Gogh … undetected for years in the basement of the museum, until it was spotted by an expert.
3 Matilda always tries to avoid trouble by … to her parents.
4 There is nothing I like better than … on the beach and soaking up the sun.
5 The manager … the blame for his team's poor performance on their lack of fitness.
6 At the weekend, I … and don't get up until at least eleven o'clock.
7 It is a fire hazard to leave litter … in the forest, so please take it home with you.
8 After the accident, the victims … helplessly on the ground until the rescue services arrived.
9 The rules … several years ago and cannot be changed without the approval of the Board of Directors.
10 Wherever I … my hat, that's my home.

Guidelines

The choice of which future tense to use generally depends on the speaker's frame of mind at the time. There are few rules of the kind that apply to other tenses. The various forms are listed below with notes on their uses.

1 The Present Continuous is used:

1 when future events are certain. No doubt remains and no act of will or further planning is required.

I am flying to Spain on Saturday.
George is coming at eight o'clock.
Sandra is getting married in August.
We are having lasagne for lunch.
The conference is being held on Saturday.

2 in a question when the speaker has a good idea what the answer might be, but is not certain. He or she is checking plans or finding out the details of a plan or schedule.

Are you coming to the disco tonight?
Why is Miss Happ meeting us this afternoon?
Are the delegates being met at the airport?
Where are you getting married?

2 *Be going to do* is used:

1 also to express certainty about the future, especially where there would be confusion if the Present Continuous was used.

Look at those black clouds! It's going to rain.
It's raining right now! I felt a few drops a moment ago.

The house is going to burn down.
The fire in the kitchen is spreading.

Harriet Atboy's novel is going to be made into a film.
The filmscript is being written already.

2 to express strong logical probability.

On his present form, John Barry is going to win the match tomorrow.
It looks as though we are going to arrive on time.

3 to show intention, especially where there is a determination to succeed.

I am going to pass all my exams.
We are not going to give up the struggle.

4 in questions to check and find out about future arrangements and intentions.

When is Arthur going to sell his car?
Are you going to sign the contract next month?
Are there going to be any seats available on the next flight?

3 The Simple Present is used:

1 when a future event occurs naturally and inevitably.

The next total eclipse of the sun is in 2031.
Tina's birthday is on Saturday.

2 when a future event is part of a specific pre-arranged order, plan or timetable.

The ship sails at dawn tomorrow.
The arrangements for the visit next Friday are that the Chief Executive meets the Governor at the entrance and escorts her to the Board Room.

3 after time words such as *when* or *as soon as* in a sequence of future events.

When the sun sets, we'll walk into town.
As soon as I see them, I'll tell them.

4 The Simple Future is used:

1 to express future plans where there is an element of doubt or indecision. This doubt may be either expressed or implied in the sentence.

I think I'll have smoked salmon rather than fillet steak but both sound pretty good.
They'll be there by eight o'clock, provided the traffic isn't too heavy.
Unless there are any objections, Miss Handel will take charge of the investigation.

2 as a form of command, giving the person addressed little or no choice.

The doctor will see you now.
You will write, won't you?
Will you please sit down?
Won't you have another cup of coffee before you go?

3 to express a sense of purpose about the future, especially when there might be difficulties.

We shall overcome the present economic crisis.
Perdita will pass the exams, with a little help from me.
Cinderella will go to the Ball.

4 to express surprise or criticism when a person habitually behaves in a certain way.

Ben will leave all the important decisions until the very end of the meeting.
My flatmate will play his favourite record, Loud and Dangerous, just as I am going to bed.

5 The Future Continuous is used to express certainty about the future, especially when the action in the future has a continuous element, or when the speaker is imagining the future, maybe using a phrase such as *this time tomorrow.*

I shall be having lunch with her tomorrow.
Good luck in your new job. All your colleagues will be thinking of you.
The judges will be examining all the evidence before they reach a verdict.
This time tomorrow we'll be on the plane.

6 The Future Perfect, the future tense of *have* + the past participle, is used:

1 to describe when an action will be completed.

By this time next week, Peter Ratten will have finished his fourth novel.
At this rate, Trencherman will have eaten all the food in the house before the shops open.

2 to describe the length of a period of time, from a time in the past to a time in the future.

In October, my parents will have been married for thirty years.

7 The Future Perfect Continuous, the future tense of *have* + *been* + the present participle, is used to describe the length of a period of time, from the past to the future, when the speaker wishes to emphasise either the length of time or the continuous nature of the action.

By the end of this year we will have been living in this house for forty years.

8 Note the following points on the use of *shall* and *will.*

1 The general rule is that *shall* is used with the first person singular and plural (*I* and *we*) and *will* with second and third person singular and plural (*you, he/she/it* and *they*).

In modern usage this rule is not strictly followed. *Will* / *'ll* and *won't* are often used in statements with the first person. In question forms, however, *shall* cannot be interchanged with *will.* (*Shall* in questions is often a form of offer.) For example:

Shall I open the window?
Shall we have dinner together?
Will they arrive on time?

Further practice

Complete each of the following sentences with a verb in the appropriate form.

1 When you arrive at Oviedo airport on Thursday, the local representative … you and drive you to the hotel where you … the night.
2 According to the forecast, the winds … very strong by tomorrow evening and could cause structural damage.
3 Look at the black clouds! It … at any moment.
4 My aunt … the most extraordinary clothes when she comes to visit us. I'm sure she only does it to shock my father.
5 Cordelia … lunch with Hudson Ford, the film director, next Thursday. She always gets the lucky breaks.
6 After I've had this coffee, I … the composition I started this morning.
7 By the end of this week, Andrew Nelson … in prison for ten years, even though many people have always thought he is innocent.
8 … we … the old lady who lives two doors away to our party?
9 Good evening, Miss Raver. My sister and I … a party tomorrow night and wondered if you would like to come.
10 If the bus does not come in the next five minutes, I … at this stop for exactly an hour. What a ridiculous waste of time.
11 Ron Knee, the ruthless manager of Neasden Football Club … his star player from the team to play Pinner Athletic next Saturday, because of his poor performance.
12 Provided there are no technical problems, the space probe … the planet Venus by the end of next year and can then start sending back photographs.
13 A partial eclipse of the moon … next week but only people with powerful telescopes … to see it clearly.
14 I can't possibly eat this meat; it's far too tough. I'm … to see the manager. Waiter!
15 In order to pick the winner for the best TV drama series, the judges … over a hundred hours of programmes between now and the end of the month.